King of Pawns

King of Pawns is a work of fiction. Names, characters, places, incidents, and dialogues are the product of the author's imagination or are used fictitiously. Any resemblance to actual events or persons, living or dead, events, or locales is entirely coincidental.

2019 Promotion Publishing Inc

Copyright © 2019 by Promotion Publishing Inc

All rights reserved

Cover design/Chess photography: Demi Bom
Ig: @demibom

Cover photography: Thomas Johnsen
Ig: @ thomasjohnsenphoto

Editor: Travis Feelds
Ig: @ foriegnfeelds

TO

Mitko Bombata

KING OF PAWNS
Contents

SLAVENA 1
THE SINNER 5
MISSION 16
ROVISH 28
CHIEF OF STATION 37
JARO 53
CLEANSING 60
SNOW WHITE 75
ALEXANDER 85
ARCHIE 98
TRADE 109
EAGLE 117
EMBASSY 130
THE ADMIRAL 139
KNIGHT 151
PITCH 160
MARINES 175
PLAN B 189
EXPOSED 206
NAVY 211
QUEEN SACRIFICE 219
VELINA 229
BULLET CHESS 243
BLOWN 255
DRAGAN BOYCHEV 263
COUNTER ATTACK 267
INVITATION 283
BLACK KING 293
DOUBLE GAMBIT 299
CHECKMATE 312
HEARTBEAT 322

SLAVENA

Slavena Ivanova was on the run.

She would have been dead by now if she was not properly trained by the Central Intelligence Agency and if she didn't break every rule in the book. Adrenaline was still in the bloodstream as a reminder of the things she had to do to survive.

The sound of the airline jet engines went silent and everyone stood. Remaining seated, she looked out her window with a relief that she was back home. It was a big risk to enter the United States, but she had no other place to go.

She was feeling the strain of the travel as she entered the terminal. Her efforts to rest during the flight had betrayed her. Fear was clouding her mind, costing her the sleep she would need later. She couldn't lose the memory of the night before. The shadows of her killers prowling in the dark, looking for her and they'd found her. But she surprised them like lightning in the middle of December. None of the gunmen lived long enough to hear the thunder. It was as easy as her sniper instructor used to say: "Shooting is just muscle memory."

Back at the Farm, they made everything sound simple.

KING OF PAWNS

Like the escape plan where you were supposed to flee to your safe house and call for support. The CIA had one lined up for her, but how could she trust them now after everything that had happened in Bulgaria? She couldn't. That was why she had to do the one thing they didn't teach her at the Farm: to flee back home.

The passport control lines at JFK Airport were long but moved quickly, making her heart drum even faster. She visually swept the environment with a heightened degree of alertness that would make the difference between life and death. She made the calculated decision to join the line in which the officer—a polite, older black man—asked little or no questions. Before her in the line was an Indian woman, wrapped in a bright red sari with an exposed midriff and engulfed in the aroma of exotic spices. In her ski bib and a blue ski jacket, Slavena felt as if she almost belonged here in this line of foreigners.

To her right was the line for US citizens. That would have been her line if things hadn't gone so wrong in Bulgaria. She had her American passport safely tucked inside her purse, but it was essential that she entered the country unnoticed. Nobody needed to know where she was. Not even her boss—the Chief of Station—and not until she found out who was pushing the pawns across the board.

With her peripheral vision, she observed a family of five, two parents and three children, all visibly exhausted by their journey. They looked like a well-to-do American family on their way back from a European holiday. The dad wore an old football jersey, baggy jeans, and a worn baseball hat. The mom tried hard to replicate the stylish look of an average European woman: a seemingly expensive cashmere coat, topped with an exquisite floral scarf around her neck and a face full of makeup. It would have worked, if she was still on the French *Cotê D'Azur* with a cocktail in her hand and the expanse of the Mediterranean in her eyes. Not at JFK Airport with its infusing smell of Dunkin' Donuts and coffee. Behind all the makeup stood a tired woman, who held tightly onto the family's passports, knowing well that her sanity depended on them. Slavena could bet money that all the family members would have given anything to be back home right now. Parked on the couch, in front of their 46-inch TV, fighting for the remote.

Slavena sympathized. She also wanted nothing more than to be on the other side of the immigration booth, walking briskly towards the baggage claim area.

The American family got their passports back without questions. Slavena watched them disappear out of view. The older, black officer called Slavena forward. *It's now or never*, she thought. She hoped it was now because she wasn't ready for never.

"Passport, please." The officer's smile was a good sign.

Slavena smiled back and rummaged in her bag before handing her Bulgarian passport over. She could've gotten her passport ready while she waited, but she wanted to have a genuine reason to appear flustered. Not finding what she was looking for, gave her that excuse.

"Here. Sorry!" She brushed her hair off her face and tried to relax. She wasn't going to do anything she hadn't done a thousand times before. Lie through her teeth.

The immigration officer leafed through her passport in search of the US visa. Slavena held her breath. The visa was in there, all right, but the expiration date was in less than two weeks. For any immigration officer that would be an obvious red flag.

KING OF PAWNS

He gazed at her visa with his eyes narrowing slightly.
"Reason for your short trip?"
He had noticed. Damn.
"Business."
"What type of work do you do?"
"Environmental cleaning."
He studied the visa again, taking his time, touching her nerves. He nodded and stamped her passport.
"You're in the right city for that," he said. "Welcome to the United States of America."
Those were the exact words she had desperately hoped to hear for the past ten hours on her flight to New York.

THE SINNER

Stefan Nikolov was shouting into his mobile phone as he stepped out of the Bentley limousine in front of nightclub Sugalips, the newest hot spot in Sofia, Bulgaria.

The line of dressed-up, ordinary people waiting in front of the club's entrance followed him with timid eyes. Most of the men in the line dreamed of becoming the next Sinner, as he was popularly known on the streets; a few wanted to work for him and some eventually would, fully aware that the job of a gangster's watchdog was dangerous and underpaid.

"What do you mean there was a problem?" Nikolov exploded into his phone, oblivious to the attention of the people standing around. "Is he dead or not?"

Inside the car, Mitko, Nikolov's chauffeur, swelled with pride. Who else would have the balls to admit in public that he was up to no good but his boss! The Sinner was invincible. So was Mitko, by proxy.

"He is dead!" the voice on the other end said. "But the bitch got away."

"Say that again?" Nikolov said as he looked down at his brand-new shoes. They were Valentino but strangely reeked like hell.

"The bitch got away," the man repeated. "But that's not all."

Nikolov lifted his foot and hissed with disgust at the sight of dog feces on the sole of his shoe. A blindingly strong urge to kick something, or somebody, overpowered Nikolov, but knowing the crowd was watching him, he continued walking while carrying on the conversation.

"If she got away, then what else could there be that I care about?"

"You want to know this. She may be CIA."

"What?" Nikolov raised his voice again. "How do you know?"

The man cleared his throat. "She killed all my men. Only a well-trained CIA officer can pull the trigger like this."

Nikolov paused by the door. That was big news indeed. He needed to make a few calls, but first, he needed to clean his shoe.

"I'll call you back."

Nikolov hung up and walked inside the club with his four guards.

The red-haired hostess rushed on her six-inch stilettos to greet him. She pointed him towards the VIP room. The memory of a $1,000 tip she'd gotten once just by doing that was the happiest memory she held.

Ignoring her, Nikolov turned left passing the cloakroom — used primarily for snorting cocaine and quick, casual sex — and walked into the black-and-gold men's room.

Once inside, he secured the stall door, sat on the toilet seat, took off his shoe and kicked it to his bodyguard to wash it off. While waiting, he stared at his shoeless foot and thought of the CIA woman. Nikolov had been suspecting for some time that it was the Bulgarian Secret Service behind the serial killings of the mafia bosses in Bulgaria but the CIA never crossed his mind. Now with the new information, everything made sense.

America wanted to build a few military bases in Bulgaria to fight the war on terror, but Bulgaria's organized crime was too serious of a problem to execute the plan. And since the Bulgarian government did nothing to tackle the problem, it seemed the US decided to wipe out the mafia themselves. By sending an assassin with no name, nor history, but the skills every hitman coveted.

If she was really CIA, as his gunman suggested, he wanted to meet her face-to-face. If she was pretty, he would be kind to her at first. He took a morbid pleasure in seeing women on their knees. At the thought of a CIA officer begging for mercy, his eyes flamed with excitement. Finally, something to revive him from the cardiac arrest his life had been lately.

In the past two years, things had started going his way a little too easy. His wife had given him a second son. His new mistress had just got breast enlargements, and now her breasts were as big as melons. He'd grown tired of her and would've dumped her if only finding someone new didn't seem like too much of an effort. What was the point? The new mistress would also have breasts that needed enlarging, cellulite that needed massaging at $100 dollars a session, and hair that needed dyeing and retouching every couple of weeks. Nails, clothes, haircuts, make-up. It was all the same in the end.

Not that he minded investing in women. He was now the richest man in Bulgaria because he was the Sinner. That is what they began calling him and his business partners, rest their souls, on the day Security Insurance National, known as SIN for short, became licensed by the state after the communist regime collapsed.

He remembered that day very clearly. All the people on

the streets, waving their flags, and flowers with smiles full of hope for a brighter future, while behind their backs the former communists stuffed their big red suitcases with all the cash from the Bulgarian national reserves. By sunset, 11 billion dollars disappeared from the Bulgarian horizon along with the last ray of sunlight.

Among the Bulgarians in the crowd who was never to see another day of sunlight was Nikolov—a former Olympic bronze medalist with the drive to be the best wrestler in the world. Only to find out his government's promise for life-long financial support expired along with the communists, thus crushing his dreams for gold. But then something better than gold dazzled him when Pavel Dobrev—the former captain of the Bulgarian National Wrestling team—told him and a select few other Olympic wrestlers about the master plan.

The rest was history. The old communists needed protection to keep their stolen wealth in plain sight. SIN emerged as the largest Bulgarian security firm, making Nikolov and his former wrestling teammates millionaires overnight. Everyone on the lucky team, including Nikolov, was rewarded with luxury and respect in exchange for their protection of the new oligarchs. SIN's tentacles quickly expanded to other illicit businesses, including loansharking and racketeering.

Over time, Nikolov took leadership of SIN and became known as the Cardinal Sinner and his assassins. Or the mafia for short. Nikolov didn't care what they called him as long as he was treated as the elite and right now, he didn't feel like one.

"Am I going to be waiting for my shoe all night?" He barked to his guard.

"I think I got it all washed boss," His guard tiptoed on

the floor as if he was stepping through a minefield and quickly slid the clean shoe underneath the stall.

Nikolov put his shoe back on and walked to the bathroom sink. He splashed his face and sprayed himself with extra *Dolce and Gabanna Pour Homme*, which he always had in a tiny travel bottle in his breast pocket. He hated bad odors. His childhood had been full of them—pickled cabbage, rotting fruit in vats for homemade moonshine, sweat and bad breath. Now, the paired scent of Provence lavender and cedarwood gave him the perfect balance of tenderness and power. Even his nose could tell how far he'd come in life.

The music in the club was booming and pulsating throughout his body. The lights shook and swirled making him dizzy. He hated nightclubs, but that was where you were expected to be seen these days. He had no choice but to put in an appearance.

Upstairs in the V.I.P room, the music was less loud. Nikolov spotted Sergei Petrov from afar and walked towards him with an outstretched hand. Sergei, a legendary figure from Russia—Nikolov also liked to think of himself as a legendary figure—shook Nikolov's hand and asked him to sit at his table.

"Hey, Sinner! Long time, no see!" Sergei said and lowered himself down on the sofa.

"It's not like you've been around. Aruba?"

Sergei took a sip from his mojito and took his time. "Yeah. How did you know?"

"I know some people there."

A nearly-naked woman with a minuscule tray in her hands appeared by the table and discreetly hovered at the edge of the group. She wore a tight miniskirt and no top. The top half of her torso was spray-painted in gold.

"Korbel on the rocks," Nikolov said and the woman

vanished.

Next to Sergei sat another man. Nikolov didn't know him and couldn't be bothered to be introduced. All kinds of people swarmed around men like Sergei and him. Only the survivors were worth remembering, and proving you are one of those took time. He would learn this person's name in due course if he was worth it.

It was the same with women. They were interchangeable, like car tires. Some brands were better than others, but they all served the same purposes—to be ridden fast and hard.

Opposite Nikolov, completely still, sat a beautiful woman, who obviously belonged to Sergei. She looked too expensive for the other man. Out of his league. Her long legs were perfectly arranged at an angle that best showcased their perfect shape. Nikolov couldn't give a rat's ass what her name was either. Why should he care? He suspected he would never see her again.

All Sergei's women behaved like fucking statues. Never saying a thing; never drinking or going for a piss. What Sergei saw in these beautiful mummies was beyond him. Who would want to fuck a corpse? Not Nikolov for sure. He liked his women moving about, moaning, and even fighting back, if he got a bit rough.

The nearly-naked waitress placed a glass on the table in front of him. Nikolov appreciatively stared at her bare breasts painted in golden colors. They chose them well here, he thought, but the quality would decline soon. He'd seen the pattern before: a club opened with the best interior design, the newest technical equipment, the freshest girls and the classiest drinks. The owners were motivated to do well but running a club wasn't easy. When a year later the interior of this club gets topped by a new club, the equipment ages and the owners can't be bothered to fork out money to replace it, the customers move on. The owners lose interest. Then the bartenders, unsupervised, start diluting the drinks. After that, only common boys and fat girls come in. Then the club disappears. The club circle of life as he knew it.

Nikolov put an ankle on top of his knee and relaxed, letting his head fall backward. The sofa was comfy and the ceiling was spectacular. Hidden by clouds of cigarette smoke, it was covered by an exact replica of the information boards of the Wall Street Stock Exchange with the intention to affiliate the club with money. But also, Nikolov mused, it revealed the dark side of greed that hung above them all.

"Jesus, man!" Sergei couldn't stop the snide remark. "What's up with your shoe? It reeks."

Hearing this, Nikolov boiled with anger but hid it well. He didn't need to be reminded of the shoe disaster, but Sergei brought it back to the foreground.

"Stepped on some dog shit outside. You know how it is in this shitty country."

Nikolov's mood was ruined. He had wanted to socialize and boast tonight. Squeeze a couple of waitress's asses. See where luck would take him, but now he had to go. He didn't feel like talking to anyone anymore. He finished his drink in one gulp, chucked some money on the table, and called for his car.

As he exited the VIP room, the eyes of the two men followed him.

"Why did you bother with the smell? The Sinner isn't a man you want to have as an enemy." The stranger at the table asked Sergei. "You know how vain he is."

Sergei picked up his glass and slurped through the straw the last dregs of his mojito. "Didn't you hear? The word on the street is that he is the Last Sinner to walk on Earth."

KING OF PAWNS

Outside, the night had gotten colder. As Nikolov stepped out of the club, a shiver went through his body. He rubbed his arms around himself to warm up while one of his guards waived patiently at Mitko. The car was stopped at a traffic light about a hundred yards away from the club entrance. Nikolov stepped to the edge of the curb to wait for him.

He was distracted by what had happened in the club. Sergei had never before disrespected him so blatantly. Nikolov was annoyed but also worried. Disrespect, especially in public, wasn't something he could tolerate. He would have to think of a way to get back at Sergei, and fast.

A young woman stepped out of the shadows and asked him for a light. He gave her a thorough once over. Everyone knew asking for a light was just a pretext to chat. If he was to give this young woman the time of day, he wanted to make sure it would be worth it.

She was on the pretty side, although a bit chubby and with smaller breasts than he usually liked. He put his hand in his pocket to fish his lighter out. She'd have to do for tonight since his hasty exit from the club had curbed any other prospects. He lit the lighter intentionally low, so she'd have to lean over to light her cigarette. As she did so her top gaped and he had a good look at her lacy bra and the breasts encased in it. *Yeah, she'd have to do,* he thought. If she stuck around — you never knew — he might pay for her to have them done up. She had a mysterious vibe to her and long blonde hair that played with the wind. She deserved a nicer pair of tits.

DEMI BOM

He heard the motorbike before he saw it. The roaring of its motor registered at the back of his mind a little too late. When the motorbike was only a few feet away, roaring at full volume, Nikolov turned his head and caught a glimpse of its dark shadow cutting through the night without its headlight on.

Sensing the danger, the four guards were fast to form a wall of flesh around their boss to protect him. But they weren't fast enough.

The submachine gun in the outstretched hand of the biker registered in Nikolov's mind when it was fired. Light came from its muzzle and bullets ripped through their bodies. Nikolov died instantly from a wound in the forehead.

In the car, Mitko saw what was happening. He put the car in gear, charged forward, nearly missing a drunken pedestrian. He was less than a second too late to shield everyone with the car from the bullets. The bike sped on and was out of sight before Mitko managed to come out of the car and crouch next to the six, now lifeless, bodies.

Two Years Earlier

"Play the opening like a book, the middle game like a magician, and the endgame like a machine."
– Rudolf Spielmann

The Opening

*"I, ♙ , do hereby affirm
my allegiance to the United States of America
and, likewise, disclaim any partiality toward Bulgarians
by virtue of having blood relatives living there until
my mission in Bulgaria is complete."*

MISSION

The buildings in Langley were just as impressive and intimidating as Slavena remembered them from her first days on campus. The original CIA headquarters building was a perfect example of the Brutalism style that had dominated American architecture in the '60s. It was a solid block of concrete with ends jutting in and out, creating the illusion of infinity. The never-ending rows of identical and forbidding windows reminded her of a bee colony. She approached the main building with the trembling a new worker bee must feel when returning to the beehive. She wanted to get in more than anything, yet was unsure if she could produce enough honey for the queen bee—the Director of the CIA.

To add more fuel to her anxiety, it was her last week in DC and she'd been dealing with an endless list of chores to complete prior to her permanent change of station, the CIA vernacular for an assignment abroad. Despite the name, she knew there was nothing permanent about it. It was just a mission to get her feet on the ground until the next one came up. If anything would be permanent in her line of work, it would be living on the brink and losing her friends.

On such thoughts, she went back to the night when she'd

had a farewell dinner with her friends. She'd told them she was picked up by the State Department to work overseas as a Consular Officer and they cheered for her, confirming her first objective was achieved. If she could fool the razor-keen ears of her friends, then she was off to a good start.

And off to a bad start, considering she was running late for her first assignment briefing. She looked at her cell phone with panic before she handed it over for the security check. She had only ten minutes to get to her briefing and the corridors in the building were notoriously long.

Eventually, she entered the conference room and was relieved to discover she was the first one in. Slavena chose the seat away from the head of the table and sat quietly for a moment to silence her brain. Any minute now, she would be a pawn with a mission. A pawn to be pushed around the board until the end. What if it was too dangerous? It was possible, but it was the unknown that made her anxious the most.

At least the waiting was nearly over.

Two officials, she'd never seen before poked their heads around the door carrying coffee mugs and manila folders with large boldface "TOP SECRET ORCON" coversheets.

"Good morning," one of the two men piped cheerfully and advanced his stout body her way. He had white hair, more plentiful than you would expect from a man his age, and deep-seated eyes that were serious despite his smile. "Welcome to the team! We've heard nothing but glowing remarks about your performance at the Farm."

"Thanks!" Slavena was immensely grateful for his kind words and it put her at ease. The man must have seen more than a few Junior Officers being briefed and was probably aware that it was a tough spot to be in.

The other man—tall and sullen in his dark suit—said

nothing. He merely put his mug and folders down and aligned his pens carefully on the table before taking his jacket off and sitting down a few chairs away from her.

"Now, we are just waiting for the division chief to join us and we'll start with our brief." The chatty man's voice was brisk.

The tall man opened his folder and wrote down something. Slavena wondered what his part in all this was. It struck her that despite being at CIA headquarters and having just qualified for one of the most desired jobs in the country, everything remained the same. The conference room, the people with their hot drinks and insincere smiles were just like the meetings back in her old job. Ordinary.

After the extraordinary experience at the Farm with its parachute jumping, wilderness survival, unarmed special combat, silent strikes, surveillance, and the assembly and disassembly of small arms, she was now back in the real world. She hoped whatever was to come next was going to fully use the skills she'd picked up.

A third man appeared at the door, dressed the same as the other two.

"Well, hello everyone! Sorry, I'm late," he said charmingly, dropping more classified folders to the table and sitting in a chair opposite Slavena. It was like there was a competition for who could bring the biggest and most classified folder to the table. The interim supervisor had brought three; the white-haired extrovert had only two — loser — and the guy who sat tall and took more notes even while no one was speaking had four. Slavena put him in charge of the room despite the fact that he hadn't said a word yet.

"So, how was the Farm?" The division chief directed his attention to Slavena as he arranged his folders on top of the table.

Finally, Slavena started to feel at ease. The Farm was something she could always talk about, especially because other CIA employees were the only ones, she could talk about it with.

"Overpopulated with deer and children if you ask me."

The men laughed at her comment.

"Ok Slavena, my name is Devin Becker and you already know why we're here."

Slavena straightened her back and nodded. The allocated time for chit-chat was apparently over. She swallowed hard. She was about to find out what her mission would be. Where she'd be sent to spend the next months or even years of her life.

"You probably already guessed we're sending you to your home country." Becker studied her face for an initial reaction, but Slavena didn't have one. Mixed emotions swirled inside her head. Relief - she already knew the place she was going. Disappointment - it wasn't one of the front lines in the war on terror and, perhaps, a tiny bit of curiosity: Slavena hadn't been back to Bulgaria in nearly a decade and she wondered what her home country would be like now. "But, of course, Bulgaria is no longer your home country, right?"

Slavena mentally frowned at the comment. It was delivered with a slight sarcasm but it was a telltale that Becker and the Company still needed validation from her of her loyalty. She had renounced her Bulgarian citizenship, pledged allegiance to the United States of America, and agreed to defend it with her life, but clearly, that wasn't enough. Perhaps that was why they were sending her back? To plunge her deep into the life she'd left behind and see how she'd react.

Everything was a test with the CIA.

"You'll operate under non-official cover. An illegal."

Yes! She rejoiced mentally. She had joined the CIA to become a NOC and here she was getting her wish. Then again, she was about to start a life in which she'd deceive and lie to everyone she came in contact with. As a NOC, the US Government would not bail her out if her identity was exposed. She was on her own, and she would have to get used to it.

Becker was still talking. "Your cover will be working as a psychotherapist with a private practice and a taste for high culture. As such, you will frequently attend high social and cultural events to identify government and business leaders in Bulgaria susceptible to influence and exploitation. Because you're a novice, you'll be playing only a support role as a case officer." He hesitated before continuing. "This means you won't be running any sources, but rather identify potential sources or agents. Once you spot a potential agent, you'll make recommendations to the Chief of Station, who will take it from there…"

The black arts of espionage, Slavena thought. None of this was a surprise to her. She had a Bachelor degree in Psychology and although she was not a licensed psychotherapist, the subject wasn't alien to her. Coupled with the training on tactical questioning and elicitation, she'd been given at the Farm, she reckoned she could shovel nice gems of information out of the enemy and friend if given the chance.

"…additionally, you will be the in-country cavalry for the Company. You are on-call for operational support for other programs when needed."

Slavena nodded light-headed.

"Now that we've got that covered, let's move on to the primary focus of your operation in Bulgaria, and the real reason for non-official cover."

There was a moment of silence and all the men in the room were looking at her now.

Here we go, she thought. *This is where they tell me what they really want from me.*

"You'll be using your cover to establish an election campaign network for one of our agents who stands on the brink of a brilliant political career. Your job is to get him elected. But before I reveal his identity, let me ask a question. Why do you think the United States is interested in Bulgaria?"

Becker watched her from under his thick eyebrows and waited for the answer. She was glad she had a tall cup of coffee before the meeting. It gave her the edge to answer fast.

"Bulgaria is more pro-American than some of our long-standing allies in Europe and its geographic location has strategic importance for the United States." She said.

"Elaborate."

"Bulgaria is at the crossroads of the Mideast and Europe and it provides great access to the US military to engage in the global war of terror. If Bulgaria succeeds in joining NATO this year, the US will almost certainly seek military basing rights. Sea, land and air."

"Anything else you want to add about the geography?"

Slavena knew he was interested to hear about Russia. With the CIA, it was always about Russia and so she answered point-blank: "Bulgaria also borders Russia across the Black Sea. If America forges close ties with Bulgaria, it can limit Russian influence in the region and provide a leap pad for the US military into the Middle East."

Becker smiled with approval in his eyes. "And if that

happens, US can influence Bulgaria to invest in modernizing its military primarily with US military hardware. Now that we covered our mutual interests and the real reasons why we are trying to cultivate a deeper friendship with Bulgaria, let's move on to our agent. We recruited him in 1993. At the time, he was a top graduate from Stanford University and, since he came from a Bulgarian family with significant political influence, our agent is now a Deputy Minister of Interior. We are grooming him to become the next Prime Minister of Bulgaria."

That's more like it, Slavena knew the CIA would not let her down. Her mission sounded more exciting than she ever hoped.

"What we need from you is to build popular support for him by conducting a western style publicity campaign for his upcoming election. Your main objective is to influence domestic public opinion and undermine any viable political opposition. This is why you're going in under NOC. If you're compromised, which is very unlikely, the US cannot be seen as mingling in the democratic elections of a friendly country. Here is his full profile." Becker slid a thick folder towards her and Slavena looked at the folder.

"And this is our man," Becker said, waiting for the screen on the wall to flicker to life.

Slavena looked up and saw a close-up picture of a man in his early forties. The face was muscular and expressionless with an aura of self-importance that was detectable even through a picture on a screen.

"His name is Dragan Boychev." Becker pronounced his name perfectly and her world tilted fully on its axis.

She knew the name. In fact, she knew the name too well. After so many years since her sister's death, Slavena couldn't believe she had to hear the name Boychev again.

The memories from the day her sister died, flooded so swiftly into her mind that for a moment it felt like she was drowning from inside out.

The three men sensed something was amiss and pinned their eyes on Slavena. She knew they were waiting for her to say something. Anything. But talking appeared to have become impossible, just like thinking and breathing.

Finally, after what felt like hours but was just a minute, she managed to speak.

"I've heard a lot about his dad. They say he's shadier than the dark side of the moon," she said. "Now I understand why his son went to Stanford."

The three men glared at her face as if they'd just seen Slavena for the first time and she wasn't what they were expecting.

"Please expand on that," Becker said, watching her with his attentive eyes.

"His dad was the former head of the Secret Service during the Communist regime, and after the collapse, he stole millions of dollars from the Bulgarian reserves. Then he cashed in his status and became the Director of the Bulgarian National Police. That's how he could afford to send his son to Stanford. But of course, you already knew that."

"Yes, we do know about the dad. He's one of the most powerful men in Bulgaria."

"And the real Al Capone," she said, regretting instantly the slip of her tongue.

Becker smiled. "Regardless, people in Bulgaria love him."

"You mean the common people?" Slavena raised her eyebrows. "Sure, they love him for his promises to fight corruption and the mafia. But the educated Bulgarians, and the ones who vote know the real truth." Slavena decided to say no more. She was certain the CIA knew everything about the father. Formerly a Secret Service agent, Boychev Senior became Director of the National Police with an empty promise to fight the mafia. His promise was nothing more than sending minor league gangsters behind bars while the big mafia lords became his buddies. Yes, the CIA knew all this but didn't seem to care. She was beginning to taste the true flavor of her new employer.

"I'm not surprised you know about his dad." Becker's voice was soft. "But his son is our mission. Your mission."

She couldn't take her eyes off Boychev on the screen. She scanned the capricious pouting mouth betraying the man's vain and cynical nature. The broad forehead. The strong, dimpled chin. The sloping brows over predator's eyes. She disliked the man, but she knew one of the essential elements in this trade was to keep her personal emotions to herself while doing the things she had to do. It was also the hardest part of her job.

"I just hope he's not like his dad. A dirtbag." She tossed her words like pebbles in a lake, causing serious ripples.

"A dirtbag is not a dirtbag if he is our dirtbag!" Becker's words verged on patronizing now and he knew it, but couldn't stop himself. Had he been alone with Slavena, he'd have given her a lecture on how things worked around here. He'd have knocked out a few illusions. But he didn't want to be condescending towards Slavena in front of an audience. Life in the clandestine world had taught him that officers moved around the world to advance U.S. interests. You could never predict where someone would end up in the hierarchy of the organization. One day his life might depend on Slavena, and he didn't want to make an enemy out of her at their first meeting.

"And it's your job to make him not look like a dirtbag!"

"Yes, sir." Slavena swallowed hard and kept her emotions in check.

"In this folder, you'll find your new Bulgarian passport with a working visa for the US to explain your absence from Bulgaria. Make sure you get your working visa reissued every six months for your cover, and only use your US passports when we ask you to travel."

"Yes, sir."

"You'll also find an identification card, driver's license, and lastly, a fabricated professional license to practice psychotherapy in Bulgaria along with papers for a Doctorate in Clinical Psychology. The credentials are from the University of Sofia. According to university records, you did your residency with Dr. Ivan Pavlov for three years and then opened your own practice following a clinical exchange in Washington DC. Any questions?"

She wanted to ask with what resources and army of staffers she would have at her disposal to win a national election. But knew she'd already dug the first shovel of dirt into a hole. A hole she did not want to dig any further.

"No, sir." She took the folder from the table.

"Have a safe trip and send a budget request through Station for your mission requirements. In my opinion, this is one of the better missions I've seen for a rookie throughout my career. Don't screw it up."

Slavena smiled. "Thank you." She pushed back her chair and stood up.

The three men did not move. Instead, they followed her with their eyes as she walked towards the door. She paced with a stride full of purpose, but deep inside she felt like a powerless pawn on the chessboard. She was left to decide how far she could go before losing her moral high ground. There was no doubt that her task was distasteful, but she had to admit it served the purpose of the United States. If Boychev was a joey in the US Government's pouch, and they wanted him elected so he could become an undisputed leader and an ally to the United States, she could help them with that. She already had a deep understanding of the obstacles she would have to encounter to get him elected and her job wasn't going to be easy. But she was skillful and highly capable of achieving the objectives of the CIA. She reasoned if she successfully developed her campaign and built her sources, the rewards in status and peer respect would be high enough to ignore the ethical pitfall of working for Boychev.

Even a pawn can become a queen one day.

At the thought of this, her confidence slowly pumped back into her veins and she closed the door behind her with dignity.

♟

In the silence that settled in after she left the room, the three men exchanged glances. The photo of Boychev was no longer visible on the screen, forgotten.

"Did you provision for this, Devin? With her history, you must have anticipated some kind of reaction." The third man finally spoke and Slavena had been right: he was in charge.

"We did, but nothing like this. Clearly, our agent triggered something inside her and it concerns me." Becker made a motion with his hand and a piece of paper got dispatched to the wastebasket.

"We need her there, you know. Things are heating up."

"You're telling me."

"But we can't rush this. We need to find if there is something that should concern us. Devin, go over her dossier again and look for something that we missed. In the meantime, contact Rovish. If anyone can figure it out, it's her recruiter."

ROVISH

The second Slavena walked into her hotel room, her phone rang and she answered it right away. It was her recruiter, Dr. Peter Rovish, and his voice was tinged with concern: "Is everything all right?"
"They got to you fast. They're good!" Slavena said bitterly over the phone.
"I'm just concerned about you," Rovish responded.
"About me or my mission?"
"Both!"
Slavena remained silent.
"You there?" Rovish asked.
"Yes, I'm listening."
"If there is something we need to know, you have to tell us," Rovish continued. "And if it's serious enough, we may have to change your mission. You do understand that, right?"
"I do!" Slavena's voice was low, determined.
"It has happened before, you know? I rejected a mission once. But first, you need to build rapport with the Company before you question your mission or they won't tolerate it."

Slavena said nothing, but this time Rovish gave her some space.

"We have to talk," she said at last. "But not on the phone."

"The sooner we talk the better."

"Old Glory on M Street. Give me an hour," Slavena said.

"I'll be there," Rovish said and hung up.

Old Glory was an over-the-top American BBQ restaurant, renowned for its spareribs and rooftop patio. Slavena had been there many times. She loved the bar and atmosphere on the patio. Today, however, was too cold and windy to sit on an ill-shielded rooftop. She knew that Rovish would never talk mission details anywhere else. She wished for a warm drink and a nice, cozy booth, where she could sit and spill her guts to him. She didn't need wind to chill her to the bone. Her thoughts of what she was about to tell him were stormy enough. But it was necessary to tell him what he needed to know.

Slavena walked into Old Glory a few minutes later than agreed. Rovish was nowhere to be seen. Slavena sighed and climbed up to the dreaded patio. She was positive he'd be sitting upstairs nursing a beer by one of the flimsy plastic windows.

Rovish was indeed on the patio, but Slavena had been wrong about his drink of choice. He had a glass of whiskey in his hand and an empty one by his elbow. He was having an early start, Slavena thought. It was just past 3 pm and the patio was empty. The lunch crowd was already gone.

Slavena approached the table and sat in a chair opposite Rovish. He took a sip of his glass and looked at her with a faint smile on his face.

A cheerful waiter approached the table with a couple of menus. "I'll have what he's having," she pointed to Rovish's glass. "That'll be all for me," Slavena said, remembering she hadn't eaten anything all day. She'd been too anxious before her briefing in Langley and too upset afterward to think about food.

Once the waiter left the patio, Slavena looked at Rovish. He was still looking at her, waiting.

Images of what she was about to tell him flooded her head. It had been a decade ago, yet as soon as she recalled her sister's face in her mind's eye, she felt faint. She largely remembered Boyana's face from the photograph in her wallet. All other memories were mercifully veiled over and buried by time.

"What is it that you're not telling me?" Rovish finally asked.

She placed her hands on the armrests, like a schoolgirl called to the principal's office. All Rovish wanted was to know her connection with Dragan Boychev, but the task of having to exhume her memories from that period of her life paralyzed her. She felt like a train wreck survivor that was being forced to remember the exact moments that had blown up her life.

"I didn't come here voluntarily, you know. To this country," Slavena heard her voice coming from outside her head as if someone else was using her vocal cords and not doing a good job of it. "What I mean is…" She swallowed and faltered and then started again. "Everything I had back in Bulgaria was wiped out in one night. So, I escaped. Here. The further, the better, I figured. Nineteen of March, I'm never going to forget that day. I was seventeen. My sister, Boyana, was eighteen. She was the beauty in the family. I was the challenger. It'd been like this from the moment I was born. She surpassed me in everything: height, charm, boyfriends, wit...but she was naive. I had one advantage over her: determination."

Slavena made a long pause and Rovish thought she might not have the strength to carry on, but she did.

"That summer she became distant and she didn't come home one night. In the morning, two police officers came to the house. I wasn't allowed in the room where they talked to my parents, but I listened in. I wish the walls had been thick enough so I didn't hear anything, but I did. I heard all of it."

Slavena looked into Rovish's eyes intently. "They said my sister was dead. Murdered. Raped and dumped in a forest close by. Her car had been spotted crashed by the road and someone called the police. Her body was found close by. Naked and—"

The waiter brought the whiskey and once he caught up with the mood on the table, he quickly disappeared.

Slavena's throat was dry, unlike her eyes that were moist with tears. She took a long sip of the chilled liquid and then looked at Rovish. "You didn't know?" She said. "But you recruited me."

Rovish didn't say anything and kept his eyes on the amber liquid in his glass. To his defense, he cased Slavena thoroughly prior to recommending her for personnel action, but he failed to look closer into the details of her sister's death. Back then, he thought the death of her sister would only make Slavena more resilient. A better candidate for the CIA.

"Slavena, I'm sorry for your tragic loss. I really am. But you can't ruin your future because of what happened in the past."

"I know," she said.

"Were there any suspects?" he asked, watching her for her reaction.

"It was a gang-rape. So there were many suspects."

"This is awful. I understand now why you don't want to go back," he said as softly as he could.

She lifted her eyes up at Rovish, filled with tears and the pain she'd been carrying around for years. He marveled at Slavena's strength. To have been inflicted with such a horrendous wound so young and to have found the strength to keep going. That was a badge of honor.

They kept silent for a while after that. Rovish was at a loss what to say, but the Company wanted their information. Rovish went over the conversation he'd had with Becker this morning: *"She gives the impression of a professional, but when she saw our man's picture on the screen, she looked as if we gave her a shovel without a handle,"* he'd kept on hammering his point. *"So, if there is anything between her and Boychev, it's better for her to tell us now than later on when we are deeper into the mission."*

"So, she knows him?" Rovish'd asked.

"That's for you to find out, buddy. If I knew I wouldn't be calling you. We suspect she knows him, but can't be sure. We found out they both came from the same city, but that is not enough to conclude anything. Find out what that connection between those two is and let me know."

Now it was Rovish's turn to do some thinking of his own: CIA knew about Slavena's sister's murder, that was a given, but not the circumstances. And certainly not its potential connection with the prospective prime minister. She gave the polygraph machine a *flush* when she answered questions about her sister but Rovish didn't think too much about it. Many other applicants lied to the lie-detector when they were asked uncomfortable questions about their siblings. Who would think that Slavena's *flush* would come back at him like a boomerang and slap him in the face? Now that he knew there was more to the story, he was furious Becker didn't brief him properly before he agreed to meet with Slavena.

"Slavena, has anyone been convicted of your sister's death?" he finally asked.

Slavena took a sharp breath and straightened her shoulders. "No. Nobody."

So, the murder was never solved. He needed to be careful not to sound too obvious in his belief there was a link between Dragan Boychev and her sister's killing, but there was no other way. He had to ask. This is what the Company wanted from him.

"Then how is Boychev connected to all this?"

"He's not," she lied. "He has nothing to do with it. His dad, though, was the head of the police at the time, and the police did nothing to investigate my sister's case. It was under his dad's watch when the big criminals escaped justice and prospered as the biggest mafia lords in Bulgaria. This is exactly what I escaped from. The injustice of it all," she said quietly.

"Do you know Dragan Boychev personally?"

She shook her head. "No. I never met him."

Of all questions Rovish could have asked, he'd asked the wrong one. She never met Dragan Boychev in person. That was true. But she knew a great deal about him and his dirty past. Boychev was infatuated with her sister and when Boyana rejected him, he threatened her on numerous occasions. Then she got killed and Boychev suddenly disappeared. Now she knew that he got dispatched by his father to Stanford University.

Those were the exact memories she was terrified of recollecting when she walked on the patio. Now she loathed herself for being too weak to admit the truth because of her intense desire to become a successful officer in the CIA. They gave her a decent mission and she didn't want to disappoint them. Or disappoint herself. But it quickly turned into a slippery ground and she had to make sure she didn't fall down.

Don't get caught lying, she reminded herself for hiding the truth. *Or Rovish will go down along with you.*

Her hazel eyes glanced at him one last time before she turned away. She was afraid of him noticing the shadows of betrayal that layered her eyes. Rovish drained the last sip in his glass and stood up.

"I need to make a call," he said. "I'll be right back."

Slavena didn't acknowledge his words. It was clear for both of them that there had always been a third party in their conversation: him, her, and the Company. They needed to be informed if their mission was vulnerable in any way.

It wasn't.

Rovish took the stairs to the nearly empty dining room on the ground floor. He didn't stop there but carried on and was satisfied his conversation would remain private only when he walked out on the street and into the parking lot next door. There was a secluded spot behind a First Bank and he huddled there against the chilly wind as it picked up speed and dialed Becker's number.

"It's not what you think!" Rovish said assured.

"Does she know him personally?"

"Negative!"

"Are you certain?"

"I am. She never met the guy."

"We couldn't find any connection either. For the last 10 years or so, they lived on two different continents. There is no way they could have met. But the rage in her eyes when she saw his picture makes me cautious!"

"Can you blame her? She tried to escape from a corrupt system and now she is asked to go back and support it? On top of it, she's going to revisit the brutal rape and murder of her sister. Thanks for briefing me about it, by the way. It's nice to know the Company has my back."

"I couldn't do it and you know it. She needed to know you are on her side. If you knew about her sister upfront it would've been like you were in the room with us in the morning. Her against us."

Rovish had to agree. He had a point.

"Did she tell you anything about Boychev?"

"If I was you, I wouldn't worry about him so much. If anything, she hates his corrupt daddy for letting the murderer of her sister walk away from justice."

Becker went silent. He needed Slavena in Bulgaria. They did not have enough field officers to do their job right. But he didn't like it when he had to give in to pressure from newcomers. Slavena had only completed the clearance investigation and her training at the Farm, for Christ's sake. She wasn't even properly in the CIA and was already questioning her mission.

"So, she has principles all of a sudden? She should have thought about it before she joined the Company!"

"What's wrong with having a bit of integrity? I admire her for having the courage to stand up for herself, unlike some of us, who wouldn't even blink an eye if they are asked to betray their own family."

"Peter, I know she's one of yours and I know you're fond of her. But she fits the stereotype of the officer with a foreign background who pledges allegiance to the United States and the moment they land on home soil, they start shoving their own beliefs and political agendas down our throats! Enough already!"

"That's why we don't send them to their home country."

"I have no choice, Peter. Right now, I need more operatives there."

"Then you may have to turn a blind eye on what happened and keep her on the books for now. She is strong and she will do whatever it takes."

"I just hope you vouching for her is not going to bite me in the ass one day."

"Devin, don't drive yourself into nervous exhaustion. She has an intense interest to succeed in the Company and she won't let us down. And don't forget she speaks five languages and shoots as good as you do."

"She is deadly for sure." Becker, who was a former Ranger chuckled. Rovish knew how to tickle his ego. "All right. You convinced me. I'll make sure her orders are in place first thing tomorrow morning?"

"I'll let her know."

Without further pleasantries, Rovish closed his cell and walked back to the restaurant to tell Slavena the good news.

CHIEF OF STATION

It had been a year since her plane touched down at the Sofia airport and spat her out into a city that was beyond her recognition. Slavena remembered Sofia as a sad and shabby place full of equally sad and beaten down people. The streetlights never worked. Rations for everything, especially gasoline. Queues outside dark and dingy shops stocking only Turkish delights and toilet paper. People with drawn faces in Russian cars on their last leg, crawling down roads covered in potholes.

Fast forward ten years and Sofia was beautiful. There were cafés and restaurants on every corner. On the small street where Slavena now lived, she counted five restaurants that were worth a stop. One of them, a low-key diner nestled in a small house covered in ivy was her go-to place for late dinners. Its name was the Green Dragon and it served the best salads in town.

The fleet of cars had changed as well. There were still old cars on the roads, but they weren't Russian made anymore. They were American, French, Italian, German, and even Japanese. The cold war was officially over and the USSR had lost the market.

There were also fancy new cars—big, black sports utility BMWs and Mercedes-Benz limos—that flew down roads defying gravity and basic driving safety standards. They were habitually driven by thick-necked mobsters or *moutri* as the Bulgarians referred to them. The *moutri* or the nouveau riche, who fought fire with fire to maintain their status in society as the top dog. All the contract killings, racketeering, money laundering, and drug trafficking were controlled by them. The force protection team briefed her on the dangerous places and people she needed to stay away from and for the longest time she thought she was safe until recently.

"Girl? Girl!" Slavena heard behind her but didn't turn around. She pretended she didn't know the high-pitched voice of the old lady, who was calling her.

Another old woman stepped out of a hole-in-the-wall shop and poked her in the arm. "I think she means you."

Slavena had no choice, but to turn around and face the white-haired woman, who had been following her for days. "Yes?"

"Are you the one who feeds the cats with food leftovers?" the woman asked, peering shortsightedly from the door. "Do you live here?"

This lady had asked her that same question three times last week and her eyes had been following her everywhere she went since the day Slavena gave her dinner leftover to a begging stray cat.

Rookie mistake, Slavena thought and heard the echo of her instructor's voice from the Farm: *Don't do anything out of the ordinary or the two people watching you today will be five people watching you tomorrow.* Great advice indeed, but how would she have known that by *out of the ordinary*, her instructor meant feeding cats? She only fed the damn cat once and these were the consequences. A bunch of old women finger pointing at her because they had too much time on their hands. Between the daily reports of their bowel movements and their obsessive knitting, they had to inject catty remarks to spice up the monotony of their last days. In Slavena's mind, those were the real spooks she had to worry about. It was a good thing they didn't remember a thing the next day. All thanks to dementia. And a bad thing, that they sneaked on her everywhere she went.

Slavena hadn't known what to expect when she arrived in Bulgaria. The CIA threat briefs focused on the dangers of foreign intelligence services and gave her no warnings of the constant prying eyes that crowded the old town.

She imagined Sofia would be like Southeast Washington DC, where a casual stroll after dark could render you dead. Sofia was nothing like it. Here, the old ladies, or *babichky* as they were known, were on top of the food chain. Nothing and nobody got past them. If they weren't pleased with you, they'd chase you down with the tenacity of a pit bull chasing prey. They had the time to make your life a living hell. Nobody messed with *babichky*.

"I live here," Slavena admitted. "But I didn't feed the cats."

For some bizarre reason, the first line of Bob Marley's song popped in her head.

I shot the sheriff
But I didn't shoot the deputy…

These old women were driving her nuts!

"Hmm," the old lady wasn't satisfied with Slavena's answer. "If I see you feeding the damn cats again, I'll ask my nephew to poison them all." The old woman's voice followed Slavena down the road. "He's already poisoned four, you know!"

Slavena nodded and turned back on her way to her

office. She was already running late. Every morning she walked from her apartment, located on Vitosha Boulevard, towards Malusha Street, where her practice was located in a new glass and steel office building. She had leased a spacy apartment there and furnished it tastefully. She couldn't risk a wandering patient knocking on her door and blowing her cover.

Slavena pushed the heavy glass door of the office building closed and was glad to get away from the noise outside. She looked across the street at the homeless man in the corner. She had noticed him simply because he had a healthy glow on his face. Trained to spot surveillance, she observed and analyzed everyone in her surroundings, including homeless people. Her impression of them was that they were all plagued by health problems and chronic alcoholism. This man, however, was relatively young and healthy to be living on the streets. At the Farm, she'd heard tales of spies disguised as homeless men and it concerned her. This man could be one of them. His poor disguise could easily be explained. He was either in a hurry or perhaps he thought Slavena was too green to notice him. Either way, she realized she couldn't linger in observing him any longer. It was too risky if he noticed her watching him.

She quickly turned around and climbed the stairs to the sixth floor with anxiety. Before she'd become a CIA officer, she rarely paid attention to her environment. Now, every shadow in the dark or footstep in the distance had to be weighed and examined from every perspective.

She stormed inside her office, opened a desk drawer, pulled out her binoculars and peeked from out her window. To her relieve the man was still there, giving her the perfect opportunity to inspect him more carefully. He was sitting on the ground with his legs crossed, waving an empty jar with his left hand. She studied his hands with particular care. His fingernails were clean and polished and there were thin tan lines on his fingers. Her binoculars moved to his upper body. His white T-shirt was spotless as navy whites and the shape of his arms suggested that he was in excellent shape. He was certainly not getting his muscles from waving his jar.

All those were red flags.

"Damn it!" She mumbled as she moved to his face. He angled his head upwards to thank the person who just threw a coin in his jar. Immediately she zoomed her lenses and was relieved to see his dull, dilated pupils. The guy was as high as a kite. He was a brand-new drug addict and it explained the tan lines on his fingers. He had sold his rings. She felt sorry for the guy and was tempted to go out there and get him off the street. Maybe help him straighten up his life, get him clean, and help him find a job.

Then a voice echoed inside her head. *"If I see you feeding the damn cats again, I'll ask my nephew to poison them all."* The old woman followed her around even in her thoughts. But the old woman had a point. Whether feeding homeless cats or guys, it would lead to no good.

Her heightened counter-surveillance was slowly evolving into paranoia.

She switched on the coffee machine in the kitchenette and waited for it to warm up. One thing was for certain. She'd been aching for human contact lately. She hadn't been out of her office since she arrived. Her work called for seventy-hour weeks and she was too tired to go out. Her nightlife consisted of writing reports and falling asleep right after she hit the Send button. For the longest time, since Allan, her ex left her, she had no desire to be with another man. But she was getting lonely. Work became her diversion, and luckily for her, it grew a lot more interesting and occupied all her time for unpleasant thoughts like these.

She put a white porcelain cup with a double espresso by her PowerBook. She used it mainly for open source analysis and networking for her propaganda. She flipped the computer open and scanned through her emails. She had an operation to run. For the past six months, she was actively involved in the recruiting of new agents: a taxi driver and a journalist who was also a public relations expert. They both had one thing in common—greed—and greed always brought excellent results.

Konstantin, the taxi-driver, was the easiest to recruit. She'd found him at a party and learned about his breed: A starving actor, who would do pretty much anything to feed his gambling addiction. He drove her around town without suspecting the CIA was planting drops in the back seat. He never asked any questions and she expected him to be that way as long as he had an addiction.

Most of her emails were from her other agent who was running public relations campaign. Her name was Velina Mentova. A beautiful woman in her early 30s, who prowled through the streets of Sofia to fulfill her need for male attention and complete tasks on the go. She was the epicenter of her propaganda mission. Extremely efficient at providing quality information and the latest rumor when Slavena needed it the most.

It took her six months to shape Velina into a trustworthy agent. She was the political section editor for Vestnik, the largest and most influential newspaper in Bulgaria. She decided what stories to print and what gossip and libel the people of Bulgaria believed. Thanks to Velina's insatiable hunger for a glamorous lifestyle and a steady flow of CIA money, Velina's bias on the upcoming prime minister election was skewed in favor of Boychev. The Vestnik newspaper published story after story of how Boychev would modernize the stagnant Bulgarian economy. End corruption in politics and most importantly declare war on organized crime.

As she sipped her coffee, she noticed an email in her "draft" folder. The Chief of Station kept his communication secret by writing his emails as drafts in their shared Gmail account. It was one of the many ways to conceal their email trafficking by preventing the records of the transmission and the IP addresses on either end. The text was also in Korean. Such encryption helped confuse prying eyes and was another way to fool any curious ease droppers. Since she didn't know any Korean, she copied the first line, *Sah bum nim key,* pasted it into Google translate and waited for the translation. It came as *face the master*. Knowing her boss who used Taekwondo terminology in a cryptic way to talk through a secure line, his *face the master* was his way of asking for a briefing. The next line *Bah ro 10* was everything she needed to know. She looked at the clock on the desktop. It was 9 am.

She slammed the computer top, grabbed her backpack and shot out of the office.

Slavena was staring at herself in the bathroom mirror of a cafe. She had cloned a blond wig with long wavy strands, large sunglasses, a baseball cap, and typical American sneakers. Nobody would recognize her like this, but she was anxious nevertheless.

Whatever the issue was for the urgent briefing, it must

be important enough to break the normal communication silence that came with being a NOC. Bringing her into the US embassy was a serious risk of blowing her cover. But her disguise should take care of that.

Once safely inside the compound and past guard post one, Slavena proceeded to the Defense Attaché conference room, the only Sensitive Compartmented Information Facility (SCIF) in the building.

There was nobody else in the conference room. Just her and the Chief of Station, who was sitting by her side, fidgeting with his pen and patiently waiting for the screen to load. His name was Gavin Boyd. Judging by the enormous dark circles under his eyes, he was not getting much sleep lately and Slavena had an idea why.

Gavin was a walking 48-year-old cliché in the midst of a bad midlife crisis. He was sleeping with a subordinate intelligence analyst, Catherine Hunter. Her last name was not a coincidence. She was a femme fatale par excellence who was endowed in her capability to hunt the men with the most seniority on their shoulders.

Slavena stumbled upon their affair during her in-processing at the Embassy. She'd just finished one of her briefings and on her way to Gavin's office, she noticed Catherine exiting the boss's office with a surreptitious smile. Inside his office, Gavin's messy hair and the wide, gaping collar was a sure giveaway they were doing more than just chatting, but better the analyst than the prostitute down the road. With the analyst, his pillow talk did not cost people their lives. Too many operatives in the shadow world had been burned by loose talk following casual sex.

If nothing else, Gavin was a dedicated case officer that worked long hours and his marriage had broken down years ago as a result. Neither his wife nor his two children wanted anything to do with him. In their minds, he was solely the sponsor.

"We've just stepped into the ring and we've already taken the first jab in the nose." Gavin's opening line was in his usual cryptic way and Slavena wondered how long it would take her to talk like a sour cipher-maniac.

"Are we talking about my mission?"

"Yes."

"Do I need a new cover?"

"No. But you'll need to get out on the street," Gavin carried on. "And do some *real* tradecraft."

Slavena suddenly felt tightness in her neck: What did he mean by *real* tradecraft? She'd been putting in seventy-hour work weeks since the day she arrived. She recruited two worker bees, her agents, in less than a year to deliver the propaganda honey to the queen bee, the Director of the CIA. And here was Gavin telling her that the CIA received nothing from her, but a cavity.

"This is Alexander Orlovsky," the screen on the wall flickered to life and a picture of a man's face emerged on the screen—young, ruthless, expressionless, and striking. He had sharp gray eyes that glittered on his tanned face. A small scar stretched right above his left eyebrow. That was the only flaw as far as Slavena could see. The face was of a man in perfect physical shape. He was sitting at a café, on a French-style white metal chair and was looking straight at the camera.

"Mr. Orlovsky appears vigilant in this photo."

With a click, Gavin filled the screen with a new photo. It was of the same man with his right hand and middle finger pointing to the sky. "Whoever took this photo," He added, turning back to her. "was lucky to walk away without a bullet in his head."

"And why is that?"

"Because Mr. Orlovsky is a specialist in the art of the distant kill. He is a hitman."

A hitman. Slavena studied the face on the screen. She was both intrigued and repelled by the man. Orlovsky's sculptured muscles were clearly visible under the crisp, white T-shirt he had on. He looked like your typical hitman, except for his eyes. Cold as glaciers but hot with rage. She wouldn't want to be this man's enemy.

"All his history is in his file, but I will go over the highlights. Half Bulgarian, half Russian. Moved to Bulgaria with his mother after his father's death, excelled during his compulsory military service at the Navy and later was selected for a naval Special Forces unit Vulni. After the collapse of the communist regime, his unit took ownership of four Bulgarian Naval and Army bases that housed some exportable military hardware. They sold the equipment to African warlords and Middle East radicals and became millionaires overnight. That is how Bulgarian Assets Management or BAM for short was formed. Soon after it was legalized by the state, Orlovsky was paid out his share and headed to work for the Russian mafia."

This alerted her. "What does my mission have to do with him?"

"He has been sent to do a job here in Bulgaria," Gavin continued. "And because his *target* is of such a high value for the Company, you have to first establish close and personal contact with Orlovsky. Then you will monitor him carefully until we find out who had ordered the hit. As of right now, we think it's Russia."

Slavena wanted to ask who the target was but she knew the answer would come later if Gavin thought it was mission essential. So, she proceeded with the less immediate question, "Do we know for sure he's working for the Russian mob?"

"We don't have enough recent data in his dossier to conclude anything. He has been quiet in Russia for a couple years."

A real pro, Slavena thought. "What about the name? Any relation to Peter Orlovsky?"

"Yes. Alexander is his son," Gavin said with an air of finality and Slavena swallowed hard. Peter Orlovsky was well known in the intelligence community as the KGB officer who had carried out one of the highest profile assassinations of the Cold War: the UMBRELLA case. He'd been a tremendously talented spook but had died of alcoholism at a young age.

"So, he's a son of a KGB spook and a hitman? Are you sure I'm qualified for this, sir?" she asked, realizing her words came out with an edge.

Gavin didn't miss it: "What we *do* know is that his father died when he was only thirteen, so although he was born with silver espionage spoon in his mouth, he was way too young to learn any tradecraft from his father."

"But that only makes it worse."

"How so?"

She turned her eyes back to the screen. "Thirteen is a vulnerable age to lose a parent, and if I recall, one of the psychological impacts of such event is a strong drive for overachievement."

"What does that mean?"

"That the son is potentially more lethal than his father."

Gavin tried to twist his wedding ring, forgetting that it wasn't on his finger anymore.

"Possibly, but that's just an assumption."

"True," she said. "What did Langley say?"

"That you can handle him. They're firm on their decision to send you." He gave her the impression that he knew more than what he was ready to tell her, and Slavena wondered if by them he meant Rovish.

"If his target is of such a high value for the Company, then why can't Langley just take him off the street?"

"Because it's more complicated than it looks."

Isn't it always the case with the CIA? Slavena asked herself.

"Let's put Orlovsky aside for a second and talk about the European Union and Bulgaria's accession to it. Any update?"

"Last I heard is that Bulgaria received the green light to join next year on the condition the country intensifies its fight against organized crime and corruption. So far the Bulgarian government has failed to tackle any of those problems."

"And to ensure the entry, I will take it from here," Gavin said. "There was an exclusive order placed to exterminate the mafia leadership. The rumored code name for that is CLEANSING."

"Noted. It's kind of ironic," Slavena smiled.

"What is?"

"The code name. It refers to cleaning up Bulgaria's image, but if the mafia's tentacles get cut, wouldn't they regrow on the next day?"

"Oh sure, but that's none of our concern. What we want is Bulgaria to become part of the EU in 2007 and if the CLEANSING speeds up the entry, we will be in full support."

Slavena took a sip from her coffee and asked, "So, Orlovsky is the chosen hitman for the CLEANSING?"

"That's right!" Gavin said. "And our future prime minister is one of his targets."

Slavena swallowed. "How did *he* earn his spot on that list? I thought it was reserved for the mafia only."

"We don't know that yet, but our analysts seem to think it's Russia's way of securing the seat of the prime minister for one of their own before Bulgaria enters the EU."

"It makes sense, but doesn't it sound a bit too aggressive?"

"That's how Russia likes to tinker, but as I said we don't know this for sure until you confirm it."

From what Gavin was telling her, Russia didn't oppose Bulgaria being part of the big European family as long as they looks."

"And if I confirm it? What happens next?"

"We'll have an account lined up and on stand-by for negotiations. But we'll discuss that when you reach the meat phase of your operation." Gavin clarified and pushed a thin folder towards her. "Here is Orlovsky's profile. I suggest you study it in detail. When you make contact with him, you better know this man better than he knows himself. He is a tough nut to crack and you would need all the information you can get your hands on. This is just the start. The rest you'll have to gather yourself."

"Will I have full support?"

"Absolutely. Everyone has already been briefed."

"Guns?"

Caught by surprise, Gavin froze. "You *do* know the provision for that. It carries too much risk if you get caught."

"I'll take the risk."

"That's too much red tape if you ask me."

"Langley can't expect me to babysit a hitman without a gun!"

It took Gavin a few seconds to think. "I'll look into it but if things get out of control, you'll have the East Europe and Caucus A team on stand-by."

That was his closing line. He'd done his brief and would have to let her stew on it a bit. He smoothed down his trousers and walked towards the door.

As she stepped out of the conference room, she felt her chest contract with unfamiliar tightness. She was no longer in a good position on the chessboard. But good positions didn't win games. Good moves did and Alexander Orlovsky was one of them.

♟

On her ride back home in the embassy car, she looked at the folder. It contained no more than ten pages. Not a lot was known about a man who'd been at work for almost two decades. He was either good at avoiding attention or the CIA wasn't telling her everything. Either way, she'd have a lot of groundwork to do.

Orlovsky's profile photo brought her back to when she was a student back at the Farm. She'd been sitting along with the other students in the auditorium and listening to their instructor: "If you joined the Agency in the hopes of meeting a Hollywood-lookalike agent in the field, then you might as well pack your bags tonight and go home. Because I'm here to tell you that perhaps, only one of you in this room will be lucky enough to meet such a gem."

I must be the lucky one, she thought with a smile as she continued to look at the picture. His features, magnetic and cruel, his dark hair, and his piercing gray eyes were overpowering. Orlovsky was certainly a gem—great to look at—but at what price?

There was only one way to find out. By learning everything about Orlovsky. She leafed through the first few pages and it was the fourth page that cut her breath like a knife— "...*routinely worked with its Soviet sister unit, KGB's Spetsnaz unit Directorate "B", better known as Vympel.*" She read the next sentence with narrowed eyes. "*Deployed to Afghanistan from November 1986 to February 1989 while assigned to Naval Special Forces unit Vulni, attached to Russian Spetzgruppa 'V', more commonly known as Vympel.*"

"Son of a gun!" she mumbled and opened her tinted window just enough to get some fresh air. She needed to think: Not only did Orlovsky know the tradecraft, but he knew it well and he learned it from the best. Vympel was the legendary KGB Directorate "V" paramilitary group, both admired and feared within the global intelligence community. She wondered why Gavin downplayed this important detail about his past.

Was he afraid to admit it to her face?

And what did he mean by establishing close and personal contact with Orlovsky? She looked at the picture one last time before she closed the file. Orlovsky was very attractive. There was no doubt about that. But could she sleep with him if she had to? Gavin's explicit hints suddenly reversed her excitement about meeting Orlovsky. It was strange how psychological reactance worked: push me and I will resist.

The car pulled five blocks away from her apartment and the Embassy driver gave her a moment to scan the area for any potential surveillance. She opened the passenger door and exited with a polite smile. With her backpack on, she walked to the nearest park to make a phone call. She dialed the number of her local analyst and the same woman Gavin was sleeping with.

"Cat, I need a huge favor."

"Anything for you doll!" Catherine said cheerfully in her southern drawl.

"I need a copy of the UMBRELLA case and the psychological profile of the man behind it," Slavena said. She reasoned the best way to get to know Alexander Orlovsky was through his dad.

"I'll arrange for a brush pass," Catherine was already "briefed" by Gavin. "Are you staying in town this weekend?"

"No, heading for a little sunshine—"

"The Black Sea?"

"Yes," she said now confident there was no one watching or following her. "Sunny Beach," Slavena said determinedly. She wasn't authorized to go on vacation, but as the NOC she was obliged to go anywhere without approvals if her naked feeling told her to do so. If they wanted her to confirm the CLEANSING, then Sunny Beach was the place to be. Where all the mobsters vacationed in the hot August weather.

"You're going during the hurricane season?"

Hurricane was code for an infiltration.

"Yup. That's why I need an *umbrella*." Slavena stressed on the last word and Catherine understood.

"I'll get you that umbrella," she said, but the only sound Slavena could register was the wind rustling the branches of the trees.

The hurricane season had already begun.

JARO

A young man dressed in black stepped forward as Slavena was about to enter the hotel elevator. "Do you need a hand with your luggage?"

She was tempted to decline his offer. Her pathetic suitcase weighed no more than 20 pounds but she realized the man's income depended on tips, so she let him pick it up and carry it in.

Once in the room, she tipped the bellboy $10 and in exchange, he slid a flash drive inside her palm and left. The surprise element of the brush pass tingled her nerves. She anxiously slid the little piece of metal inside her pocket while scanning around for any cameras and closed the door.

She found herself in a room furnished by surreal Salvador Dali décor. She touched the silky sheets on the king-size bed and eyed the misshapen clock on the wall above it with amusement. The mobsters obviously liked their hotel décor distorted, just like the twisted world they lived in. Slavena couldn't blame them: everyone needed validation for whatever reality they created in their heads.

Mobsters were mere humans despite what they liked to think of themselves.

She walked to the balcony and slid open the glass door. The view was spectacular. The reflected sun rays glittering on the sea and the cries of seagulls soaring over the golden strip of sand. Slavena was pleased with her investment. What better way to collect information about mafia lords than to lay your towel on the beach right next to their wives and kids.

The private beach in front of the hotel was separated in two large sections by a long straw-roofed bar planted divisively in the middle. Bars were the hub of gossip and a perfect starting point for her. She changed into a swimsuit and tied a sarong over it. She chucked sunglasses, sun cream, her wallet and keys in a bag and walked to the beach.

Tanned and fit bodies laid on the beach like colorful confetti sprinkled in the sand. Slavena sensed the oval-shaped bar separated the beach in half for a reason. Not wanting to pick a side just yet, she took a seat at the head of the bar. The bartenders flashed her a smile but didn't approach her right away. She was certain she was wreaking havoc in the strict hierarchy of the mafia world, but in order to find a place in it, she needed to make a hole first.

From a distance, one of the bartenders approached her.

"What can I get you?" He asked in clumsy English. His face was sunburned.

"A mojito, please."

"Which side are you sitting on?" The bartender indicated with both thumbs pointing to the left and to the right of the bar.

"I'm sitting right here." Slavena tapped her fingertip on the polished wooden bar top. "Which is good news for you."

"Why is that?"

"Because you don't have to walk on the beach to bring me my drink."

"Oh, so you noticed my burned nose?" He smiled. "Mojito, it is then!" He turned around and walked away. Slavena hid her eyes behind dark sunglasses and watched the bartender's muscular back while he made her drink. Ever since her last briefing, she realized her thoughts had increasingly become sexual in nature. Alexander Orlovsky had woken up her dormant sexuality and she was wondering how she was going to stuff it back in the box again. She was a bit disappointed in herself about that. She'd thought herself tougher, choosier. Instead, she was eyeing the bartender.

"Here you go." The bartender put a tiny white serviette on the bar top and positioned a tall glass in the center of it. Inside, a couple of ice cubes swam along some dried-up mint leaves. Slavena took a sip and realized the only thing they didn't skimp on in this bar was the alcohol.

"Cash or room number?"

"Cash please."

While they exchanged notes Slavena asked a few casual questions.

"So, what's the deal with the two sides of the beach?"

"Have you been here before?"

Slavena slurped her already warm drink and shook her head. "Never."

"I figured."

"How so?"

"Why did you choose this hotel?"

Slavena wasn't pleased that all her questions were answered with questions, but this wasn't new to her.

Bulgarians were notorious for being inquisitive and discreet all the same time. She figured that's why she got recruited by the CIA.

"I stumbled upon the hotel online. The photos and the reviews were very appealing."

"I see." The bartender was skeptical and for a reason. Very few 'normal' Bulgarians would spend a month's salary for one night's stay here. And that excluded food and drinks. Slavena had to find a better explanation if she wanted to sound credible.

"My boyfriend from Germany booked the vacation, but work held him up. I didn't want our vacation to go to waste, so here I am. Alone." She shrugged.

"I knew you wouldn't be paying for it yourself."

"I guess so," Slavena said, thinking of the CIA.

"In that case, you can go to either side of the beach," the bartender leaned forward, close to Slavena's ear and carried on in a low voice. "You must have realized by now what kind of Bulgarians we have here?"

Slavena nodded. "I have. It's obvious, although it wasn't mentioned on the website."

The man smiled.

"On this side," the bartender inclined his head left, "are the wives and kids. And on that side are the mistresses."

Slavena's eyes widened with disbelief. "You serious?"

"Perfectly. Neither side acknowledges the other nor do they intermingle." The bartender gave her a wink and disappeared to serve a new customer.

Slavena pulled back in her chair and looked at the women and children on the beach. The wives' side appeared busier than the mistresses' side, mainly because of the shrieking children and middle-aged women, presumably nannies, chasing them around with bottles of sunscreen. The wives, easily recognizable amongst all the fuss for their deliberate idleness, looked exactly the same as the mistresses, only older.

Choosing sides wasn't easy. Which side would provide her with more information? The mistresses would undoubtedly be the mobsters' more favorable companion and would know the most current information, but the wives had been around longer. Also, they were bound to be bitter about being cast aside and more willing to talk.

The generous amount of alcohol in her mojito and the bright sun made her head slowly spin. She walked back to the foyer of the hotel when she spotted a couple of bulky men standing by the restaurant's entrance. In their hands, cradled like babies, were a pair of MP5s.

At the sight of the assault rifles amongst near-naked bodies and barefooted children, Slavena felt she was in an alternate reality universe. What were these people doing here, so heavily armed? She did a subtle double take on the scene with her eyes of the scene and was surprised to see a woman sitting alone inside the restaurant. A naked boy of about two crawled at her feet. Were the MP5 men guarding her? The woman pulled out a jewel-encrusted cell phone from her purse, looked at the screen and then at the entrance of the restaurant. It appeared that the armed men and the woman were waiting for someone. And he hadn't arrived yet.

Slavena walked past the scene and out to the restaurant's patio by the pool. She chose a table that was close to the wall and took a seat where she could see the reflection of the woman's table in one of the glass doors. It wasn't a perfect visual point but enough to surveil her and find out for whom she was waiting. She was attractive but looked tired,

Slavena observed, and strangely human among all the pointy tits and swollen lips that were everywhere.

Suddenly, there was a flurry of activity inside the restaurant. A few more thick-set men passed by the tables and surveilled the patio and the swimming pool area outside. They paid no heed to Slavena who pretended to be engrossed with the blank screen of her phone. She noticed that all of the bodyguards had little pig-tail cables running behind their ears and into their T-shirts. The kind of security that cost a lot of money. Slavena waited with anticipation.

A man dressed in a white linen shirt and knee-length blue chinos walked in and sat at the woman's table with his back towards Slavena. She cursed inwards at her carelessness. She should've chosen a spot with a good view of the empty chairs around the table, not just the woman. Now she couldn't see the man. She was too far away to hear whatever the conversation was about. Her snooping was useless. She wouldn't get anything out of this.

Yet, she kept on watching the scene reflected in the glass door. The man's back was broad, like those of the men guarding him, but the intensity he emitted was of another kind. His bodyguards who were spread out with their MP5s kept their eyes open and alert.

Determined to see his face, Slavena decided to risk it and casually walked through the restaurant, to the bathroom. The bodyguards didn't try to stop her.

Walking deliberately slow, Slavena passed by the table in the center of the restaurant. The man was looking down at the crawling toddler.

"Goddamn it, Sylvia!" He swore at the woman as Slavena passed by. "Put a fucking diaper on this child."

"I'm potty training him," The woman said quietly.

"Do it when I'm gone then."

"That's what I am doing, Jaro, you are always gone."

At the sound of his name, Slavena's nerves jerked and she hurried her steps. Jaro was a high-echelon mobster from her hometown Plovdiv and because of it Slavena already knew a lot about him. He was a former Olympic wrestler, known for his incredible luck.

The story of Jaro's most glorious days of him winning his first Olympic silver medal had circulated in Plovdiv for years. Slavena was only eleven back then. He won silver in the 1988 Seoul Olympic Games in the Greco-Roman light heavyweight class by pure luck. His Russian opponent, Mikhail Vladimov, fell ill to a virus right before the finals. The same viral infection struck Jaro a week prior to the games. He lost significant weight, qualifying him for a lower weight category. He easily rode into the Olympic finals and won silver.

He was a legend in Plovdiv and liked by many. But she despised him since the day he was found "not guilty" for the murder of her sister.

CLEANSING

Slavena woke up from the sun rays that were streaming in the room. Bright and overly-cheerful, completely at odds with her sour mood. She walked towards the balcony and watched the Black Sea from afar. It was just past 9 am, yet the air was already heating up and rising above the mellow waves. It was going to be another hot day by the sea.

She skipped breakfast and after a long run on the beach and a swim she settled down in the wives' section of the beach. Save for a middle-aged woman and a screaming child, the section was deserted.

"They say it will reach 40 degrees today," the middle-aged woman said to Slavena without preliminaries. "I can tell you're not one of them," the woman carried on. "You read books, not gossip magazines. I've never seen anyone in this hotel with a book and I've been here for a while."

"Well," Slavena played along. "Since I don't have any children, I have plenty of time for everything."

The old lady was right.

"Huh! You think they look after their children? That's left to old hags like myself. All they do is party at night and take manicures, pedicures, hairdressing, make-up, and massages. Anything, but to spend time with their children."

The wives started showing up around noon. All prepped up with glossy hair, make-up, and well-oiled skin. They requested the children be taken indoors, fed, and put down for afternoon naps. Once the kids were gone, the beach filled up with a different kind of chatter. The wives leafed through magazines, shared gossip over screeching chats on their cell-phones, admired each other's nails, and ordered cocktails. They discussed the side effects of plastic surgeries—ranging from total loss of nipple sensation to life-threatening deep vein thrombosis—and exchanged references about surgeons.

But mostly, they bitched about the women on the other side of the beach. The mistresses. The competition. The segregation of the wives' side of the beach from that of mistresses was clear for all to see and strictly enforced. Wives did not interact with mistresses and vice versa, but both parties knew the other was there. The wives' fixation with the mistresses of their husbands sounded pathetic to Slavena. There were no men around, all seemed too busy with running the "business". In their absence, all that was left to do, for both sides of the beach, was to obsess with the other side of the beach. And obsess they did. Every detail, every overheard word, and minor incident was dissected with gusto.

And Slavena's surveillance cameras caught it all, video and audio.

In the late afternoon, the situation escalated when two women approached the mistresses' side of the beach. They were holding hands and they were both stunningly beautiful, but one drew particular attention to herself. She was a spectacular specimen of her kind—tall, graceful and perfectly formed. Her face was hidden under the brim of a black, floppy sunhat. Her swimsuit was cut so low it bordered on scandalous. *So much for the art of seduction and leaving it to the imagination,* Slavena thought.

As the woman approached, Slavena noticed that the top of her two-piece bikini wasn't made out of cloth at all. It was two metal snakes that wove themselves around the woman's body and circled her perky breasts. The heads of the snakes rested on the nipples.

"Fucking cunt!" Grumbled one wife to another. "Showing off her new tits paid for by my husband!"

"She is doing it on purpose, Niki. Don't you see that? She wants to piss you off."

Slavena noticed that the wife's lips were trembling. The woman was on the verge of tears. That was the first genuine human emotion Slavena had witnessed since she'd arrived the day before.

"I'll go check out what's the new gossip," another wife suggested. Seemingly, she didn't have a rival in the other camp and she was quite smug about it.

The woman stood up and donned a see-through tunic with a Versace logo print scattered all over it. It showed off her shapely legs while covering up the angry-red cesarean scar below her belly button. It seemed to Slavena that everyone here was trapped in a catch 22: a woman needed a child, or children, to tie a man up. But as soon as she gave birth and became less attractive, that same man found himself a shinier model. The mistresses wanted to become wives only to be entangled in the same paradox a few short years later. The only consolation both sides had was the deep pockets of their husbands.

Slavena realized she was getting no useful information here, so she abandoned her listening post and went for a cocktail at the bar. She needed to find a better way to integrate herself with the *moutri*. She sat at the bar, which was busier than usual, but Milo, the bartender who served her the day before, came towards her right away.

"Mojito again?" Slavena remembered the strong cocktail from the day prior and shuddered.

"I'll have a beer if it's cold."

"Corona ok? I don't have anything else. Beer isn't exactly popular around here." He gave her a playful smile.

"Corona is fine," she said, returning his smile. "Thanks."

She sat facing the mistresses now and wondered if it was worth trying that side out tomorrow. She felt she was wasting her time here. She was surrounded by brick-brained bodyguards and anorexic women escaping reality. She wasn't in the right place, she knew. Spy craft was ninety percent trying out tactics that never paid off and extreme amounts of patience. Something she was already beginning to lose. But how do you penetrate this elusive mass of people? How do you get to where the decisions were made and fast?

"What did you get him?" a skinny man sitting next to her asked another man with a protruding beer belly.

"A painting. I heard he appreciates art."

"As long as it's not religious. Last time Little Christ got him an icon, Jaro burned it in the fireplace." The chubby guy snickered and took a sip from his glass.

Slavena had never heard of Little Christ before and made a mental note to search reporting on the name later. Jaro, on the other hand, was a name quite familiar to her. She reasoned he was here to celebrate his birthday, finally giving her the information, she needed.

"Did you hear the Sinner is coming to the party?"

"Is that right? I thought they didn't see eye to eye."

"Nobody misses Jaro's party. You never know when the last one is going to be" The men chuckled.

Slavena mentally chuckled with them. She had read up on key figures in the Bulgarian mafia before leaving for Sunny Beach. If the Sinner — the most powerful mobster in Bulgaria and Jaro's biggest competitor — was coming to the birthday party, then the party would be more business meeting than celebration. The moutri were getting together to discuss something important and she bet it was the CLEANSING.

"What time do you plan on showing up tonight?"

"About ten. Was thinking of having a drink first on my balcony and keep an eye on the party. I'm in 403 if you want to join me?"

"You're right. Nobody will show up downstairs at nine o'clock. Let's do it"

Slavena's mind was racing. She'd give her right arm to be a fly on the wall at that birthday party. It was the perfect opportunity, yet there was no way she'd be allowed access. She finished her beer and walked quickly back to her room to call Velina.

"Where are you?" Velina was concerned.

"Buried with work. What can you tell me about Jaro?" Slavena asked, hoping that Velina wouldn't ask too many questions.

"He is the Vice President of the BNB. The Bulgarian National Bank." Velina clarified and carried on. "Rumor is he's going to Sunny Beach to celebrate his birthday with his friends, and by friends that means his enemies too."

"Is Little Christ a friend of his?"

"He is Jaro's pet. A cocky little rat," Velina said. "Do you want me to find out more details about the party?"

"No. I assume it's going to be private."

"Private and well-guarded," Velina confirmed. "I'm afraid there is no way you'd be able to slip in uninvited."

No way, unless you're a CIA officer, Slavena thought and smiled big in the privacy of her own hotel room. Then she saw the clock and her smile quickly evaporated. It was already 5 pm. That party was her chance to get as much information out of the mobsters as possible, yet she had less than four hours to find a way in.

Under her feet, at the main hall of the restaurant, the preparation of the party was underway. She could hear the scraping of table legs dragged across the floor. She heard the rapid exchange between management and staff about what and how things should be done through the open window. Slavena guessed any performance less than perfection could get someone fired, or worse. Bulgarian mobsters were notorious for being demanding and cruel.

Slavena tried to slow down her racing brain. Yesterday, while observing the scene between Jaro and his wife, she'd also gotten a good look at the layout of the restaurant. She needed to delve in her memory and find a plausible way in. She closed her eyes, brought up the scene at the table in her mind, and devised a plan.

She pulled out the kit that Travis, her tech guy, had given her right before she left Sofia for Sunny Beach. She ripped the plastic red line with her teeth and spilled the contents onto the bed. It was an arrow that was so small, she barely noticed it. She picked up the piece of paper and studied the instructions. Then she looked at her watch and her mind swirled with panic. There was no time for plan B. Not even time to sit down and think. She had to move fast.

Slavena glided to the reception desk carrying a glass. "Where can I get some ice?" she asked the receptionists.

"Ice?" One of the women that had been staring at a computer screen was now watching Slavena with a perplexed expression.

"Yes, ice."

"Of course, we have ice." Slavena heard a man's voice from behind her. "It's in the kitchen's freezer. Come with me!" It was the bellboy.

"But I'm afraid nobody is allowed—"

"She is with me," he said as he flashed his charming smile at the receptionist.

"Great!" Slavena smiled back. "Finally, some ice in this hotel."

The receptionist regarded them with her big brown eyes and opened a hatch in the reception desk to beckon them in. Slavena couldn't believe her luck. She rushed past the other receptionist who wore an alarmed expression. Women here had developed predator's instincts towards impostors and Slavena was still new scenery to the hotel employees.

She followed the bellboy and walked behind a door that led into a small office Slavena didn't know existed just a moment earlier. "Kitchen is this way." The man gestured down a long corridor brightly lit by fluorescent tubes. "I'll wait here and if anyone comes, I'll deal with the situation. You have to trust me. You won't be disturbed, but you only have five minutes!"

"I like roses," she replied.

"You mean orchids?" He smiled and she smiled back. Knowing the code meant he was properly briefed by Gavin and he was to be trusted. Whether he was a CIA operative undercover or a well-placed, well-paid agent was unclear. Slavena didn't care either. She had the access she needed to get the job done.

Slavena walked slowly in the direction of the kitchen and passed a sign that read *Authorized Personnel Only*. She pushed the swinging hinged door, like all doors designed to be opened by waiters carrying heavy trays and found herself alone in the private VIP room of the restaurant.

The VIP room was already prepared for the party. The joined tables were covered by a giant tablecloth in dramatic black with gold Versace logos. A lonely, fat bottle of 15-year-old Dimple sat in the middle. Tiny glass bottles of water were arranged next to wide crystal glasses. The room was simple, yet luxurious.

Without missing a beat, Slavena kneeled to the floor and shot up to the ceiling. The little arrow with the microphone lodged into the marbled plaster by a lamp and disappeared from view. Slavena exited the room without a second glance.

"You got it?" The bellboy asked.

She nodded and together they walked back to the reception.

When her watch showed it was close to 12 am and there were still no sounds in her earpiece, she was ready to give up. If there had been anything else, she could have been doing to collect information, she'd have abandoned the project—cursing Travis and his Chinese-made piece of crap equipment—but there wasn't. So, she waited.

She must have nodded off at some point because suddenly there was laughter in her ear and chairs scraping on the floor. A group of men had entered the room, talking all at once. Slavena sat up in alarm and adjusted the earpiece back in her ears.

"Thanks, everyone for coming to my birthday party and to this meeting."

Slavena recognized the voice. It was Jaro.

"Some couldn't make it," there was bitterness in Jaro's voice. "The Sinner isn't here. Bankov is also missing."

"The Sinner couldn't make it," another voice barked. "He's test-driving his new toy."

"You mean his new mistress?" someone in the room joked and sporadic laughter followed.

"Shut up, Little Christ!" The voice was agitated. "His new toy happens to be a brand new Azimut-800, sitting in the Marina Yacht Port in Saint Vlas."

"Well, I have a name for his yacht," Jaro inserted. "How about the *Last Sinner*?"

This time there was no laughter, only nerve-wrenching silence. Upstairs, in her bed, Slavena was also silent, waiting for more words to come into her earpiece.

"Soon he'll regret his absence," Jaro carried on. "But that's his loss. Not mine!"

"I heard he's planning to retire in Cape Town."

"Even better!" Jaro's voice rose. "If anyone wants to join him in Africa and peel his bananas, leave now. The rest of us businessmen need to make a plan right here, right now."

By the lack of scraping chairs or response of any kind, Slavena concluded everyone stayed put.

"Nothing is carved in stone," Jaro continued, "but Bulgaria will join the EU in 2007. Mark my words. And when that happens, the EU will think they can come in here and control Bulgaria. But this is our country and we are the Government. Last elections I gave two million euro for political campaigns. I'm safe for now, but that'll be the last time. The political parties have been told to clean up their act if they want Bulgaria to be part of the big European party. And they will."

"Meaning?"

"Get rid of us," Jaro said.

"How? They can't put us in prison. We own the police, the judges and all the prisons."

Murmurs in agreement reached Slavena all the way upstairs.

"Exactly. They're going to kill us," Jaro said.

"Kill us?"

Another wave of laughter followed.

"Yes. Kill us. And my source tells me soon they will try."

"Wait a minute. Are we talking about government sanctioned killings?"

"Possibly."

"Who is your source?"

"A politician I trust," Jaro said. "He told me there's been a list of many contract killings of powerful men like us. They're calling it the CLEANSING. There was a payment wired to a Swiss bank account. My man didn't know who was on that list or how many. But he knew five million dollars had been paid into that account as a deposit. You tell me how many will be killed for that much money."

"Who got the list?"

"A single hired gun."

"You mean one person is supposed to kill us all?"

Laughter again, but this time it was uneasy.

"Yes," Jaro said so quietly that Slavena almost missed it.

"No one could pull that off. We're too well protected"

"Maybe. But I warn you, the time for squabbling is over. Tighten your security. Put out feelers. Release your hounds. Among us, we know all the hired killers around. We must be able to find that son of a bitch."

The mobsters carried on talking. Slavena listened to their conversation in her headphones until the end, but her mind was racing. The CLEANSING rumor was true, and thanks to Langley, she knew who the hired hitman was. Now more than ever, it was important to make contact with Orlovsky.

Easier said than done. Orlovsky was a dangerous man and she feared him. On the surface, he was her enemy, but deep down Slavena saw him as a natural ally against the parasites that were sucking the blood from Bulgaria. The same men that had murdered her sister.

♟

She checked out early in the morning on Sunday. The only person minding the desk that early was Bea. Slavena already knew the names of the receptionists.

"You are leaving two days early?" she asked Slavena.

"Yes. I can't sleep here! It's impossible with the noise and everything." Slavena completed her rant with a heated gesture she'd copied from some of the women on the beach.

Bea smiled thinly but said nothing, just kept on typing on the computer. Slavena turned her back to the reception to cut off further questioning. She looked towards the pool area visible through the glass doors. The usually immaculate patio looked like a mess. Upturned tables, broken glasses, and cloth napkins littered the ground.

Slavena shivered with disgust. These people were animals. You give them a perfect piece of nature, the best food and drinks money can buy, and what did they do with all that? Ruin it in every possible way. She was glad she was leaving.

"Ms. Taneva!" For a split second, Slavena had forgotten her alias. She kept on looking at the pool area and frowning. She turned to face the receptionist.

"Yes?"

"Here is your ID and an envelope arrived for you."
"Thank you."
"Do you need help with your luggage?"
"No," she said but handed her a significant tip with the keys. "For your help yesterday."
Bea looked at the cash and her manner became subservient. "Thank you! Have a safe journey home. We hope to see you again."
"Ciao!" Slavena picked up her bag and walked out.
Slavena's Toyota had been parked in a corner of the parking lot so remote and overgrown by weeds that it looked disused. The front parking area was reserved for posh cars like Ferraris, Lamborghinis, Bentleys, and one Aston Martin. Her Toyota didn't meet the mark so it was banished in the corner. Slavena drove off feeling relieved to be alone at last. How people thrived in packs like these — the moutri and their entourage — was beyond her. She was exhausted after only a couple of days.
Inside her car, she opened the envelope and read: *Check your glove compartment.* She unlocked the glove compartment where a Glock 26 Gen4 laid inside invitingly. She took out the gun and opened the chamber. It was full. She moved the catch to "safe" and sat holding the gun with a smile. She never asked for his name, but the bellboy executed his mission brilliantly.
Gavin didn't let her down.
The streets of Sunny Beach were deserted on Sunday mornings like no other day. The only people out and about were dog walkers and heavy smokers out on the prowl for cigarettes after a heavy Saturday night partying.
As soon as she left the resort and hit the highway to Sofia, the fog in her thoughts lifted. The sprawling sunflower fields on both sides of the road, backed up by tall mountains in the distance, provided perfect grounds for her

imagination to wander. She turned on the radio, put the volume up and started to make plans on how best to catch Orlovsky's attention.

Other than the file Gavin had provided her, she hadn't done any baseline work on him yet. From Orlovsky's dossier, she knew a great deal about him already such as the places he favored. His schedule from the moment he had his cappuccino in the morning at Caffeinated till dawn when he drank scotch at his favorite bar, Amnesia. According to his profile, he was a loner and had no friends. He hardly ever slept with the same woman twice and almost always picked up his women at clubs. She figured the women were attracted to his bad-boy demeanor and they clustered around him like ants around a honey jar. And just like honey could be deadly to ants, Orlovsky was violent with them. She imagined women leaving his apartment licking split lips and sporting angry red marks on their limbs.

Slavena shivered and turned down her AC to the lowest setting, but she knew it wasn't the cold air that chilled her to the bone. It was Orlovsky and his raging eyes that made her nerves crawl. The worst thing about it was her self-doubt. Somebody in the Company thought she was cunning enough to deal with this predator when in reality she was the prey, curled deep into her hole, too afraid to sniff her way out.

"What the hell were they thinking?" she mumbled and turned off the music to focus on her thoughts: Langley knew she wasn't experienced for this, but they rallied her into a tight hole anyway, because they either had no one else to run the mission, or they had full confidence Slavena could handle a man like Orlovsky.

She liked to believe that it was the last. The Company knew she and Orlovsky had a lot in common. They'd both lost their closest family member at a young age. They'd both moved away to a foreign country shortly after and learned to operate on instincts, live in a state of constant readiness, spot every potential danger, and take advantage of every opportunity. Their own tragedy turned them into lone wolves with keen survival instincts.

But for an instinct to form, there needed to be panic in the air. And there wasn't any until she came to the resort. That's what drew her to Sunny Beach. Not only to confirm the CLEANSING rumor but as a mental exercise to fire her nerves and prepare her operationally for what was to cross her way: A man with a knack for shortening human life. A skill he inherited from his father, one of the most famous KGB assassins ever.

The more she read about the dad, the more intimidating her mission seemed. The UMBRELLA case was the real reason why she decided to cut her holiday short. She could have spent another day or two to devise a plan on how to stalk, infiltrate and pitch her way into Orlovsky's brain, but there was no time for thinking up her next move. Not now when her opponent — Alexander Orlovsky — was raised and trained by the Grandmaster. And his dad was exactly that.

A Grandmaster.

From what she read already, Peter Orlovsky was a sophisticated high breed of KGB officer. Having cut his teeth in the jungles of Nicaragua, leading teams of Sandinistas guerrillas in the '70s, Peter Orlovsky gained his status as the KGB operative who mortally poisoned a BBC journalist with an umbrella on London Bridge in broad daylight. The UMBRELLA murder became known as one of the highest profile assassinations of the Cold War.

Orlovsky Senior's resume was indeed impressive, but what unnerved her the most was his psychological profile. He was a narcissistic sociopath with a history that would terrify any psychiatrist. Slavena was convinced this trait trickled down to his only child — Alexander.

Realizing this, the thought of her meeting the son excited her even more. She would finally get to use her Psychology degree to exploit a target, but her knowledge wasn't enough to outwit a man like Orlovsky. He was probably too good at his game since he'd been doing it all his life. She figured the only way to go against him was to learn everything about him. How he operated. The key to his inner life. What hid behind his larger-than-life psyche? Everything! But the most important part, and possibly the hardest, was to attract him.

That was the plan.

She turned the radio back on and toyed with different scenarios about making his acquaintance. She thought of paying a couple of guys to pretend to attack her in the parking lot of Orlovsky's favorite bar. He could conveniently come out just on time and "save" her. No man could resist helping a damsel in distress. And if he saw her as a victim, he wouldn't be threatened by her.

But then it'd be difficult for her to convince him she was his equal later on, so they could maintain contact. It was vital for her mission for them to stay in touch. She needed to think of something that would make it possible for her to approach him with ease but allow her to hold her ground.

She was beginning to know Orlovsky and with her mind engaged with his, Slavena managed to reach Sofia.

SNOW WHITE

It was 12 am and nightclub Sugalips was already buzzing with people when she entered it. Slavena approached the hostess and asked for her reservation in the VIP room. The hostess curved her petite body towards the stairs and Slavena followed her while taking notice of her frail back, molded in a see-through dress.
Too young to be working here, Slavena thought.
"First time here?" The hostess turned around to ask and Slavena nodded, saving her breath for later when she would need to talk over the loud music. She had to make sure she didn't end up with a hoarse voice during her first meeting with her target.
On her way to the second floor, Slavena caught one last sight of herself in a full-length mirror. Ninety-five percent of the VIP crowd were mobsters with their mistresses and she knew to blend in with them was not an easy task. She wondered if she looked expensive enough. Sure, her outfit cost her a whole paycheck, the equivalent to the annual income of the average Bulgarian family, but in her mind, that was not enough. What she needed for a proper display were diamonds and she didn't own any. Luckily those were the easiest to fake in the dim lights of a club with the right

choice of dress.

She rocked a black Hervé Léger dress with a cross-side fake ammunition belt that revealed the hourglass figure of an assassin femme fatale on her mission to seduce. The only thing missing from the picture was her two 9mm Glocks in both hands. She only carried one Glock 26 Gen4 concealed in her inner thigh holster where no one could see it. To complement her dress of a killer, she wore Jimmy Choo sandals with skyscraper heels that made her toned legs look endless. With those shoes, she thought, she could only kill herself.

She was betting the dress was Orlovsky's style, with his attitude—*don't talk to me or I will fucking kill you*—written all over it. The kind of dress a woman would wear as a repellent, hoping to intimidate every bug in her surroundings. And the club was full of them—the ordinary men, who had nothing to offer her.

Right before she entered the VIP room, she adjusted her fake diamond earrings with her hand to soothe her nerves. Inside the room of opulent extravaganza, she was relieved to find out the type of people who could buy real two-karat diamond earrings as easily as a pack of cigarettes was not there.

The VIP room was empty.

Or she thought it was empty. The smell of expensive cologne gave away the group of men sitting in the far corner, conveniently hidden from the entrance. She identified one man right away. It was Little Christ with his gang. She had built profiles of all the important mobsters after her trip to Sunny Beach and she was glad to see her efforts paying off. As she continued to follow the hostess to her table, she heard the men appraising her silky legs as if they were for sale. And they were that night but only for one man and that man was Alexander Orlovsky.

Unfazed by their predatory stares, she sat on a leather sofa, crossed her legs, feeling the handgun between them as a reminder of who she was — a well-trained CIA officer who was capable of protecting herself. With that thought, she ordered a drink and prepared herself for an interesting night.

She took a few minutes to settle down before she effectively scanned the crowd and registered Orlovsky. He was sitting at the main bar with his back to her sipping his drink. She stared shamelessly at his muscular torso imprinted inside his tight, black shirt and imagined how his muscles moved when he was in action.

"Your Kafka martini." The waitress placed her drink in front of her with a big smile. Slavena returned the smile and realized immediately her own mistake. She had invested so much time and money into getting the right outfit but it had slipped her mind that attitude was the most important accessory of her disguise. It was simple, but a vital mistake that could crumble her cover. Then again what was already done was done.

She sipped her drink and turned her gaze to the dance floor.

Most all the men had their eyes glued to the women dancing. Orlovsky instead sat at the bar with his back to the crowd, focused on the screen of his phone. This worried her. If he expected company — especially a woman — that could complicate things, and this was her best chance to make first contact with him before the CLEANSING began.

She continued to observe him for ten minutes before sitting back in her seat. Thus far, she was puzzled by his behavior. Her image of him as a player had faded in her books. He showed no signs of being the aggressive predator his psychological profile suggested and that highlighted further the possibility he was expecting someone.

Downstairs, the crowd had doubled. She noticed a group of high school girls, dancing all tribal right behind Orlovsky's back. The most beautiful one of them coiled every inch of her gorgeous body towards Orlovsky and that annoyed Slavena. No doubt she was the most attractive woman in the club and if she didn't get the attention of everyone on the prowl for the night, she did now after the DJ announced: "Let me hear the BIRTHDAY GIRL make some NOISE!!!"

Hearing this, the same pretty girl screamed out and everyone looked in her direction. Everyone but Orlovsky. He remained stoic and Slavena assessed he was disinterested in the world around him. Or he had already collected every detail about his new prey—age, height, levels of vulnerability and whether she was going home with him.

Slavena looked at her watch. It was already past two in the morning and she was running out of time. She zeroed in on the birthday girl who looked barely eighteen. *So young and naive*, she thought, *just like my sister*. The girl's seductive dance subconsciously brought Slavena back to the night when Jaro and his buddies raped her sister. Boyana was also provocative, like this girl, and Slavena had for the first time a glimpse of how it all started. Her sister dancing in the club and seducing the wrong type of guys. She wondered if things would have been different if Boyana hadn't gone out that night.

Lost in her thoughts, Slavena drifted back to Orlovsky, who was now aiming his phone directly at her.

She froze.

Was he taking photos of her? The possibility of it made her want to sink her body deep into the sofa like a deflated doll, but he would have noticed. He was a professional and was watching her every move. Instead, she remained still and continued to keep the same visual. With her nerves tightening and her mind racing, she took a large gulp of her martini. Was it time to approach him? The answer was no. He was surveilling the VIP room now and his target was likely not her.

At the realization of that, she turned to face the same group of men in the VIP room that were catcalling her earlier. If anybody was a potential target for Orlovsky, it was Little Christ who sat in the middle of a big leather couch. She knew he was Jaro's right hand and the same man who gave Jaro an Orthodox Christian icon for his birthday. Despite his publicized piety, she had found out Little Christ was a notorious gang rapist, who converted to religion to wash away his sins.

Little Christ winked at her and her skin crawled. Didn't seem religion changed him one bit. Disturbed by his predatory behavior, she turned back to Orlovsky, who was now paying his bar bill. Seeing that, Slavena immediately signaled the waitress for her own tab only to find seconds later, the waitress brought her another drink instead.

"Compliments of the gentleman in the corner," the waitress said while placing an exotic blue cocktail in front of Slavena.

"The man in the middle?"

"Yes. Do you know him?"

"No," Slavena lied. "Does he come here often?"

The waitress nodded. "Great tipper, but a nasty piece of work. If he wants something, he always gets it and if I were you..." she lowered herself close to Slavena to take the empty glass and whispered over the DJ's music. "I would be *very* careful."

Slavena knew what she meant. Little Christ was a notoriously dangerous man, but her concern shifted to another urgent matter. The birthday girl was successfully seducing Orlovsky with all the right moves—whispering, touching, sticking her chest out—and Slavena became convinced that Orlovsky was going to leave with her. Her observations corroborated with his CIA dossier that he picked up his women from clubs. She knew she was too late to stop it.

"Damn it!" She cursed under her breath while reaching for her purse.

"Your tab is taken care off," the waitress said and walked away with the tray.

Her eyes darkened. Her interesting night had suddenly become dangerous. She was no longer concerned with Orlovsky. Little Christ posed an immediate threat that needed to be dealt with.

Slavena opened her purse and pulled out a box of cigarettes. She was not a smoker, but she knew all mafia mistresses, known as the moutressi, shared one thing in common—smoking. To complete her cover as a confident moutressa, she needed to acquire the nasty habit of smoking.

She lit a cigarette, inhaled slowly until the smoke filled her lungs. She nearly coughed but controlled it. There was no room for mistakes. Not here. Not now. She exhaled a dense cloud of smoke, giving her the needed disguise to resume her observation of the men in the corner. There were seven of them.

"You got the wrong Snow-White you fucking dwarfs!" She muttered at the irony. Only those men were not the harmless dwarfs from the fairy tale. They were trolls, with thick necks and big heads who knew all too well how to protect their boss.

She put out her cigarette in the ashtray slowly, watching her perfectly steady fingers. Fear had not yet entered her mind. If anything had, it was the feeling of raw power over the men who kept on looking at her as an object, thinking they were entitled to her body because they were powerful and rich. Little did they know, this object they were staring at, was an expert marksman who held the type of grudge that only a machine gun could wash away. Lucky for them, she only carried a handgun tonight.

Then logic settled in. She knew the odds of defeating seven armed men were bad enough to signal for backup support. But she was a NOC. And NOCs didn't operate with backup.

Different exit strategies ricocheted inside her head, but none seemed doable without blowing her cover. She couldn't take any chances. If she wanted to get out of this unscathed, she needed to make a deliberate move. She picked up her purse, stood up, and suddenly felt light-headed and weak like a newborn colt taking its first steps. It was immediately clear that her last drink was laced. The Rohypnol, which was the date rape drug they probably used, was entering her bloodstream and hitting her brain with full force, releasing the first wave of panic. She cursed herself for drinking the cocktail. No matter how well she would open the game, her opponent had already placed his pawns in a superior position.

But the CIA had taught her how to keep composure under the influence of alcohol and truth serum-like drugs. She was prepared to avoid this date rape. She made about ten steps, towards the exit when one of the bodyguards — the youngest and the least experienced in her impression — stood and closed in on her.

"Where do you think you're going with those legs?" he growled.

"To the bathroom. Do you mind?" She went to move past him, but he blocked her again.

"My boss minds," he lashed. "He wants me to tell you

nothing will save your holes tonight."

"Wow. How chivalrous of him, and who's your boss?"

"Little Christ"

"Never heard of him." She lied.

"Never?" He raised his heavy eyebrows and laughed with a crooked smile. "Well, you'll get to know him tonight."

"I don't think so," she said. "Tell Baby Jesus my boyfriend is atheist and doesn't respect the Christian faith. Can you remember all that?"

"And where is your boyfriend now?"

"He's tucking his wife into bed."

He looked at his watch. "Did you mean fucking his wife? It's almost two. Which means he's not coming tonight."

He's right. Nobody is coming to save me tonight, she heard her subconscious voice growl in survival mode, already plotting her next move. She tilted on her high heels and gently touched the back of his thick neck with her right hand. She wasn't able to get Orlovsky tonight, but at least she learned from the birthday girl a few good moves to soften a man.

"You may be right," she said while eyeing Little Christ, "My boyfriend may not be coming but is your boss psychotic enough to risk his life for one fuck?"

"Who the fuck is your boyfriend?"

It's about time you asked asshole.

"The Sinner! Have you heard of him?"

The bodyguard exploded with laughter, but knowing he was being watched by his boss, he quickly returned his composure to serious.

"Nice try, but the Sinner prefers his women blonde with no brain and huge tits."

"Thanks for the compliments, but there is a first time for everybody!"

"If you belonged to him, as you say, the Sinner would have sent his guards with you."

"Why would I need guards when I have this?" She pressed the muzzle of her Glock to his chest and then for exactly five seconds, she counted, he stood still. She leveled her eyes to his and smiled. The roofie they gave her was making her fearless and aggressive.

Sensing the tension in the air, Little Christ jerked his head and two of his guards stood up. Judging by the size of muscles and the number of prison tattoos on their arms, these were his most experienced ones.

"You're outgunned bitch!" the young bodyguard said self-assured, knowing support was on its way.

He's right about that too, she thought. If she fired her gun and blew open his chest right in front of everyone, the rest of them would rip her apart like a pack of hyenas. She knew bluffing was her only way out, so she carried on. "I'll take my chances."

"Bitch, you're not just gonna get raped tonight. You're gonna die."

His breath blew hot against her face and her muscles trembled with tension.

"I told you. I'm taken," she said while looking at the two bodyguards slowly coming towards her. She still had room to negotiate, although its walls were contracting by the second.

"Little Christ won't buy it. You're not the Sinner's woman."

"Oh but he will," she said recalling the conversation from Jaro's birthday party at Sunny Beach. "He'll realize his mistake when you tell him the Sinner didn't appreciate his nasty joke about test-driving me on his yacht." She pressed on with her bluff.

"What model is the yacht?"

"Azimut 800, sitting in the Marina Yacht Port in Saint Vlas. Any more questions?"

Hearing this, the guard eyed her with less confidence and stepped away to call off his colleagues before they made a grave mistake. She'd got the timing right. Relieved, she smiled and lowered her gun to her side. Convinced the danger had passed, she gathered all the grace she could muster and floated towards the exit. On the way out, she locked eyes with Little Christ and winked at him before his ugly mug disappeared from her sight. Little Christ finally understood that despite the Rohypnol, the only consent she was willing to give him was a bullet in his head.

She walked out of the club as a chess player and not the chess piece they thought she was.

ALEXANDER

Alexander Orlovsky woke up late. With his arms tucked under the pillow, he laid on his stomach watching the well-lit bedroom window. It was partially obstructed by his muscular shoulder. The tattoo of a bull skull on his arm was visible just below the windowsill.

The girl from last night also had a tattoo. The wings above her delicate shoulders made her look like an angel in disguise. He had found her in a dance club. A beautiful blonde with bold blue eyes and sinuous scent lacing the air. She was quite a dancer, *this angel*, teasing him with every move she had, but she couldn't wing him the way she had hoped.

He recalled sitting on his bedroom couch, stark naked, watching her crawl on all fours. Her perky ass and heavy tits moving in unison as she worked her seduction. The whole performance was funny rather than erotic, but he didn't expect much from a girl half his age. When she finally got on top of him to ride him like a cowgirl, she slapped his face. Not hard, but enough to provoke the post-traumatic demon inside him. It was when she slapped him for the second time that he reacted subconsciously by punching her back. She'd given him a wounded stare, picked her clothes from off the floor, and ran away.

And here he was now, in his bed with a painful erection, picturing her beautiful curves and wishing she was still around. The only reminder of the *angel* was her heavenly scent that lingered on his pillow with the saying "May angels guard you through the night and keep you safe till morning light."

"Fuck angels!" He stood up with a growl. "And hello demon," he said at his reflection in the mirror. His tanned post gym muscular physique complemented his short chestnut colored hair, clear, attentive gray eyes, and perfect teeth. But his most attractive feature was his focused confidence. In a way, the bitch had done him a favor. He needed his sleep now more than ever because he needed to be in shape—both mentally and physically—for his new job. He was hired to pull the trigger on some leading figures of the Bulgarian criminal world and this required his full concentration.

He sat on the bed letting his feet drop to the cool floor and blessed the man who created the air-conditioner. He despised the hot August weather, and if it wasn't for his new job, he would have been gone by now. And not to the crowded beach resorts where all Bulgarians went for their summer vacation. Instead, he'd go somewhere rainy, vast and cruel. Normandy perhaps or Holland where he liked the red-light district and the coffeehouses.

He looked outside his window at the city panorama and stretched with a big yawn. The only thing he liked about August was the empty streets. Gone were the obnoxious mothers with their snotty children crawling all around. Gone were the teenagers drinking on the streets. Everyone was gone to the sea. He pictured the people at the beach, laying on the sand, towel to towel, ass to ass, like greased-up sea lions frying in the sun, and shook his head with disgust.

"Fucking idiots," he mumbled. There was no doubt in his mind, Sofia was the better place to be in August. While doing his morning stretches, an object in the kitchen caught his eyes. It was the half-empty scotch bottle on the kitchen counter. He stopped his stretching abruptly with his brow knitted in a frown. Who was he kidding? The weather and the people were not the problems. It was his idling around, the waiting, and the anticipation for his work to start that made him start drinking again. He was becoming like his father — a restless alcoholic.

He stormed towards the bottle, grabbed its neck, and dumped the amber liquid into the sink. The muscles on his face loosened with each drop. Once empty, he threw the bottle in the trash. The loud shattering of the glass silenced his thoughts that he had done exactly this every morning for the past month. Only to buy a new bottle the next day.

Today, he was convinced things were going to change.

He turned on the stereo and with a few swift movements back and forth to his fridge, he made himself a protein smoothie. He gulped what he could. The rest, he dumped into the sink and started his coffee machine.

At the sound of cappuccino streaming down the cup, he went to his closet. He put on a white linen shirt, a pair of navy blue shorts, drank his coffee on foot and sprinted down the stairs to his garage. He never used the elevator. Ever since that time in Kiev, when he planted his first bomb in the elevator of the Sheraton hotel in downtown. The memory of the explosion made him proud. It took the recovery team a whole week to find all the pieces of flesh scattered in the rubble of the building. Since that day, the stairs had become his best friends.

Once his Range Rover peeled out of his garage, he sped towards the gym. He had a Titan T3-X at home, but lately, he had increased his workouts to a whole-day routine, including massages and swimming. That could only be accomplished at a gym.

The health club he frequented belonged to the diplomatic corps in Bulgaria during communist times. It was a complex of low buildings and tennis courts on the slopes of mountain surrounding Sofia. It had an Olympic-size swimming pool, saunas, Jacuzzis, outdoor hot tub, individual changing rooms, but best of all—it was always empty. It accepted only a certain number of members per year and was chiefly used by them for networking, not exercising.

Today, like most days, there was only one car in the members' parking lot. A luxury edition Chrysler Jeep that belonged to a tiny blond who only used the Jacuzzis.

"How are you this morning, Mr. Orlovsky?" The gym receptionist had flirted daily with him for the past two weeks now.

Orlovsky stopped before the desk and rapped on the surface with the knuckles of his right hand. He hated small talk.

"Here is your key. Room 29." The woman smiled again.

After he left his changing room, he warmed up with a hundred alternate hammer curls. The repetition usually put him in a determined frame of mind, but today his thoughts drifted. The memory of a different woman from the club kept popping in his head and distracted him. She sparked his interest from the moment he saw her shadow upstairs. The woman, whoever she was, had observed him from the VIP room on the second floor of the club and was suspiciously attentive to every move he made. He couldn't see her face in the dark, but there was a certain vibe around her that caught his eye. Her self-reliant pose, strong shoulders and down to earth mannerism convinced him that she was not just another indulged moutressa. He could spot moutressi from afar. They crawled like worms, enduring all sort of humiliation just to be seen in the luminous salons of the elite.

She was definitely not one of them and she was in the club by herself. In fact, it was her solitude that made her that much more appealing. No woman would have dared to sit alone in the VIP room unless she was well protected. He would have approached her if it wasn't the *angel* who pleaded with him using her big innocent eyes.

Murphy's Law, he thought. Now that he had his mind-set on his new job, women—beautiful women—were coming from every corner to distract him.

He moved on to deltoid raise and aimed at a two hundred. By the time he was done, his shoulders were screaming in pain but his mind refused to engage.

"Damn women!" he muttered while wiping the sweat that was getting in his eyes. He had to stop thinking with his dick if he was to complete the deal that was coming his way.

Frustrated, he picked up his towel. He was done for the day.

Back to room 29, he took a hot shower, masturbating under the solid water stream. He came with a groan but realized he was just as unsatisfied as before he started. He watched the water carry his semen down the drain with mixed emotions of relief and anger. He needed to get back to work. It'd been too long.

"Mr. Orlovsky! Leaving so soon? Is everything all right?" The receptionist's face displayed surprise but her pose—

three-button deep neckline and a visible tits-crack—told him that she had known he'd be coming. There were spies everywhere, including this gym. He was used to being watched. He walked on without a word.

He drove to the city center and stopped for coffee at his favorite place called Caffeinated. It was close to lunchtime. Caffeinated didn't serve food, so he didn't expect a crowd anytime soon.

He ordered a double long espresso and while he waited for his coffee, he observed a couple arguing a few yards away on a park bench. The woman had jet-black hair pulled back and the same color expression on her face. The man was a bum in a cheap suit with a guilty expression on his face. Whatever the woman accused him of doing— cheating, lying, stealing—Orlovsky could bet she was right. He'd always been a good judge of character. It was important for his work.

A taxi pulled up on the other side of the park and a sleek brunette came out of it. Orlovsky wouldn't have paid any attention had it not been for the eye contact he and the woman made all the way across the park.

Another fucking woman, Orlovsky thought as he watched her close the door of the taxi and walked down the park's alley towards where he was sitting. She was athletic and walked with confidence. Orlovsky liked athletic women but too often they became beefy and stiff. This one had everything going for her—muscles and agility. She smiled at him.

"Your espresso!" The waitress said. "Would you like anything else?"

Distracted by the question, Orlovsky turned to face the waitress. When he turned back, the woman in the park was gone. He scanned the alleys and the benches, but couldn't see her anywhere. He grunted a "no" to the waitress and took a sip from his coffee while sitting back in his chair trying to relax in the sun. The taxi woman appeared by his elbow.

"You are here early," she said with a smile. "That's nice of you!"

"What?" Orlovsky said, frowning. Her undetected appearance by his side unnerved him. Nobody snuck up on him. He did that to other people.

"You are Alex, aren't you?" The woman said. She shifted her weight from one leg to the other on her high heels.

Orlovsky stared at her face. Who was this woman? How did she know his name? He was certain he had never met her before, although she seemed familiar. She wore glasses and wasn't strikingly beautiful, like his usual groupies, but her hazel eyes captivated him from the start. They were alert and observant like the eyes of a lioness, well too aware of her surroundings. Her lips were full but nude as if she was hiding them from predators like him who had discovered plump-lipped women were better at lip service.

The woman smiled down at him as if she already knew him, but it didn't escape him that her expression was somewhat guarded.

He gave her a once over sliding his eye down her body that had sparked interest in him a few minutes earlier. She wore a white silk top under which her perky breasts were well contoured. He liked the size and shape. Her legs reminded him of the professional tennis player he'd banged once. The best pair of legs to go around his midriff, as far as he was concerned.

"How do you know my name?" He asked at length.

"From your profile on the website." She laughed. "How else could I've learned it?"

"What profile? What website? What are you talking about?" His instincts were urging him to flee. Yet the woman, in her high heels and black pencil skirt, didn't represent any kind of danger he'd come across before.

"I don't understand," she said. Her vibrant smile began to crumble. "This meeting was your idea, not mine. I was against it."

Orlovsky shifted in the chair. He was used to being two steps ahead of everyone at working out complex situations. Not knowing what was going on right now made him uneasy.

"You are not making any sense," he told her. "Start over."

The woman took the chair opposite Orlovsky.

"I have a blind date with a man that looks like you and is called Alexander. What are the chances?" She said. Then she put her black leather bag on the table and whipped a Blackberry out. Her thumbs crawled fast over the keypad. "I'll show you."

Orlovsky watched her. One thing was for certain—she wasn't after his money. Often women spotted his Rolex Yacht-Master II and tried to chat him up to sponge off him. This one was different. For a start, she had a cell phone half the population of Bulgaria coveted after but which had the dents and scratches of a well-used item, not a display prop. For another, her shoes were brand-new and expensive. She either didn't walk a lot or had many pairs of shoes. Either way, he approved.

"Look," she turned the display of the Blackberry to him. It was showing a profile on a dating site called EliteDate.com that had his name and picture on it.

"I don't believe this; what kind of bullshit is that?!" Orlovsky grabbed the phone from her hand and scrolled down. The woman was right. He'd been chatting her up for some time. Who would set him up like that? And what was the point?

"I'd love to look into those hazelnut eyes of yours in person," Alex from EliteDate.com had written. And "I'm positive we have lots to give to each other." Was that cheese love drivel or was it a hint? Was this woman here to give him the first name of his CLEANSING list? It was fucking twisted but in his line of business, people were rarely straight thinkers.

She took off her glasses and placed them on the table with a defiant gesture. He looked up at the woman fully for the first time, admiring the proportion of her features. Without her glasses, he realized, she looked as dazzling as a New Year's Eve sparkler—her features were spirited and arresting. The cheekbones were perfect, the eyes large and bright and the tiny freckle above her upper lip was intoxicating to look at. The woman was certainly full of surprises and knew how to command his attention. But it wasn't her looks or her confidence that piqued his interest. It was something else that he could not define quite yet and it made his breath stand still.

Was she a present from someone? In his experience elite escorts made a lot of money. She could easily buy phones, cars, and shoes for herself if she was an elite pro. But if she was an escort, she was a damn good actress. Sure as hell he could see she wasn't impressed with the situation they were stuck in either.

He handed her back the phone. He'd decided to stick around and find out more. He was interested where it would all lead.

"What's your name then?" He asked, already knowing the answer.

"Alena. Listen," she put her hands down on the table. "Someone is obviously playing a prank on us. I should be going."

Before he could say anything, the waitress appeared at the table.

"Nothing for me, thanks," Alena said.

"No," Orlovsky interrupted her. "She'll have a cappuccino."

Alena gave him a puzzled look.

"We'll talk this over," he said.

Alena inclined her head. "A cappuccino, then."

Orlovsky wasn't ready to make it easy for this woman. Alena, as she'd called herself, looked suspiciously comfortable in the presence of someone she knew had been a fake acquaintance, and she'd consented to a drink with him too easily for him to respect her.

He prided himself on knowing people but also on knowing women particularly well. They were a specialty of his, a hobby, a research field. He no longer knew how many women he had been with, but the number ran into the hundreds. He was proud of that, although he wasn't ready to acknowledge that for some of the women the experience hadn't always been pleasant. Last night included.

He knew Alena was here for a reason. He could tell she was hiding something from him and he didn't like it. He decided to be provocative in an attempt to shake the truth out of her.

"Bring lots of sugar," Orlovsky said to the retreating waitress. "Alena here needs to sweeten up after a bitter disappointment on the dating front."

He watched Alena's face carefully for traces of any emotion, but there was nothing. Her eyes narrowed as he spoke, but she didn't show any sign of anxiety. She was just as confident as when she'd approached him. She was either good at hiding her feelings or he was the one being pranked. He would need to dig deep to find what this charade was all about.

The waitress came back placing a cappuccino before Alena and dumping a bunch of sugar packets in the middle of the table.

With the sugar, lying on neutral grounds, Alena and Orlovsky played a staring game. Both knew that whoever looked away first would be one step behind on the challenges up front. Alena was sitting back in her chair comfortable looking at him and smiling faintly.

"I know the reason you're here," Orlovsky said eventually.

Alena inclined her head to one side. "Do you now? And what is it?"

He picked up the sugar packets from the middle of the table and ripped them open—all fifteen of them. He spilled the sugar on the glass surface.

"Spell the name." He told her. "Use your fingers."

Alena picked up the cappuccino cup with both hands and tasted the temperature of the liquid with her lips. She was calm and precise, Orlovsky noticed, not rattled as he'd expected her to be by now. She was enjoying this and it annoyed him.

"Come the fuck on," he urged her.

Alena smoothed the sugar over and began to write with her long index finger. The letters she wrote were upside down for Orlovsky, so he had to crane his neck to read them.

"*WTF*," she wrote and leaned back in the chair.

"W... T... F?" Orlovsky pronounced the letters in a deliberate manner as if testing the flavor of the sounds. As soon as he said it, a thin smile flashed across Alena's face. Recognition darkened Orlovsky's features. "*What the fuck?*" He said with acidity in his voice.

"Yes. *What the fuck* do you want from me?"

"What do *I* want from you? I'm not the one sitting at a stranger's table and drinking coffee with a dude I chatted up online..." Orlovsky scoffed. He finally figured out what he liked about her. It was the quality of her courage. This woman wasn't afraid of anything and he imagined the things he could do to make her heart race fast.

"And I'm not the one with a tattoo on my shoulder that symbolizes pigheadedness and a tendency to promiscuity." Alena was looking at the bull skull visible bellow his short-sleeved top.

"What are you? A fucking psychic?"

"Precisely. I can read you like an open palm, Mr. God's gift to women. And you know what? I don't find arrogance attractive. Your appeal of a callous narcissist might be hard for women with dependent personalities to resist, but I couldn't give two shits about it. If you'd excuse me I have a life to live and patients waiting for me. Good-bye!"

Alena's bright hazel eyes flashed at him in a final glance before she got up. She threw some banknotes on the table, grabbed her handbag and swung if off the table. She walked across the park and waved to a taxi on the street. Once inside she gave the address to the driver and relaxed for the first time in days. As the car moved on, she leaned back and closed her eyes.

"And now I wait," Slavena mumbled inside the taxi.

Back on the table, Orlovsky watched Alena walk away with narrowed eyes. Nobody spoke to him like that, least of all a woman.

Bitch.

He watched the defined muscles of her legs contracting while carrying her away. He fiddled with his car keys, trying hard not to look at her, but she took a hold of him like the kind of woman who had the knowledge of a man at her fingertips and knew how to use it. It was when her taxi sped away that he recognized her silhouette.

Orlovsky chucked some money on the table and left the café with a confident smile. He didn't need to find her after all. The woman from the VIP room came to him first. But the question now was why? What was she after? And how soon can he put her in tears?

There was one way to find out. He dialed a phone number.

"Archie you free?" He asked.

"No," a sulky male voice answered.

"Too bad. I'm coming over."

Orlovsky hung up.

ARCHIE

Archie lived with his mother in a boxy and cramped apartment in a part of Sofia bearing the melodramatic name "Freedom". Freedom from what exactly wasn't clear, but it was obvious what the neighborhood wasn't free from: concrete. Anywhere one looked the ground and adjacent lands were covered with that grey and crumbling material. It gave the appearance of a graveyard.

Orlovsky parked his Range Rover on the street by the building where Archie's apartment was. The fifteen-story building was soaring up to the sky like the middle finger of a rebellious teenager. Orlovsky looked up towards the bright blue balcony on the twelfth floor, where he was heading. All balconies of the monolithic building looked identical: grubby and stuffed with junk. Archie's balcony was visible all the way from street level because of the half-finished paint job on the outside. Shortly after the communists became Democrats, nineteen-year-old Archie decided to paint the balcony of their apartment blue. It was supposed to be a hallmark of his opposition to "the reds" as the communists were popularly known. His enthusiasm had lasted only an afternoon or half a balcony, and the result of this was still visible some fifteen years later.

Archie's real name was Archangel, but nobody called him that. Some of his recent acquaintances didn't even know he had a real name. His name was short for archiver since Archie was one of the first Internet search engines created back in the 1990s.

In the shady world of Internet porn lords naming themselves the *Devil's Crew* and *Dark Stud*, Archie's civil name was a minority. He had a fierce reputation among the most reputable hackers of Eastern Europe as the man for break-ins. There wasn't a website or web-based database he couldn't find an entry point to. Mostly for fun. Orlovsky was one of his few paying customers and Archie resented him for it. He resented anyone his age that had enough money to afford their own place, away from their parents. That was pretty much everyone. If it hadn't been that Orlovsky and Archie were in the same Navy unit, Vulni, they would never have met and Orlovsky would have been forced to use a different, less talented hacker.

Orlovsky entered the cool interior of the building and shivered with disgust. The building was inhabited by forty-five families and looked like the floor hadn't been cleaned in years. *Lazy pigs*. Orlovsky's mouth curled with the thought. He sprinted up the twelve flights of stairs. He hated elevators.

On the twelfth floor, the lightbulb had blown, so Orlovsky made his way in the semi-darkness. He kicked an empty fuchsia-colored plastic pot and it rumbled down the corridor with a gritty sound against the dirty floor. Before he could ring the bell, Archie's mother opened the door and poked a mousy face above the door chain.

"Alex, is that you?" she peered at Orlovsky shortsightedly. "You've put on weight at last. Not a skinny bum anymore, huh?"

Orlovsky hated that Archie's mother knew him from the time he had been an awkward skinny sailor.

"Is Archie home?" he grumbled.

"Don't be stupid. Of course, he's home. When has he not been in?" Archie's mother spoke with a certain tenderness about her son that always irritated Orlovsky. She let him in.

Orlovsky crossed the short corridor to Archie's room and walked in without knocking. The hacker's room was pitch dark that smelled of stale clothes. Archie sat in a chair before three computer screens, all of them showing a woman's vagina from up close. Archie's fingers were working fast on the keyboard and he didn't lift his head up to see who had come in.

"Not hungry, Mom," he said. "I'll wait till dinner."

"Not your mom." Orlovsky slapped Archie's bony shoulder and knocked him against the middle screen. It wobbled unsteadily and made the vagina on it to appear to be moving.

"Eagle! You got here fast. Wait until I finish this frame." Archie's main source of income was editing porn movies. It didn't pay well but he got to watch all the latest stuff before it hit the Internet. "Done." Archie swiveled his chair around to face Orlovsky. "What do you want?"

"Got to break into a dating site." Archie showed no surprise at the request. He'd heard weirder from Orlovsky before but was still curious.

"I haven't got much time. Got to deliver this to the States before their workday starts, which is…" he turned back to the three screens. "Now!"

"Five hundred dollars." That was more than Archie's mother made in a month as a nurse in the local clinic.

"All right," Archie conceded.

"EliteDate.com"

Archie entered the name and pressed Enter. A login screen popped up. A man and a woman in a light embrace in the background.

"Someone has created a profile in my name. Need to find out who and when."

"Password must be between eight and twelve symbols." Archie was reading, already fast at work. "One uppercase, three base digits, two no alphanumeric characters. Of course. We are not idiots."

With few clicks, the picture of the vagina was replaced by a light blue screen and sequel server computer code. His fingers danced on the keyboard and eight minutes later the fake profile was cracked open.

"This profile has only chatted with one chick," Archie's fingers hovered over the keyboard. "Alena Balkanska. Not bad looking. Wait. That's strange."

"What?"

"She only chatted with your fake profile. Her profile must be fake as well."

"She's real enough." Orlovsky murmured. "When were these profiles created?"

Archie searched the information tables. "Only a week ago. Both on the same day and same hour. Could dig deeper, but I would put money they were created from the same IP address."

Orlovsky pointed at Alena's smiling face on the screen. "What info has this bitch given?"

"Work address and a cell phone. Everything you should not put on a dating site." Archie printed it out from a black desktop printer in a corner.

Orlovsky looked at Alena's picture with an angry face. What was she after? It annoyed him that he couldn't figure it out. He picked up the paper and folding it in quarters stuffed it in his back pocket.

On the three screens, Archie had already brought the porn back up and resumed working. Orlovsky threw some banknotes by his elbow and walked out without another word.

His thoughts were full of Alena, not only because of the unanswered questions that surrounded her. The chick was intriguing. If she was playing some game to get his attention it was working.

Out on the street, he was walking towards the car when his cell phone vibrated in his pocket. He raised the phone to his ear but gave no courtesy or greeting. It was a trademark of his to not indicate he had answered but only listen instead. Usually, it rattled whoever was calling surprisingly well.

"Hello?" A female voice said. "Hello?" The voice betrayed confusion. Frustration. "Anyone there? I can't hear anything."

Orlovsky sensed the woman was about to hang up. "Who are you?" He said.

"Hi. The connection is bad."

Orlovsky said nothing.

"I have something for you," the woman said.

"Not over the phone," Orlovsky warned. "Where do we meet?"

"Hotel Diplomat. It's on—"

"I know where it is. I'll be there in half an hour."

"I might not make it that—"

"You better make it." Orlovsky got in the car, chucked the phone on the passenger seat and sped off.

A name at last. He could hardly wait.

Hotel Diplomat was built only a decade ago but already looked worn out and haggard. The building was ill-conceived—heavy on the top to compensate the lack of ground space—and appallingly executed. Inside, the unauthentic posh interior had patchy walls, peeling railings, and crumbling floor tiles.

Orlovsky knew the hotel well because it was a well-established pickup place for prostitutes. Even now, in the late afternoon with no customers around, there were quite a few women lounging about in overly provocative outfits. From high bar stools and corner sofas they eyed him appraisingly, but sensing he wasn't interested, they didn't bother to approach him. Orlovsky took a chair at the bar that had a direct view of the revolving door he'd just come through.

"Johnny Walker Blue neat," he told the bartender who rushed to prepare his drink. While he waited, he took out the piece of paper with Alena's pictures and read the text. The address she had given was in the city center, not even five minutes away from the hotel he was sitting in.

On the picture, she wore a pink Ralph Lauren shirt that complemented her sun-kissed skin. She was smiling with her perfectly even and white teeth. She looked glowing and confident. He liked that. Alena Balkanska, it said underneath, twenty-eight years old. Single, no kids. Profession: psychotherapist. A smile spread on Orlovsky's lips. That explained her self-confidence—she thought that by understanding how people minds worked, she was better than anyone. That could make for an interesting game. He anticipated having a lot of fun with this one.

He folded the paper and put it back in his pocket. His cell phone indicated the conversation with the woman had happened twenty-seven minutes ago. She should be here any moment. Just as his drink arrived, a girl walked in the hotel and looked around.

She was very young and thin. His employer liked them almost criminally young like most all-powerful men did. Powerful enough that he wanted the women around him to be young and frail, so when standing next to them he'd appear a superhero. Judging by the shabby two-piece suit — short skirt, tight jacket and boots reaching above the knee, this one couldn't be high up the food chain. She was probably just a toy for his bodyguards. A small patent leather purse hung from her shoulder on long thin straps, which the girl clutched in her hand like a life raft. Everything about her — the thinly plucked eyebrows, cheap-and-cheerful lipstick, and long luscious hair carefully combed back and pinned to one side with a strawberry hairpin, screamed new in the city. The boots and short skirt were supposed to make her appear worldly but reeked of insecurities all the way to where he was sitting.

The only thing the girl had going for her, Orlovsky thought, was that she was pretty. She had clean translucent skin, full lips, and big blue eyes that still had an innocence about them. Orlovsky loved innocent girls. When he humiliated them, they were the ones who suffered the most.

The girl spotted Orlovsky by the bar and her face visibly relaxed. She walked to him and leaned on the bar.

"I thought I was late," she said. She obviously had no idea who he was or what he did for a living.

Orlovsky stared at her heavily made-up eyes. She tried to hold his gaze but eventually had to look away. To keep her hands busy, she brushed her hair to one side and stroked it. Her wrists were so slender he could break them with his bare hands. Like twigs.

"Want a drink?" Orlovsky asked.

"Yes. Why not. But first business. You'll find your mark in this," The girl said, handing him a copy of Vestnik newspaper.

Orlovsky took the magazine and signaled the bartender to pour a second glass.

"Ice?" The bartender asked.

"Yes, please," the girl replied.

"You don't drink single-malt with ice," Orlovsky grumbled.

"I know, but I can't hold my liquor. It's better for me with ice." For a second, Orlovsky felt sorry for her. She was as innocent as a white dove on a wedding day. She had no idea. Still, it wasn't his fault she was ripe for the picking.

"You a working girl?" he asked and took a sip from his glass.

"I have a boyfriend," the girl pouted as if the question insulted her.

A boyfriend my ass, Orlovsky thought. "Can I be your boyfriend for an hour, then?" He asked.

The girl became disturbed. The buoyancy she had when she walked in was gone. Her lips were trembling. She licked them with her pink tongue, trying to calm her nerves. "I don't do this kind of stuff."

Orlovsky was enjoying himself. "I'm not asking it for free. I'll pay you well."

The girl stared numbly at his face. Eventually, she decided to drop pretenses. "I don't do kinky. Just sex, ok?"

"Whatever," Orlovsky said. Once in the room, he could make her do whatever he wanted. "Go get a room while I pay for the drinks."

The girl left and Orlovsky watched her walk to the reception desk. Something in the way she walked — her perky ass, her shapely legs reminded him of Alena earlier today. He had also watched her walk away, but while Alena had gotten away, this one wasn't going to.

Why was he still thinking of the psychotherapist woman when he had a perfectly good piece of ass to look forward to? He paid the bill and walked away from the bar.

He needed to get that Alena bitch off his mind.

The girl turned out to be meek. Sex with her brought him no relief or pleasure. After the first few minutes of struggle, she had accepted his domination with no real enthusiasm. He craved a challenge. A hot-blooded woman that would stand up for herself and give him a decent fight for his money.

When Orlovsky came out of the hotel Diplomat, it was already dark outside. The busy, hot and humid streets of Sofia were finally calming down after an intense day. Orlovsky got in the car and drove to a bar not far from the hotel, called Amnesia. He could have walked there, it would have taken him less than ten minutes, but no self-respecting Bulgarian walked the streets. Being seen arriving in an expensive car was everything. He struggled to find a parking spot and finally parked his huge black Range Rover across the pavement obstructing everyone's way. Orlovsky didn't care. People daring to question his right to park there were more than welcome. He was spoiling for a fight.

He ordered bourbon this time and tried to collect his thoughts. He opened the magazine the girl gave him and looked for the name. He listed page by page, looking intently at every article, but he found nothing. Frustrated, he listed through the magazine again in his last attempt to see something that he didn't notice before. He finally saw it. The tiny red dot on the forehead of the man that was on a picture of the second page. The name was interesting if not unexpected: Pavel Lozanov, the owner and the president of the Bulgarian National Bank (BNB). He was the richest man in Bulgaria, rumored to be worth two billion dollars. Oligarch! A former nomenclature turned businessman, Lozanov had established himself as a respected and prominent citizen with legitimate business. But, like every oligarch out there, Lozanov had a weakness: he liked fashion models. His current girlfriend, a gypsy beauty with an infectious smile, was the best-kept secret in the mafia world. Orlovsky had fucked her sister years ago and would have liked to have the set, but Nadia belonged to Lozanov. *Not for long*, Orlovsky thought, if he did his job properly.

What was it with oligarchs and models? They gravitated around each other like tidal waters and riverbanks: they would pull away only to be back for more the next day. Personally, Orlovsky couldn't care less about fashion models. Most of them had these blank faces and malnourished bodies that he found unattractive. They only took care of their hair, nails, and clothes but not their bodies. At least not the way he liked them: toned, healthy, and feisty.

He thought of the legs of the therapist. He hadn't seen a pair of legs like hers in a longtime. Every muscle in them well-defined. Every joint working with the ease and flexibility of a professional athlete. Orlovsky tried to picture the therapist naked. When he felt his penis stir, he came back to his senses. Why was he still thinking of that woman? He had a killing to plan, yet all he could picture was a pair of legs walking away from him. Orlovsky looked out of the bar window in despair. It had started to drizzle and the streets were deserted. With a jolt, he realized that unwittingly he'd chosen to have a drink in a bar close to the therapist's office. He drained his bourbon, paid the bill and got in his car again. Less than a minute later he parked in front of the office building the therapist had given as her office address. It was late but he hoped she might still be at work.

It was time he confronted her about the setup of those fake accounts; and for him to see if he can stick his prick in something firmer than the cunt this afternoon.

TRADE

There was a knock at the door. She looked at her watch puzzled. It was way past 10 pm. She closed the lid of her laptop and went to get the door.

Outside stood Orlovsky. His eyes bloodshot; his hands in the pockets of his jeans. Her surprise at seeing him so soon was so genuine she could never have faked it better.

"You…" she said but couldn't continue. Orlovsky forcefully pushed her inside the room, walked after her and closed the door.

They stood in the middle of her office facing each other. Orlovsky looked around. His gaze jumped from the Alberton upholstered chair standing on its tiny brass castors to the bookcase that took up a wall and went from floor to ceiling. He glanced over her books with a faint light of distrust in his eyes. Only a few of the books were from the time she'd gone to Georgetown University, but he had lingered longer over them, likely because they were in English and that concerned her.

"I guess I'm in the wrong business," he said slowly as he turned to examine her Bulgarian Doctorate's diploma hanging on the wall, confirming her gut instincts that he found the contents of her office suspicious. "If you could make enough money to buy all this by chatting to people, I want in. Then again, you can't make me read that many books by putting a gun to my head."

"No?" Slavena turned around and walked to the chair behind her desk. "I took you for a reader." Her voice was playful, but she was scared by his cagey mood. She knew she was sticking her hand in the cobra's basket and it was only a matter of time before his razor-sharp fangs sank into her flesh.

"And I took you for a college student and not the Doctor your degree says you are."

Slavena's eye twitched, but she carried on calmly. "What do you like doing in your spare time, then? You never said on EliteDate.com."

Without a word, Orlovsky leaped behind her chair and put an arm around her neck, choking her. All Slavena could do was dig her fingernails deep into his skin, struggling to draw a breath.

"We can play this game all night," Orlovsky whispered in her ear. "I have time."

"What... do you... want?" Slavena's brain was in panic mode. She had seen this coming, but not so suddenly. All she could do was get a few words out of her mouth.

"I want you to tell me why you set up those fake accounts? What do you want from me? And I am warning you, do *not* toy with me or else you won't be able to see another client ever again. Or anyone else for that matter."

"I... have... a motive," she said. Orlovsky loosened his grip on her throat and she took a few desperate rasping breaths, slumping forward in her chair.

"What is it then?" He hissed.

With trembling fingers, she opened a drawer and pulled

a thin folder out. She handed it to him.

"I want him dead," she said.

Orlovsky opened the manila folder. It was a profile of Jaro.

"What for?" he asked, surprised.

"Does it matter?" Slavena found it in herself to ask. Orlovsky gave her a threatening look and she swallowed hard. "Fine. He… hurt somebody I loved."

Orlovsky studied the few pages clipped in the folder. Then closed it and looked at her.

"I don't work for free."

"I know."

"How much?"

"All I have is $50,000."

"For a guy like Jaro, I would get at least half million."

Bullshit, Slavena thought, but she knew there was no winning this argument.

He leaned over her in the chair taking in a long hard breath through his nose.

"Interesting," he said. His breath smelled of alcohol. "You are not as scared as I expected. You can take more."

Slavena's stomach contracted. She was determined not to react to his provocations, but if he continued to assault her, she would have to defend herself and risk exposing her real identity. No therapist could fight back the way she could. While she pondered her next move, Orlovsky stood up.

"I will do it," he said. "On one condition."

"What?"

"Free sessions."

"But I thought all I did was *chat* with people."

"I changed my mind. Now that I know you want somebody dead, I'm more willing to chat with you. We have something in common." Orlovsky dropped the file on her desk. "You can keep this. I know this fucking asshole better than his own mother."

Orlovsky headed for the door, but thought of something and turned back.

"Why didn't you write the name when I asked you today?"

"I needed to be sure about you."

"And are you now?"

Slavena answered timidly, "Yes."

He took a step forward and slapped her across the face so hard her ears rang like bells. Her neck gave an alarming snap and her nerves vibrated from the shock.

She stood up and looked at him with rage in her eyes. "What was *that* for?"

"*That* was for your rotten attitude earlier at the café. I don't tolerate unprofessionalism."

"And I don't tolerate aggressive employees."

His cruel eyes were now millimeters from hers. They stared at each other silently.

"In case you don't know. You are not my employer. I only consider an employer someone who can pay the price I ask for a job. Understood?"

"Yes," Slavena said, handing him her phone number, still in shock.

He took the slip of paper and walked towards the door breathing hard, like a caged animal. When he was out and the door closed behind him, Slavena touched her lip and saw blood on her trembling fingers.

"What the hell have I gotten myself into?" she mumbled to herself, feeling defeated in her chair.

The night after the encounter with Orlovsky, she couldn't sleep. It was rare for her to lose a whole night of sleep. At the Farm, she'd slept through broken fingers, mock interrogations, and severe storms, yet Orlovsky had rattled her so badly she'd laid awake until the sun came up. And it wasn't just the violence that rubbed on her. The way she felt about Orlovsky puzzled her. He reminded her of oysters — an acquired taste that many people were reluctant to try. A small part of those who did, became addicted to it. Slavena loved oysters, but right now she hated Orlovsky's guts. How could she not after what he did to her? Yet as the night progressed other emotions surfaced, like oil spills in the Mexico gulf: black, sticky and hard to get rid of. She remembered his smell when he'd stood close by. She admired his confidence, his self-reliance.

In the morning she decided to follow Orlovsky the old-fashioned way — driving after him and waiting around.

Orlovsky lived in a new and compact building in one of the up and coming gated communities around Sofia. There was a porter by the main gate and CCTV set up all around the high stonewall. And if that wasn't enough security, the apartments in Orlovsky's building were only accessible through the parking structure underneath the building. A couple of times, Slavena had surveyed the complex through the bars of the gate, pretending to be a cyclist stopping for a sip of water. She had watched Orlovsky's car disappearing down the ramp of the underground parking and a metal grid sliding behind it. The access into the building was only possible if you knew the code to open it or if Orlovsky allowed her in his lair himself.

She parked her car a block past Orlovsky's street to observe from a safe distance as she didn't want to test the porter's vigilance by watching too close by. Her telescopic digital camera compensated for the distance, but it risked missing his car if Orlovsky went the other way.

It was nearly lunchtime and there was still no sign of Orlovsky. Slavena dug deeper into her thoughts while touching her lip. The pain lingered as a raw reminder of Orlovsky's brutality. It went against all her instincts to get closer to the man, yet that was exactly what she would have to do in the next few days.

Slavena turned away from the wheel of the car and looked towards the mountain hills visible at the end of the street just in time to see Orlovsky's car speeding towards her.

"Shit!" She said and grabbed the key in the ignition. By the time she pulled out to give him chase, Orlovsky was taking a right turn onto a primary boulevard. "Shit. Shit. Shit!"

Slavena drove as fast and as recklessly as she could, cutting corners and taking right turns on red. That was illegal in Bulgaria, but still, it was the safest rule to break when in a hurry. She managed to tail Orlovsky for close to ten minutes when at a traffic light a car cut in front of her and stopped on yellow.

"Fuck!" Slavena shouted and blew the horn. The driver in the other car gave her the middle finger. She could do nothing but sit in the car and watch Orlovsky drive down the boulevard, take a left on the next traffic light and disappear from view. She'd lost him.

Slavena was so angry she drove aimlessly for a half an hour until her cell phone rang.

"It's time to make good on our agreement," Orlovsky

said in the receiver.

"Sure. What time?" Slavena rolled up her window to block off the street noise.

"Tonight. At my place."

"Your place? But I thought we are having a therapy session?"

"And?"

"My office is better for that."

"My place at eight. No further discussions."

"Text-message me the address, please."

"I will." The phone went dead.

Slavena slowed down to think. Conflicting emotions took over her: Joy at having made contact again. Not all was lost, she told herself. Yet, at the thought of Orlovsky possibly finding out her real motives for contacting him, chills ran down her back. It didn't bear thinking what he'd do to her.

She put on the radio to distract her from her thoughts.

"Latest news," the radio host was talking. "Pavel Lozanov, the president of the Bulgarian National Bank, was shot to death in Sofia this afternoon. Sources say Lozanov was shot twice in the head while leaving his house. The police have not yet commented on the shooting…"

Someone blew a car horn behind her and Slavena jumped. In front of her, the traffic light had changed to green. On autopilot, she put the car in gear and drove on. Gavin wasn't going to be happy.

Orlovsky had done his first kill and she had missed it.

She pressed a button on her phone to record a message for Gavin:

"Just came back from the Ferrari Motor Show where I witnessed the Berlinetta's raw power in action for the first time."

She paused briefly with a smile on her face. Gavin had been hinting for months she needed to learn how to crypto talk like him and he was finally getting his wishes. So, she carried on. *"I confirm the Berlinetta is one of the best Ferrari models ever made and because of its jaw-dropping speed, I wasn't able to tail it. Not even close. Frankly, the car looks like it's moving even when parked, but I think I found a way of how to reign the prancing horse and get into the Ferrari business. Stay tuned."*

EAGLE

As soon as he pulled the door open, he turned his shirtless back to her and walked away without a word. For a moment, Slavena stared at the tattoo that stretched across his muscular back. Adapted to his body movements, the design of a double-headed eagle, floated in midair with its mighty wings, disappearing in the dark. Whoever the tattoo artist was, Slavena thought, knew how to draw the perfect lines to please a man whose father's code name in the KGB was the Eagle. The tattoo was a visual representation of whom Alexander Orlovsky was. The son of the Eagle.

"Are you coming in?" Orlovsky's voice echoed.

She found her way into Orlovsky's apartment through a dark corridor and into the living room. It was a vast space, just as she imagined, but it was furnished in a way she had never expected. In Slavena's experience, grown-ups lived in carpeted and couched spaces. The focal point of a living room was usually a TV and the main activities included guests' entertaining and wine drinking.

Orlovsky's apartment had an enormous TV and a furry rug, but there the similarities ended. His living room was transformed into a 300-degree gunfighter gym in the middle of which he stood in a defensive position, shooting with a simulation weapon.

Slavena was familiar with this particular marksmanship training. The system had a state-of-the-art software with full HD capabilities that was used by the military to train soldiers to use real weapons with laser inserts. It used virtual simulations that replicated a realistic combat environment with hostile and split-second situations. To Slavena it had been one of the most fun memories at Camp Lejeune where she enjoyed competing with the Marine scout snipers. She never imagined anyone would have space in an apartment to use it. Unless you were a successful hitman. Then the gunfighter simulator was a perfectly acceptable living room furniture for you. She figured this was one of Orlovsky's methods to reach his cognitive and physical mastery over his environment and weapons. That was how he was keeping in shape. The man had a job to do; a reputation to preserve. He needed the simulator like a French chef needed sous vide, obviously.

She stood behind Orlovsky, observing him in action. He used a perfect replica of the M4 assault rifle. She knew from experience it was like shooting with the real thing. It recoiled fiercely and produced loud bangs, which explained the need for the secluded location of his apartment—a single-space at the top of the building. The floor and walls were probably reinforced so noises wouldn't carry. The apartment was a death trap. Slavena could be tortured and murdered here and no one would ever know.

At the thought, she shuddered but stayed put. She kept watching the precise, jerking movements of Orlovsky's arms as he shot at the men on the screen. The supple muscles on his shoulders flexed and contracted with the strain, giving an added dimension to his eagle tattoo and transforming it into a dynamic work of art. The overlapping movements of the wings created the illusion of motion and for a moment she couldn't help but think that the bird would abandon Orlovsky's skin and take flight.

The carbine was only seven pounds heavy, but she remembered back at Camp Lejeune, it had taken her all her strength to hold it steady for more than an hour. Orlovsky looked like he could go on for hours.

Absorbed by the action on the screen, his attention was not on her, so she used the time to glance around. The walls were painted in dark graphite. The only sign of humanity was the half-empty scotch bottle on the kitchen counter and the many crystal glasses gathering dust everywhere with amber dregs at the bottom. Orlovsky had inherited a few things from his father. The love of alcohol included.

The overall impression of his place was of a dog kennel of a lonely and aggressive pit bull. Slavena noticed the alarm sensors on the windows, but no cameras, which was a good break. On a metal bookshelf, in a prominent position, was a framed picture of Orlovsky at a young age next to what Slavena assumed to be his father. Judging by his age in the photo, it was probably Orlovsky's last memory of him.

The shooting ceased. Orlovsky scanned through the targets' report that had popped up on the computer screen.

"You missed one," Slavena teased. He had gotten 164 hits out of 165 targets. It was the highest score she had ever seen in such a challenging setting.

"You think you can do better?"

"I am not the professional here."

Orlovsky changed the magazine and handed her the M4. "Thirty rounds, then you'd have to reload. Let's see how you'll do."

"I've never... I can't really..." She started protesting, but Virtual Combat Zone flashed across the lit screen and instructed her to prepare for targets.

Damn it. The last thing on her mind had been playing with simulation weapons in front of Orlovsky. She needed to remember fast what it was like the first time around she'd touched a rifle when she was only 10 years old. Under no circumstances should she show any experience with this.

"But it's heavy."

"Deal with it," Orlovsky said annoyed and spilled the rest of his instructions: "As soon as the environment loads, you lock a round into the chamber like this, then turn the safety off and start shooting."

Slavena didn't listen to what he was saying. She knew what to do already. During her first time on the simulator back at Camp Lejeune, she got nearly all her targets. She remembered everything but didn't want to take a chance with Orlovsky. So she missed every target that appeared on the screen.

She could feel Orlovsky relaxing by her side. She knew her ineptitude would amuse him. So, when she attempted to change magazines, she clumsily dropped the clip on the ground and heard him laughing.

"Take your shirt off. It'll give you some agility," he said with a voice of authority.

With all the strain she was under, Slavena did not mind his suggestive remark. She held no illusions of why Orlovsky invited her to his place. It wasn't for target practice, a civilized candlelit dinner or friendly chatter but for raw sex. She knew it and did not oppose it as long as her job got done and her sexual desires fulfilled.

Without hesitation, she whipped her shirt over her head, revealing her silk bra. Not paying attention to Orlovsky's reaction, she continued with her task, determined to complete it. She felt his eyes on her half-exposed body and took advantage of his distraction by hitting five targets in a row. With her sixth one, she got his attention.

"What did I tell you, comfort is everything," he said conceitedly.

She killed five more before he embraced her from behind to assist her with the shooting. Feeling the warmth of his bare chest made her thighs quiver.

"Your targets are getting away," His gentle whisper made her dizzy with desire. She tried to refocus on the screen, but he didn't make it easy for her. He slid his hands under her skirt and fingered the edge of her lace panties. *He is doing his reconnaissance before the invasion*, she thought as she continued to shoot at the hostile targets on the screen. But in her mind, Orlovsky was the only target she needed to worry about. Orlovsky and what he was about to do to her next. She knew this wasn't going to be just sex but a dangerous match of two forces — one against the other.

As anticipated, his *invasion* began. First, it was one gentle finger. Then there were two that strummed her like a harp. Finally, when his entire hand straddled inside her panties, like an army of savages, her body snapped like a whip against the strength of his hand and she dropped the carbine on the floor. In a blink of a moment, he ripped her underwear from her body and tried to take her from behind by forcing her on all fours. Unwilling to submit to him quite yet, she sharply spun around and slapped him.

"Do you really think I'm that easy?"

"Yes," he said, pulling her swiftly by the waist of her skirt. "I think..." he unclipped her bra, "that you are a woman who is not afraid to get what she wants?"

"And what do I want now?"

His eyes moved from her face to her exposed breasts. He took a good look at them like an art collector studying a sculpture he considered buying despite its exorbitant price. Then he locked her hands behind her, and as if knowing exactly what she had been waiting for, he kissed her breasts with his tongue moving softly around her pointy nipples. She arched her back—the only sign of excitement she allowed herself to give away. The rest had to wait.

"That's what you wanted, isn't it?"

"Frankly," she breathed, feeling the limits of her willpower, "I expected more from the killer of the biggest oligarch in Bulgaria."

Provoked by her, he grabbed her by the neck with his right hand and looked deeply into her eyes with a mixture of desire and a warning. He was so close, his dilated pupils looked like two solar eclipses that darkened her horizon. She saw nothing in front of her, but the madness in his eyes.

"I hate to disappoint you," he said, tightening his grip, "but I had nothing to do with his death."

He watched her squirming body coldly. He enjoyed seeing her at his mercy with every fiber of his being. As the only self-defense she could think off, she slid her hand down and cupped the monument of his hard-on firmly until he loosened his grip a bit, allowing her to breathe.

"Are you sure?" she asked with more color to her face. "Because that's not what my polygraph is saying?"

"I didn't realize this was a hostile interrogation."

"Well, your weather vane is telling me everything I need to know," she said, looking at him. His gray eyes were studying her, memorizing everything about her. Overcome by what he'd made her feel—wanted and desired—she allowed him to hold her face like a cup he wanted to drink from.

In her euphoria, Slavena tried to keep the thought that Orlovsky was a dangerous killer who could choose to hurt her at any moment. That she should stay vigilant, on guard. Yet, even as he twisted her necklace around her neck, choking her, she had to admit she had been wanting him from the day she set her eyes on him.

In what felt like a blur, she managed to have a mind-blowing orgasm before he finally collapsed on top of her, crushing her under his bulky torso, holding her tightly. He looked at her with a smile of a man whose male ego was full of knowing how to please a woman.

Eventually, Orlovsky stood up with a sigh.

"That was exceptional, but I knew it'd be with a tight ass like yours." He walked away stark naked. He had the beautiful body of an athlete in his prime. The only thing suggesting he used it as a weapon, rather than for sports, was the half-dozen bullet scars visible over his back and legs.

Slavena raised from the floor without saying anything. She pulled down her skirt, picked up her torn panties from the floor, and swept her long hair behind her head.

"Consider this as your…" Orlovsky stopped in search of a word. "Advance."

"Advance?"

"Yes." Orlovsky poured himself a glass of scotch and took a big mouthful. "Advance."

"Very generous of you, but I'm not a hooker!"

"No?" he took another sip of his scotch. "Enlighten me, then. What are you? Because in my mind, only hookers slash therapists can be so unforgettable in bed."

Her body tensed and suddenly, she wanted to get out of his place without finishing her job. The situation was slipping away from her. A few minutes earlier she was on top of her game, but here she was now feeling like a filthy prostitute.

"You know I paid you a compliment?" Orlovsky's voice softened up a notch. "I don't call every fuck I have 'exceptional'."

"I know. Thank you." She picked up her shirt and put it on. "I'm a bit out of it. I had a long day."

Orlovsky laughed. "Not as long as mine."

Mine was long because of you, Slavena thought. Gavin had called her as soon as the news of Lozanov's murder hit all news channels and was very keen to discuss her recorded message. He had instructed her to put surveillance on Orlovsky immediately and here she was now, buttoning her shirt, tucking it in her skirt and discussing how glorious her fuck with her target had been.

"So, this seals our deal then. Right?" She finally said.

"Not even close! We haven't even started yet. That was just one of the free therapy sessions you promised me," he smirked.

It was Slavena's turn to grit her teeth. What more could he possibly want from her?

"I need a shower," Orlovsky said. "Take one with me."

"I can't. I need to go."

"Then wait for me." He sauntered out of the living room. Slavena waited in the living room until she heard running water. She hoped it wasn't a ploy to get her thinking he was in the shower but was actually snooping on her to see what she would do in his apartment if left unattended. If he saw what she was about to do, she was as good as dead.

Slavena double-checked if there were any cameras and once satisfied, she walked steadily to a side table next to the living room door, where she'd seen Orlovsky's cell phone laying earlier. She listened carefully for a second before casually picking it up. She quickly pulled out a chip from her chewing gums box, stuck it inside the cell, and downloaded the phone's data. No sign of Orlovsky. She couldn't believe her luck.

After that, she grew bolder. She took two microphones the size of peas and stuck them to pieces of furniture. One under the kitchen marble island, the other behind the big screen. She figured those were the places Orlovsky frequented most. Finally, she inserted a GPS tracker into his wallet, which she found in the back pocket of his discarded jeans.

By the time, Orlovsky got out of the shower, she was long gone.

Back home Slavena dropped her handbag in the hallway and rushed upstairs to her equipment room. She was eager to check if the newly installed bugs were working. If they were, the first phase of her mission — to get access — would be accomplished.

Her equipment room was a small windowless attic located under the roof of the same building Slavena was renting her apartment. It served as an immediate safe room in case of an emergency or exposed identity and luckily, she'd had little use of the tiny room so far. But with tonight's jackpot, she suspected she would be spending a lot more time here.

She slipped off her shoes and curled up in an old armchair — the only piece of furniture in the room — with a set of headphones on. She played with the volume control and frequency for a while, careful not to miss the tiniest sound coming through from Orlovsky's apartment. The devices were dead silent.

Slavena looked at her watch. She'd left Orlovsky's apartment sometime after 11 pm. She had gotten back home close to midnight and it was 1 am now. For these two hours, while the city slept, she waited but there had been no sound. Was it possible he had gone to bed already? She hoped he had picked up his simulator after she left, to blow off some steam. She guessed he wouldn't be impressed to discover she was gone. Nobody disobeyed the Eagle without serious consequences. She did it to ensure a follow-up. A bruised ego was the best way to get Orlovsky's attention, she knew. She took off the headphones and sat in the attic, thinking. Was it possible that Orlovsky's apartment was bug-proof? He'd gone the extra mile to mount noise canceling installation. It was logical that he would also install audio signal jamming devices or low volume white noise transmitters. But if he had done it, she would still get something, albeit illegible white noise. And she got nothing.

She grunted in exasperation. She was desperate for this to work. Ever since she missed the first hit, Gavin was on her like a ton of bricks to get her reports productive and submitted on time. Preferably before the hits occurred.

Her gut instinct told her Orlovsky was too arrogant to suspect anyone could bug his own house. *My home is my castle*, Bulgarians said and Slavena was sure Orlovsky thought no enemy could trick him into allowing access into his castle. Slavena was positive the thought that he had just fucked a CIA officer would never occur to him. Arrogance blinded people like that.

That left two options: she didn't mount the antenna properly or Orlovsky had gone to bed after she'd left. She dreaded the first possibility. What a rotten piece of luck that would be. After all, she had done to bug Orlovsky's house. The memory of his hand between her legs made her blush. Despite her better judgment, she'd enjoyed the sex. How could she not? Orlovsky was hot-blooded and seductive in a rough and dangerous way. On top of that, she hadn't had any action in ages. What happened tonight had imprinted itself on her skin to savor in the months to come. God only knew when the next time would be if the bugs worked.

She pushed the sex thoughts out of her mind and concentrated on the task at hand. She wouldn't know which way the wind blew on those microphones until tomorrow. She might as well get some sleep.

After a hot shower, she lay in bed staring in the dark for hours. She thought she would never get to sleep but was startled out of sleep by the ringing of a telephone. She looked around confused. A bright light was streaming through a tiny dot in her window blinds. The bedside clock was showing 8 am. Not only had she fallen asleep but she'd overslept.

"Shit!" she said licking her parched lips. There was a chance she'd missed Orlovsky's morning routine and that he had already gone to the gym. "Shit!"

She picked up her work phone on its fifth ring and nearly said "shit" again. "Hello," she croaked instead.

"Heads up, you are not talent spotting tonight," Gavin barked in the receiver.

She had no idea what Gavin was talking about. He always spoke like he expected everyone else to be thinking his thoughts. He had no concept that other people might have their own thoughts; their own agendas. It took her a moment to remember that she was supposed to go to a party tonight. A wine tasting at the Ukrainian Embassy with a bunch of old and grumpy hotshots.

"Then why go to the party at all?" she asked.

"The Ambassador needs a backup CAT III terp."

"A terp?" Category III interpreter was the highest "terp" category, reserved only for US citizens with a Top-Secret clearance. Slavena had the qualifications to do it. "What's it to me?"

"You are going to be that interpreter."

"What? What happened to his assigned terp?"

"Locked in a toilet somewhere. Food poisoning. Might still make it, but the Ambassador insisted on having a backup in case he bails out."

And if he bails out, Slavena thought, *this could blow my cover wide open.*

After a moment she said: "You do realize this carries high risks for me? Why would a Bulgarian psychotherapist speak good enough English to interpret at this level? And why not a US citizen? This will look dodgy."

"I took care of it, don't worry." Slavena groaned inwards. Gavin's solutions were often worse than the problems. "You are to be Jason Henderson's fiancé, the American consular. You'll get to interpret only as a last resort, as a personal favor to the Ambassador. Understand? It'll be made very clear. I insisted upon it."

Slavena thought for a second but her caffeine-deprived brain couldn't find anything to object on fast enough. "I still think it is a bad idea," she said.

"How do you say 'No' to the Ambassador?"

"The Ambassador should know better than to expose his operatives for his own agenda." She wanted to say, but she knew better than to speak her mind on an open line. Besides, she had already lost the battle. She was only hammering down pointless objections now. So she remained silent.

"Relax. It's not climate change talks, it's a wine testing for Christ's sake. You might have to translate a few bad jokes after they all get plastered and that's it."

"I hope so. Do I still need to go through the homework you gave me?"

"You mean the Embassy dossiers? Yes! And be ready to brief me if any of the guests seem dubious to you."

"Will do."

"Be there at eighteen hundred then."

EMBASSY

By 1 pm, Slavena'd given up on the bugs she'd planted in Orlovsky's apartment. She'd sat in her equipment room for five hours straight, drinking strong coffee and listening for anything that might get transmitted to her — doors opening or closing, footsteps on the floor, and any little sound that could indicate the connection was alive. The microphones had remained mute. She looked at the computer screen and the GPS tracker she had planted in his wallet showed Orlovsky was still in his apartment. Did he leave his wallet behind? That didn't make any sense.

"Come on! Move!" Her voice echoed with despair. The dot on the screen ignored her and kept blinking monotonously.

Shaky with frustration and caffeine, Slavena ripped the headphones off and chucked them to the floor. She had a party to prepare for, including having her hair professionally blow-dried. She couldn't stay in the attic any longer. She was informed that the women at the Ukrainian embassy party would be elegant with tailored clothing. She had to look the part, and that took time.

On the surface, she was pissed off at having to abandon her post for something as mundane as getting a blow-dry.

Deep down, though, she was glad there was something to take her away from sitting in a dark room. She was becoming irrational with frustration.

Inside Konstantin's taxi, on her way to the party, she clung to the thought that there was still a chance Orlovsky went to sleep last night and left without taking his wallet this morning. The bugs might still work. One of her cell phones in her purse vibrated and she hoped it was Gavin, telling her the interpreter's crisis was over.

I want to see you tonight.

She read. Orlovsky. As if she didn't have enough on her plate. She typed back. *Can't tonight. Have an important party to go to*, and then deleted the last sentence. She didn't need to give him any explanations. She glanced over the screen one last time before she hit Send. His response came instantly as if he already knew what she was going to say.

Tonight, or the deal is off.

"Here we go," she mumbled. "Petty demands to soothe his bruised ego."

"Your fiancé?" Konstantin was curious.

"Yes," she lied. It was becoming a habit of hers to lie about everything.

"I'm not surprised you're in love with a narcissist. If optometrists develop feelings for blind people, then I can see how it happen to you, the psychotherapist."

Konstantin gave her a brief smile and Slavena nodded at him thoughtfully. Konstantin was right, stomping of feet and pouting of mouth were the classic examples of narcissistic injury. She put the cell phone in her purse without replying to Orlovsky's last text message. She knew better than to give in to his demands. She was painfully aware she was testing Orlovsky and it was only a matter of time before the snake, Orlovsky, sank his venomous fangs into her. A displeased narcissist always found a way to punish his offender. As she was riding in the taxi, she realized she was watching the streets like a hawk, searching for his face.

Konstantin stopped the car. "Here you go, the Ukrainian embassy," he said.

"Thank you." Slavena paid him and got out, waving at him. The second she set her foot on the pavement, she realized how uncomfortable her high-heel shoes were to wear. Sure, they made her legs appear endless but were a health-hazard to wear. That one thing they hadn't taught her at the Farm.

Just as Slavena expected, the Ambassador's interpreter was still sick and unable to attend the party. A great fuss was made to ensure that she appeared to be invited to interpret simply because there were no other options. Slavena hoped it worked. Exposing her identity because of something as ill-advised as this was unthinkable.

The turnout was great. People chatted, mingled and drank gallons of wine. The US Ambassador spent a long time talking to the Ukrainian Minister of Defense and an Army General from Ukraine. The Minister of Defense was a short and agreeable man in a perfectly decent double-breasted suit and blue tie. His English was impeccable and Slavena sighed with relief at the temporary respite.

The Ukrainian General was a different ball game. He was crude and rude. He wore a tight black coat with shoulders peppered by dandruff and a diamond-patterned tie-in bright orange that made Slavena dizzy to look at. He swallowed every drop of wine that came his way.

"*Devotchka,*" he spoke to Slavena in drunken-slurred Russian. Slavena was fluent in Russian, but understanding the General's version of it, mixed with an unlimited supply of wine, was impossible. "Try this sour cherry brandy. It's to die for." He pressed his glass to her lips with no sense of gravity or proper etiquette. "Just like drinking vodka, never sipping. Gulp, *devotchka,* gulp." The Ambassador noticed the General pressuring Slavena to drink and led him away from the wine tasting booth while the General continued talking about Army life.

"The best time of my life," he continued in Russian with glistening eyes. "My soldiers were comrades, my best friends. There was no one but us to fight for our country. For the Motherland. Unlike now. They would let anyone in the Army—women, foreigners... Women are by far the worst. They disobey authority and complain all the time. But I'm spoiling a good party," the General said. "Let me tell you a joke. Why do women make the best soldiers?" The Ambassador shrugged his shoulders politely, waiting for the punch line: "Because they can bleed for a week and still won't die."

His coarse laugh spilled in the room and made him cough. Slavena used his coughing fit to translate the joke in her head into a more politically correct version. Then she thought against it. Only hours ago, she allowed a man to invade her body for access to information. Perhaps the Ukrainian General was on to something. Women were the worst.

After she translated the General's joke word for word, the Ambassador smiled politely and moved on. He was evidently conditioned to keep an agreeable expression at all times and she felt comfortable around him. Interpreting for him was easier than she expected and it certainly had its many pluses. Getting a drink fast was one of them. After her second glass of wine, the memory of her sexual encounter with Orlovsky washed over her like a tsunami, sweeping all her senses away with such a force, that she felt drowning into her own oblivion. She continued to translate, but in the back of her mind, Orlovsky's lips were kissing hers as if their mouths were in combat. His strong veiny arms were embracing her so tightly as if she was his very first taste of lust.

With sudden clarity, she grasped the real reason behind her obsession with the listening devices. It was her need to be aware of Orlovsky's existence—of knowing precisely what his body was doing that minute, that hour, that day.

What felt like an eternity, but was only a couple hours later, Slavena reunited with her fiancé-for-the-night, Jason, and hand-fed him with caviar. Jason, who worked as an undercover case-officer in the Consular section, licked her fingers with delight. Slavena wasn't too surprised that he was taking pleasure in playing his role. Like her, work had become his diversion from being lonely and he was eager to taste life from time to time. She smiled warmly at his affection being on display for the Ukrainian eyes, but she was dog-tired and couldn't wait to get out of the crowded embassy.

Before she made her exit, she kissed him on the cheek. "Sweetie, it was a remarkable evening, but I have to get up early in the morning. Do you really have to stay late?"

He nodded with his eyes no longer dancing behind his glasses. Like her, he'd worked all day and the night was getting heavy on him. Or perhaps he didn't want her to leave him. Either way, she had enough of this and had to go.

"I'll get a taxi and I'll see you at home, my love." She said, thinking that if there were cameras trained on her mouth and they were reading her lips in that instant, they would know she wasn't far from a possible marriage.

"Yes, darling. I will see you tonight," he said.

When she stepped outside, a taxi came by as she reached the curb and she jumped in by a habit, assuming it was Konstantin. As she closed the door, she realized that the taxi driver was not Konstantin and that there was somebody else already sitting in the backseat.

"Hello," Orlovsky's teeth flashed in the dark.

If Slavena hadn't drunk that night, her self-preservation instincts would have told her to get out of that taxi right away. But with three glasses of wine circulating in her system, her fears were fast asleep under a blanket of ridiculous confidence. It seemed to her she could conquer mountains just as soon as she got out of her high heels. She could definitely deal with the psychotic Orlovsky.

"What are you doing here, Alex? I don't remember asking you to pick me up." Slavena grabbed the heels in her hands and slipped them off. She was in pain and from here on she was going barefoot.

"I don't take no for an answer," Orlovsky said with his lips tight.

"And what if I walked out of there with a man by my side? I had a date, you know."

"Then he would have been a dead man."

To Slavena that seemed insanely funny. Her laughter startled the taxi driver and he looked at her in alarm in the rearview mirror. The woman was having too much fun, he thought and shook his head disapprovingly.

Unknown to him, a small part of Slavena's brain sided with the taxi driver. It told her she should demand to be driven home straight away. The bigger part of the brain, however, was enjoying it and refused to be sensible.

"That was funny," Slavena said when she caught her breath. "You are full of surprises, Alex."

His clenched lower jaw made her straighten her back from the seat. She snorted a couple more times before she managed to halt her giggling completely.

"How did you find me, anyway? I didn't tell you where I was goi— ah, wait. I know! You tracked my cell phone. That's clever of you." She was babbling again but couldn't stop herself. "You know what I think, Alex? I think you like me, but you should stay focused on other things. Remember the contract?"

Orlovsky gave her a murderous look that frightened her. She looked out of the window and realized she didn't know where they were going. She knew they were on the north side of town and she was suddenly alarmed. One thing was certain—Orlovsky wasn't taking her home or to his place.

"Where are you taking me?" she asked alarmed. He ignored her and kept his face averted. Chills ran down Slavena's back.

"What the fuck, Alexander?" She tried to think back when the taxi had picked her up. Did Orlovsky give an address to the driver? She didn't come up with anything. Perhaps he'd given it to him before she got in. She was at Orlovsky's mercy.

"Where are we?" Her voice sounded pleading even in her own ears.

"Where do you want me to stop?" the taxi driver asked. "At the main entrance?"

"Yes," Orlovsky turned towards Slavena. "Put your shoes on. It's gravel outside. You're gonna cut up your feet."

He got out of the car and opened the door for her.

"I don't want to go," Slavena said.

"Don't be stupid. If I wanted to harm you, I wouldn't be using a taxi, would I?"

"How do I know the taxi driver is not with you?"

"Ask him."

"Do you know this man?" Slavena turned to the driver pointing a finger at Orlovsky. The taxi driver shook his head but the unease in his eyes didn't reassure Slavena.

"Come on," Orlovsky grabbed her hand forcefully and pulled her out of the car. She staggered in her high heels sinking in the gravel. Orlovsky picked her up as if she was no heavier than a bag of cotton and carried her towards the building.

Inside things didn't get better. It was pitch dark. A strong chlorine aroma assaulted her and she sneezed. She clung to Orlovsky's body like a wet leaf stuck to the sole of a shoe. She was determined to stay as close to him as humanly possible. If something happened to her, he was going down too.

Orlovsky stopped.

"What are you going to do to me?" Slavena whispered in the dark.

"Only nice things," Orlovsky hissed back and she remembered the snake. Slavena panicked and dug her fingers deeper into his clothes. His hot breath smelled fruity and reminded her of the sour cherry brandy the General had forced her to drink at the party.

Orlovsky let her go.

"Nooooo!" Slavena screamed, hearing her own voice echoing in what seemed to be a cavernous hall.

For a second, she was airborne. Then her body hit water

and she sank. She was so shocked by the cold liquid that she didn't know which way was up. She desperately fought for air, but every way she looked she was surrounded by dark water. Her brain was blinded by panic as she inhaled a lungful of water.

So, this was how Orlovsky was going to kill her. Drowning her?

THE ADMIRAL

Orlovsky was doing laps in the pool and he couldn't concentrate to save his life. He kept over-rolling when he turned to breathe. Like an amateur. Next thing he knew he snorted water and choked, quickly shattering his desire to carry on. He cut his routine short at twenty laps and got out of the pool. He wrapped a towel around his midriff and checked his cell phone for messages.

Nothing.

Things had been going well for him in the past week if he didn't count the therapist's disappearance after their last encounter at the pool. Orlovsky was especially good on stalking, but he'd been too busy with his commissions to find her.

He'd done his second hit. The target had been Jaro's right hand—a thug with the nickname Little Christ. It hadn't been a challenging job. The fringe mafia guys were sloppy and lazy, not just with business but security as well.

Little Christ frequented a café in central Sofia that belonged to a friend of his. Like every small animal, Little Christ liked to keep to his territory. The scent of his own piss on the walls made him feel secure. Wrong. There was no hole Orlovsky couldn't dig him out of.

Orlovsky stole a priest's cassock from a local Orthodox

church and entered the café disguised as a priest. The cassock had been perfect for concealing two Colt.45 Lightweight Commanders in his inner thigh holsters. Before Little Christ and his guards could even begin to suspect there was something amiss with this particular priest, Orlovsky simultaneously released a jacketed hollow-point round into both guards, killing them on the spot. His second-round tore into Little Christ's shoulder as he attempted to unholster his Beretta M9. Orlovsky smiled at the memory of him bending down to Little Christ's face and asking him with a whisper: "Would you like to receive last rites before we find out if you can rise from the dead?" Without giving him the chance to respond, Orlovsky had released a final hollow point directly into his chest.

And now he was pleased with himself. He executed his last job well, and if only Alena texted him back, he would have been in a perfect mood. He didn't want to admit it, but he craved her since the night he threw her in the pool with her clothes on. That was really why he couldn't concentrate on swimming. It was his last memory of her in the pool. She'd screamed her head off when he pulled her above the water and allowed her to breathe. Then he ripped her wet shirt that clung to her breasts and she'd fought back, the way he wanted her to fight—fearlessly. He'd never felt so fulfilled from an act of sex. Drained of tension and anger. Hungry for her next touch.

With that thought, he walked towards the changing room. His tout muscles carried his powerful torso with ease. He could feel every ligament and tendon in his body working in perfect harmony. He'd never been in better shape in his entire life and he needed someone, like Alena to admire his body. Instead, she disappeared as if she knew just what to do to bring him to the boiling point.

While changing he heard his cell phone beep. The message wasn't from Alena, as he hoped, but from an unknown number: *Vestnik newspaper from today*. There was a link. Orlovsky clicked on it and a website loaded up with an article about leadership in crisis. The interview was given by Anton Bankov.

"Fuck," he said, scrolling down until he came to a picture of a white-haired man with piercing blue eyes and a weather-beaten face. Anton Bankov — the Admiral — was his next target.

"Fuck!" He repeated with anger and deleted the message with one swift movement.

For the first time in his life, he had been commissioned to kill a friend.

Orlovsky got out of the gym on autopilot and drove his Range Rover across the city like a speedboat breaking waves, ignoring red traffic lights and stop signs. He finally made it to Amnesia — surprisingly without an accident — and started ordering large whiskeys as soon as he was through the door. Sometime after midnight, the bartender asked him to leave. In response, Orlovsky broke his nose. It took the whole bar staff to throw him out. Two tables and a floor lamp fell victims to the fight.

In the morning, Orlovsky was still drunk but hadn't managed to forget the reason he was drinking. Anton Bankov was next on the CLEANSING list and he had been like a father to him. Orlovsky owed him his life.

After his actual father died when Orlovsky was only thirteen, the KGB moved his mother and him back to Bulgaria where they settled in Sofia. His mother worked two shifts at a chicken factory to support herself and her son. Once an Olympic gold medalist, she became a middle-aged poor widow overnight. She didn't complain, but Orlovsky was full of anger. His father had spent thirteen years filling his head with promises of apprenticeship at his employer, the KGB. He promised to teach him the tradecraft of covert activities, creative thinking, and the art of combat. Orlovsky wanted nothing else but to follow in his father's footsteps.

Two days before Brezhnev's death was announced on national television, the Orlovsky family lost the head of its household to alcoholism. The younger Orlovsky's dreams were shattered. He blamed his mother for not doing enough to stop his father's drinking; he hated his dad for dying. He hated himself for not being able to help his mother with keeping them fed and alive. But he was only thirteen years old.

The year he finished high school, seventeen-year-old Orlovsky was faced with compulsory military service. He chose the Navy in hopes of putting the Black Sea between him and Bulgaria. He was already drinking heavily, rejecting only vodka—his father's drink of choice. During his first weekend pass following basic training, he smuggled in a few bottles of whiskey, got drunk and broke the windshield of a car parked at the officers' parking lot. The car belonged to Captain Anton Bankov.

Weeks of disciplinary punishment followed. The kind of punishment Warsaw Pact militaries specialized in. Orlovsky spent the time mainly in solitary confinement. As soon as he finished the sentence of one offense, he committed another, often manhandling anyone attempting to enforce the punishment. Twelve weeks in, Orlovsky had lost significant weight and his mental health was spiraling down faster than a coin in a wishing well.

One day, Bankov walked into his cell, handed him a towel, and took him to the officers' berthing for a hot shower and a long overdue shave. Then he sat Orlovsky down in the officers' mess.

"I knew your father," he'd told him. "Discipline was his life and I'm sure he passed that on you. I see you have your father's tenacity, but you lack his character. Do you want the opportunity to become a man? Or do you wish to remain a child?"

That day changed Orlovsky's life. With the personal endorsement of Bankov, he became a professional seaman and focused his energy into fulfilling his potential, but not his father's promises. Instead of the KGB, Orlovsky followed Bankov's example and proved himself through the grueling training program for naval Special Forces operators. Orlovsky could still feel his inner pride the day he officially joined Bankov's naval Special Forces unit Vulni. Under Bankov's personal mentorship, he became disciplined, creative and an exceptionally deadly marksman. He still felt the best days of his life were spent with Vulni's Group B, conducting infiltration and key target assassinations of mujahidin in that Afghanistan. It was there that he spent almost two years fighting alongside Vympel—the elite Russian Spetsnaz unit, refining his already lethal skills.

He could still recall the party they threw in September 1988 when Bankov announced he had been promoted to Rear Admiral and Commander of the Bulgarian Naval Squadron in the Black Sea. They washed down canned meat food rations with whiskey toasts with the boys from Vympel knowing the Admiral would have operational control of Vulni when it redeployed from Afghanistan early the next year.

As revolution swept Eastern Europe in 1989, Orlovsky could only recall his exponentially growing anxiety and restlessness with garrison life outside the war zone. His country was in freefall and all he cared was to find the next conflict and continue his body count. His tension was broken when Bankov approached him alone on the main pier of Atiga. "Alexander, the world as we know it, is about to end. Revolutions are always a time of survival of the fittest. The time to defend our country is over. We lost everything defending her. It is time to be compensated."

Confused, the young Orlovsky had asked his mentor. "And how do we do that Admiral? I'm just a soldier."

"If we learned one thing from Afghanistan is that you can only rely on the man beside you. This world will eat you and shit you out if you do not seize the opportunity. The coming revolution is our opportunity to become rich beyond our wildest dreams, but we must rely on each soldier in Vulni to do his part. I need you to be my enforcer in the days to come."

With that Orlovsky was alive again as they transformed Vulni from the most elite military element in Bulgaria into a private security firm that would eventually form Bulgarian Assets Management (BAM) consortium.

As the central communist government in Sofia collapsed Orlovsky and Vulni seized the Soviet Black Sea Fleet anchored at Atiga. He still chuckled at the irony of the country struggling to control national anarchy, while it was easy for Bankov to find buyers for the stockpiles of military hardware they had seized. He recalled feeling alive again as he and his Vulni teammates provided security for arms deliveries to South America and Africa using a Bulgarian flagged Grisha class Corvette. Along with hand-selected officers of the Black Sea Squadron, Orlovsky became rich in the process.

But the money was never the primary motive for Orlovsky. Instead, he rode an adrenaline fueled high as they stormed, seized and sold the most profitable equipment of four Bulgarian Naval and Army bases. This new windfall of cash enabled Bankov to legitimize themselves and form the Bulgarian Assets Management (BAM) consortium. BAM's tentacles quickly moved to control local politics and commercial enterprises across Bulgaria's Black Sea coast.

Together Bankov and Orlovsky became respectable East European businessmen managing a multinational corporation and by the fall of 1993, they were filthy rich. The group focused on finding ways of spending their wealth on expensive cars, élite women and luxury. This bored Alexander Orlovsky.

He was a creature of disciplined risk-taking. The benefits of money and power derived from the consortium didn't appeal to him. He craved the lifestyle of a Special Forces operator.

Three years in and Orlovsky was forced out by Bankov. He'd slept with Bankov's wife, Marianna, and that had sealed the deal. Bankov paid Orlovsky his share of the company and ordered him out of Bourgas. In exile, Orlovsky killed for whatever Russian Bratva group offered the most interesting contract. He never would have returned to Bulgaria if the CLEANSING contract had not been so intriguing.

And now there was a price on Bankov's head.

Orlovsky scrambled to his apartment and slept off the booze. In the evening he cooked himself dinner and shot in his gunfighter gym for six hours straight.

Everything he was today, he owed to Bankov, but a job was a job. The Admiral had to die.

Into the silence came, at last, a sound. The blinking of a red dot on her computer screen woke her up, jerking her away from her dreams. The GPS tracker she'd planted in Orlovsky's wallet was finally working, but it was way too early in the morning for counter-surveillance. The map showed the red dot was only twelve blocks away from her apartment, moving fast, *way too fast*, towards her. Orlovsky was coming over. Suddenly the air in her room became saturated with fear. Her eyes watched the dot steadily while she developed a plan of action.

The dot suddenly stopped.

She print-screened the last location and darted out of her equipment room. As she rushed down the stairs, she remembered her instructor at the Farm telling her about different escape strategies: "Never ever use a staircase," he'd said, "when you're on the run. Thirty-eight percent of all fatal accidents in the Agency occurred when hurrying down the stairs."

In her opinion, the elevator was much worse. She slowed down her steps, but there was no stopping under the spell of the adrenaline. Her heart was racing and her thoughts were gushing out like a geyser. Why was Orlovsky coming to her home instead of her office? She never gave him her home address but somehow, he was still able to track her. Perhaps like her, he had planted a tracking device. But where?

She quickly unlocked her apartment, stormed into her double closet and keyed a code into the cipher-lock on the wall. The safe opened. She removed her Glock 19 while eyeing the bug sweeper sitting in the far-left corner of her safe. She needed to find out how Orlovsky was able to track her down but now was not the time. Now she had to run.

She closed the safe, turned on her surveillance equipment, double-bolt locked her apartment and leaped upstairs to her equipment room. Only to see the red dot on the screen had turned green. Slavena let out her tension in a deep exhale. Orlovsky had departed the *red zone* as she called it. That was an expectedly nice break. Her eyes rested on the screen for a moment while her mind plunged into a scenario. Was Orlovsky's presence in her neighborhood just a coincidence?

Her answer came in a curious fashion on her computer screen. It was a message, streamed directly from Orlovsky's cell phone to her computer and read *Vestnik newspaper from today*. She clicked on the link with bewilderment on her face. The date of the message was a day old and in the CIA technology world, any delay was unacceptable. With a light of rage in her eyes, she dialed Travis's number.

"I know, I know." Travis defended himself. "But I had some technical issues and—"

"Travis, when my life is on the line, I'd like to be informed on time."

A long pause, but she'd expected that.

"I was able to trace the text message," he finally said.

"That's great! Tell me more."

"Can't," he said sharply. "Waiting for the release authorization."

"How long?"

"Can't say, but the technology works best when it's not relied upon for actionable intelligence."

"Understood. Let me know when you hear something. Gotta go."

Slavena hung up and clicked on the link to read the article. It was a mind-numbing essay on leaders staying strong in times of crisis. She had no idea how it could be of any interest to Orlovsky until she saw Anton Bankov's name. She turned on her VPN and Googled Anton Bankov. As she expected there was little information on Bankov or his company, Bulgarian Assets Management (BAM), in the public domain. The shady company that held over fifty subsidiary companies under its umbrella was the best-kept secret in the country. There were all kinds of rumors flying around the former Admiral Bankov. Extortion, bribery, kidnapping, and even murders, but nothing the police could pin him down for personally. He'd grown so rich that he was considered the feudal lord of Eastern Bulgaria.

Switching her computer encryption and tunneling software on, Slavena continued her search on CIA's SECRET network database, the Wire. There she found a DIA personal profile on Bankov that discussed his military and criminal history in detail. It had an embedded link to a US Department of Treasury list of assets, including the recent purchase of a house for his wife in a historic district of Sofia, not far from her house.

Slavena cross-referenced the information with Google and found the address on the third hit. It was near the last location of the red dot. Orlovsky was likely snooping around Bankov's house, but she had to be sure.

She found an article about the house. The purchase deal would have gone unnoticed if the house was not the former home of one of Bulgaria's most prominent poets—Hristan Kalchev. Bankov intended to knock the old house down and build a modern structure in its place. But when local historians discovered the underhanded sale, they'd kicked up a stink in the press and the demolition of the house was halted for the time being. Meanwhile, Bankov had moved into the house and put up a high fence around the property.

Slavena thought of Travis and how he could make it up to her. She sent the print-screen of the red dot from earlier to him and waited for exact grid coordinates and the most recent satellite images of the location. Her gut was telling her that it was the exact location Orlovsky intended to conduct the hit.

But there was always another possibility. She knew Bankov and Orlovsky were close friends and former partners in BAM. Was Bankov a target or an accomplice? If the former, killing Bankov would be more personal for Orlovsky than he'd bargained for.

Slavena quickly scripted a report to Gavin about the potential new hit and that Orlovsky might have trouble handling this target due to old ties. She printed it and once she scanned over the cryptic Taekwondo language to make sure that she got it right, she called Konstantin for a ride to the supermarket. Inside his car, she planted a drop with the initial intelligence report under the back seat.

Gavin called her that evening.

"Sounds like it's time for you to do your *bang hyang bakoogi!*" He said without preliminaries.

"What does that mean in Korean?"

"Change direction. If he doesn't want to go through with this, change his mind."

So, he'd read her report and was worried that Orlovsky's ties with the potential new victim might cloud his judgment and land him in trouble.

"And what if I can't change his mind? Then what? Kill the guy for him?"

"Very funny, but you'll figure it out. Just don't take any risks. I mean unreasonable risks."

Slavena sighed. "Are you asking me to babysit Scarface?"

"Yes. Execute and keep me informed as things develop." The conversation ended.

KNIGHT

Slavena stepped out of her apartment building and felt the early morning chill on her skin. She zipped up her jacket all the way to her chin and pulled out her phone. The same phone she used for communicating with Orlovsky.

Minutes earlier, when she removed the phone out of the freezer, she had doubts about reassembling it. It was her only phone with a camera, but it was risky. Orlovsky could track her down if he woke up before 5 o'clock in the morning. Since he was never up that early, she concluded she was safe for the next two hours.

Once she turned on her data, she received an old text from Orlovsky with enough sexual context to make her heart race before she even started the run. She put the phone back in her pocket and started jogging slowly. She got to Bankov's house in 10 minutes.

As Slavena approached the house, she leaned on the eight-foot-high fence around Bankov's house and pretended to stretch her muscles. While stretching, she pulled her phone out and held it facedown to take a few pictures of the top of the fence.

From what she could see, there was no way Orlovsky was climbing over the fence unless he was a circus artist. Most likely, he was going to snipe Bankov out of this world from the abandoned house across the street. The satellite image she received from Travis had confirmed her suspicions.

Before she knew what was happening the metal gate opened and a couple of army-issue boots came out. They moved fast. Strong hands grabbed her by her jacket and pulled her in. The gate closed behind her with a crash.

Slavena was captured.

Orlovsky had just fixed himself a ham sandwich when he heard his cell phone vibrate on the table in the living room. Alena's name was flashing on the screen and Orlovsky felt a momentary sense of glee before picking up. She was finally returning his calls.

"Alex," Bankov said. "Here is a voice from your past that you thought you'd never hear again,"

Orlovsky's face froze into a mask. Alarm bells sounded in his ears. How did Bankov get access to Alena's cell phone?

"What do you want, Admiral?"

"Nice to hear from you too, buddy."

Orlovsky stood silent.

"I've forgotten your admirable people skills," Bankov sighed. "Anyway, I have someone here that belongs to you." Orlovsky heard the shuffling of feet. There was someone else in the room with him. "Ivan, bring the woman over."

The woman must be Alena, Orlovsky thought since Bankov was using her phone. What the fuck was going on?

"So, Alex, are you sending your girlfriend to snoop around me, cause you don't have the guts to do it yourself or—"

"I've plenty of guts to do anything I want, Admiral. You know that plenty well. And I haven't had a girlfriend since before I fucked your wife."

"Ouch," Bankov said in a mockingly hurt voice. "And here I am thinking you've moved on since she chose me over you. Obviously not."

Orlovsky seethed at the end of the line. He was not in the mood to out-mouth Bankov right now. Besides, he was a man of action, not words.

An opening of a door and muted mumbling could be heard over the receiver before Bankov's voice came loud and clear again.

"Here she is, your pretty little spy. Say something, love." Slavena stayed mute. "Say a few words, because this will be the last time you speak to your Eagle."

A slap followed. Then another one, but Slavena refused to speak.

"You should forgive her, Alex. She had a rough day. And she is in for a rougher night if I don't get some answers from you."

"I don't know who you're talking about and whatever bitch you brought home last night, dispose of her without involving me."

"Tut-tut, Alex. You shouldn't talk about women like this. Perhaps that's why Marianna chose me over you, you know."

Orlovsky opted for silence.

"You got her trained pretty well, your woman. She managed to knock down a couple of my guards. Nothing to worry about. A few wobbly teeth. But she botched the surveillance part for you, though. Crappy, crappy photos. I guess now you'll need a new girlfriend to cover for you."

What was Alena taking pictures of Bankov's house for? And getting captured doing it on top of it? Was she following him on his jobs? The fucking bitch! And where was she getting her information from?

"Are you fucking with me, Admiral?" Orlovsky finally said.

"Why would I do that, Alex?" Bankov's soft voice traveled to Orlovsky's ears but had a hard time reaching his brain. He was so mad right now he could wring Alena's neck if she was near him.

"Go fuck yourself, Admiral. Or fuck her if that turns you on. I couldn't care less."

Orlovsky hung up.

Bankov turned to face Slavena, who patiently waited for him to finish his call.

"He didn't send you, did he? You are using Orlovsky for information, but the question remains: why are you here?"

Slavena stood barefoot in front of him in her shorts and sports bra. She was soaked to the bone from sweat and water from them waterboarding her for hours. So far, she'd told them nothing. Bankov signaled Ivan to take her away as he dialed his cell phone.

"Sinner, I got some fresh news for you,"

"What?"

"I think the person behind Little Christ's shooting is a woman."

"You're joking? No woman could have pulled that off."

"If she was wearing a Nun's habit she might. Anything could be hidden under Nun's habit. Only the Lord Almighty knows what's under the habit!" Bankov roared with laughter at the perversity of his own humor.

"Motherfucker. You know, you could be right! How do you know all this?"

"I've got the cunt right here. Caught her snooping around this morning by the gate."

"And?"

"And nothing. Wouldn't say a thing. The silence of cunts. They're so good at keeping their lips sealed."

The Sinner laughed for a moment until there was a commotion on his side of the line.

"Move. Move. Move!" The Sinner shouted away from the phone.

"I think I hit something..." a muffled voice said in the background.

"What do I care?" the Sinner barked. "I need to get home before the wife gets all crazy on me again. Understood?"

Bankov heard police sirens in the background.

"Call you back, Admiral. I've got a situation."

The line went dead.

Bankov sat thinking in silence. Nobody was interested in the woman. Orlovsky didn't give two shits about her. The Sinner wasn't taking her seriously. He'd lost a whole morning trying to get something useful out of her and he'd drawn a blank. He concluded if she knew anything, she would have talked by now.

He stood up, dropped his cell phone in his jacket pocket and walked out of the room.

"Get the car ready," he told a pimply, bulky teen waiting by the door. "We are going to our meeting with the Mayor."

Bankov had finally decided the renovation of his house was more important than this woman who was most likely a news reporter. He would interrogate her again tomorrow.

In his apartment, Orlovsky put on black spandex tights with reinforced knees, stretching them up all the way to his six-pack. He pulled a black lycra top over his torso and strapped a multi-pocketed vest over it. It contained everything he might need for his night hit — night-vision goggles, smoke and frag grenades, laser range finder, black zip line and more.

He was going to hit Bankov's house tonight. He knew he wasn't ready. He wished he had a few more days to plan the attack, but he was out of time. The call about Alena had seriously disturbed him. He had to find out who she was. And, fortunately for her, the only way to do that was to save her from Bankov.

The situation with Alena had scrambled his brain. Who was she? Everything he knew or thought he knew about her, had to be sifted through a strainer. What was her game? Who was she working for? How did she know his next target? And the biggest question of all: was he in danger?

He walked to the front door and pulled out black army boots from a closet concealed behind a mirror in the wall. He laced them up tight and walked along the corridor a few times. He hadn't worn them in months. He preferred to do his hits in disguise — like the priest cassock — because it was inconspicuous. Walking the streets in military kit after dark, meant only one thing to onlookers. Trouble. There was no better way to attract the attention of authorities or worse, other hired killers, than dressing like you are about to kill someone.

With this operation, he had no choice. He was mad at Alena for putting him on the spot like this. He had to storm a house he knew next to nothing about and in which, knowing Bankov, two to four bodyguards lurked around.

He put more equipment in the gym bag and flew in his Range Rover to Bankov's house. He coasted the last fifty meters with the lights turned off and parked on a side street, leaving large gaps before and after his car, so nobody could block him. He put on his black balaclava, leather gloves and did a final check of his kit before disappearing into the dark.

His point of entry was at the back of the house, where Bankov's airheaded wife had knocked down a wall before the demolition was halted. The hole was currently blocked only by a dusty nylon sheet, awaiting the green light for resumption of work. It was August, the hottest month in Bulgaria and the hole in the wall didn't bother anyone. Orlovsky had spotted it on a reconnaissance trip he'd done earlier and knew he'd hit the jackpot. But that was before Alena was captured. Now with Bankov alerted, chances were, he would have more than one guard on the first floor. He would need to potentially eliminate numerous guards before he reached his main target.

The backyard was easy to access by setting up a zip line from a tree in the adjacent lot that separated the poet's house from the vast wall. In no time, he had zipped himself into the backyard. Once firmly on the ground, he leaned on the wall and listened for sounds from inside the house.

One of the bodyguards must have heard the hissing sound of the zip line and peeked from the nylon with his weapon at the ready. Orlovsky used a sword-hand to the wrist and the man dropped his gun. Then he drove a half-fist into his throat with enough force to break the cartilage. The man's eyes became wide open when he felt his internal hemorrhage choking his life away. Orlovsky grabbed his limp body, easing it to the floor, and silently walked inside the house.

It was an old house with creaking floorboards and loose fittings, but he had to keep moving even if he made noise. He knew it was a matter of minutes before the others came out to check why their colleague hadn't returned.

He crossed the room with big steps that elicited some groans from the planks and headed towards the room with the flicking blue light of a television set bouncing against a wall.

That would be the room where the night bodyguards kept a watch out. Orlovsky bent down and peeked through the old keyhole. One boy-faced thug was fast asleep on a sofa. *Jeez, was Bankov recruiting his bodyguards from the kindergarten now?* The boy's face was illuminated by the TV screen. He was a big guy. His hands crossed across his chest were like the Hulk's, minus the green skin. Orlovsky pulled a double-edged boot knife out and lowered the door handle until the latch clicked open.

Before the Hulk could open his eyes, Orlovsky had blocked his mouth and cut his carotid artery. The more the boy struggled, the faster he bled out. In a few seconds, he was dead.

Orlovsky climbed upstairs and killed what was to be the final guard with a knife into his eye socket. The guard's body dropped like a sack of potatoes onto the floor with his blood flooding the front of the master bedroom. Bankov was sleeping inside it with Marianna, his wife. She was with her back to her husband, leaving a big space between them in the large king-size bed. This made it easy for Orlovsky.

Bankov laid with his mouth open and his belly hanging out through the unbuttoned flaps of his pajama top. The years hadn't been kind to him. He looked, and smelled, like an old man.

I'm doing you a favor, old dog, Orlovsky thought as he cut Bankov's throat. *You don't want to grow any older and fatter than this.*

Marianna stirred at the sound of her husband choking on his own blood.

"Hi, sexy. Remember me?" was the last thing she ever heard.

Orlovsky made sure there was nobody else in the house before he looked for Alena. He found her in the basement, gagged and zip-tied but sleeping upright on a rusty iron bench.

PITCH

Slavena was dreaming of her sister. It had been years since she'd seen her so clearly. As time passed the image of her sister's face had faded to that of a grainy black and white photo.

In Slavena's dream they were in a café they frequented daily after school. It was a narrow, miserable place where the high schoolers, the primary clientele, shared their emerging social lives. Who cheated on what test? Who kissed whom? Who dumped whom? On and on, it went day in, day out.

Slavena dreamed of a specific afternoon in the café often. It was the last time she saw her sister alive. The two siblings had sat alone at a round plastic table, nursing cappuccinos in re-used plastic cups, sharing a packet of pretzels. The café was incredibly noisy and Slavena had to read her sister's lips to understand what she was saying.

"I told him I'm not interested. I'm seeing someone else," Boyana said and licked cappuccino foam from the tip of a plastic spoon.

"What did he say?"

Boyana shrugged. "He wasn't pleased. Said he could offer me security. I laughed in his face. Told him I had better offers than his. Then he said I should be more careful who I piss off. He told me Jaro and his gang had handpicked me for a nice ride and he would do nothing about it."

The sisters sat silent for a while.

"But isn't his dad the Director of National Police?"

"So? What's he going to do? Tell his daddy about Jaro and arrest him?"

"Boychev can certainly protect you."

"Protect me? You've been watching too many *Law & Order* episodes." Boyana smiled indulgently at her little sister.

"But what if—"

"Don't worry," Boyana interrupted her. "I know what I'm doing."

Don't worry. Don't worry. Don't worry. Her words continued to echo.

Slavena woke up with a shock. Her hands were no longer tied to the bench and someone was lifting her up. She didn't have the strength to resist. It was only when the man took her out of the house that Slavena realized she wasn't being taken for another round of interrogation and torture. She looked at the man's face.

It was Alexander Orlovsky.

It had been only two weeks since the pool party he staged for her but Alena now looked different. Laying on the bench like a broken doll in shorts and a sports bra with bruises all over her body. When he looked at her face, he almost felt sorry for her. The bruises would heal, he thought, but the experience of what he was going to do to her next would not. He planned to inflict more pain on her to get convincing and raw intelligence from her. But more than that. He was going to intimidate her and show who was in charge.

Orlovsky cut the zip tie that held her hands with the same knife he'd used to take five lives that night. He put his arm under Alena and picked her up, still unconscious. He carried her back towards the front gate of the house no longer worried about the creaking floorboards. There wasn't a single living soul left in the house to hear his footsteps. On his way out, he destroyed the camera recorder, took the hard drive, and was glad to be back on the street, a short walk away from his car. He was always glad when a job was done.

But this job was not yet complete.

Under a street lamp, Orlovsky took a second look at Alena's face. Her lips were dry and cracked, like the parched soil of a riverbed wiped out by the summer heat. Orlovsky recognized the method Bankov used to interrogate her. The dry hot sauna to dehydrate her followed by water-boarding sessions during each sauna break. She looked delirious, which was just the way he wanted her. She owed him answers and he didn't intend to be nice to her when he asked the questions.

He hurried his steps towards the car when he heard people talking down the street in loud, drunken voices. He threw Alena in the passenger seat and slammed the door. Just before the tinted windows blocked her face from view, Orlovsky saw Alena open her eyes for the first time. She didn't look like she was aware of her surroundings, but when he got to the driver's seat, she was eagerly gulping his energy drink from the can he'd left in the car's cup holder.

He stared at her and she looked at him over the can with leveled, determined eyes. Orlovsky shut the door, started the car and drove away in silence. Next to him, Alena brushed her fingers over her bruised wrists and sucked air through gritted teeth from the pain. The zip tie had cut her skin and the burning pain was unbearable.

A traffic light turned red and Orlovsky slowed down. The silence in the car became oppressive.

"What were you doing at Bankov's house?" He asked icily, tilting his head towards her.

Alena focused her eyes on her bruised wrists, trying hard to remember what happened. She knew Orlovsky saved her, but she had no concept of time. Was she captured for hours or days?

"What time is it?"

"What do you fucking care? You need to be somewhere?"

Alena didn't answer.

"I'm going to ask you one more time: What were you doing at Bankov's house?"

"And what if I don't feel like talking right now?"

"Then I'll take you to the mountains where *no one* will find you."

"I don't think so. You didn't save me just to turn around and kill me," Alena said, looking up at his face. Illuminated by the streetlights, she saw the anger etched in his features. She'd gone too far and she had to say something. "The whole thing was just a misunderstanding."

"A misunderstanding?" He banged a fist on the steering wheel. "I just killed five people because of you, Alena or whatever the fuck your name is. Go tell *them* that."

"I did not ask you to do that." Alena's voice shook as if she was on the verge of tears. If Orlovsky registered it, he gave little sign of caring.

"You're good at avoiding my questions. One. Last. Time. Why were you at Bankov's house?"

"I told you already, it was a mix-up. Something about my phone." She rolled her eyes.

"This one?" Orlovsky pulled her phone out of his vest and looked at it. "I find it interesting that I am the only contact on it."

"I don't have many friends," she said, realizing that for the first time she was telling him the truth.

"Forget the damn phone, how did you end up inside his house? I want the whole story."

She rubbed her left temple with her bruised hand. Her headache was splitting her skull in half and she had to ask. "Do you have any Tylenol?"

Orlovsky acknowledged her question but kept his eyes on the road, picturing the bottle of SP-117 inside his glove compartment. It was his favorite drug mix of truth serum and sedative that would make her tell him everything. He was tempted, but it would also make her sleep for a day or two and he didn't feel like taking care of her. He took women back to his place for sex only and that rule wasn't going to change any time soon.

"Do I look like a pharmacist to you?" He said. "Back to Bankov. What were you doing at his house?"

She looked outside her window yearning for an escape, but there was no way out. She had to tell him everything.

"I jog in the morning," she started casually as she watched Orlovsky scroll through the photos on her phone.

"Why were you taking photos?"

"What photos?" She was buying time to work out the

answer, but the look Orlovsky gave her froze the blood in her veins. "Oh, those photos!" She managed to crack a smile.

"Yes. Those photos. Why did you take them?"

"It wasn't quite like that."

"What was it like, then?"

She shrugged. "I was in the neighborhood, so I snapped some photos before the house gets demolished. What's the big deal?"

Orlovsky's jaws tightened, revealing the immaculate bone structure of his face. He didn't buy it. "Is that the story you told him?"

"It's the only story I have."

"I'm surprised he didn't kill you for your anemic lies."

"What lies?"

"This won't fly with me, you know? If you don't tell me now, I won't be as forgiving as him. I will cut your throat just like I cut his wife's throat," he looked at his watch, "exactly twenty minutes ago."

"You seemed to be quite forgiving in your last text message," she said right before his abrupt backhanded blow hit her in the face, causing her nose to explode in a gush of red liquid.

"Listen, bitch! Just because I had sex with you, doesn't mean you can play with me. This is business, you understand?"

She nodded with both hands on the bridge of her now broken nose. She didn't want any more pain. She'd received enough in the last twenty hours.

"I'm good at what I do for a reason. I don't form emotional attachments with anybody, including you. And the only reason why you're still alive is because I thought you had something for me. Obviously, I was wrong!"

Orlovsky swerved the car violently to the side of the

road. The distinct smell of the rubber burn of the tires made her sick. But it wasn't the smell that gave her nausea. It was his abrupt change of course.

The car had come to a full stop near a forested area and all she could see in the dark were the whites of his eyes. He was staring at her and her throat choked with panic. The pain from all her injuries suddenly came at her strong and urged her to tell him everything she knew. It was her own mistake to get caught. Now was her chance to come clean.

"All right." She straightened her back. "Let's talk business."

"What's your real name?"

"Alena," Slavena said. "And I'm not your enemy, Orlovsky. That much you must've gathered by now."

"What do you want from me, *Alena*?" He pronounced the name as if it was a cherry seed that needed spitting out. "You've told me you want Jaro dead, but something tells me there is a lot more to it."

"Yes. I want to talk to you about the *CLEANSING*."

Orlovsky gave her a sly, displeased look. "The cleansing? You mean detox?" He asked sourly. "Do I look like a faggot to you?"

Slavena felt a knot in her stomach. Days earlier she had scripted a pitch to negotiate with Orlovsky. It was the perfect pitch. But the circumstances had changed and anybody with a bit of sense wouldn't dare to toy with a hitman who was still high from the kill. One wrong word and he wouldn't hesitate to end her life as well. Her only rescue was her instructor's advice: "When it doesn't feel right, stroke his ego and make him a hero."

It was time to charm the Narcissist, Slavena figured, but first, she needed to calm him down. "If you want to hear what I have to say, then start listening and stop using me as a punching bag," she said firmly.

"Ok then, tell me about this cleansing thing. What is it? A *movie*?"

"A movie?" Slavena looked surprised for an instant, but her eyes lightened with hope. Orlovsky was letting her know that he wasn't comfortable talking about his work so openly, and their chat needed to be spy-coated with movie references.

Finally understanding his approach, she carried on. "Yes! It's the newest movie in production about wiping out the mafia and you were chosen for the lead role. Are you following me now?"

He gave a thin smile. "Yes. And who the hell *are* you?"

"Your best friend and I'll get to that in a minute, but first, let's talk about the politics of the movie," She said, testing the waters.

"I don't care about the politics." Orlovsky's eyes glittered in the dark, growing impatient. "Come on, get to the point."

"The point is that you're an exceptionally talented actor who doesn't care about the politics of the movie. That's why they chose you for the lead role. There are not many like you Orlovsky." She put on her act of praises to secure his attention and it worked. Orlovsky said nothing and stared at her for a full minute. He was busy doing his own thinking.

"Who is 'they'?" He said at last.

"The producers."

He narrowed his eyes. "The *Producers*? How many fucking producers *are* there?"

"Many, but I'm here to represent the most powerful one," She said feeling the sweat on her palms. Was she giving away too much information?

"Go on" Orlovsky didn't miss her hesitation. "Tell me about *that* producer. What's his deal?"

"He didn't greenlight the script of the CLEANSING."

"What the *fuck* are you talking about?" he snapped as if preparing for another face punch.

"I'm talking about a major financial risk if the script remains as it is."

"Then ask the screenwriter to edit the damn script!"

"That's the thing, nobody knows who the screenwriter is—"

Orlovsky narrowed his eyes. "What makes you think that I don't know him?"

"Because I'm well informed. If you insist we can discuss it, but as you said you only want to talk about the movie."

"I am the *fucking* movie!" he hissed and she shivered at the sound of menace coming out of his mouth. He sensed her fear and changed the cutthroat tone of his voice. "If the producer is such a big shot, as you advertise him to be, then why can't he find out who the screenwriter is?"

"Because he can't take the risk to wait that long."

"So, it is up to me to deviate from the script?"

"Yes. Since you are the lead actor."

"I don't like where this is going." His eyes blazed with fury. "If I am paid to act. I act. I don't ask questions or play politics!"

"But it's the producer who has the final say and if you cooperate—"

"Then I will get killed."

"Not if you have insurance."

"So that's where you come in? You are my insurance?"

"Exactly! I will arrange full compensation and protection

for you if it comes to that." It was partly true. Her job, alongside other things, was to make sure he did not get killed. Well, at least not until the Company ordered it.

"What about my reputation?"

"What reputation if you're dead?"

Hearing this, Orlovsky erupted with laughter, the intensity of which increased in a crescendo with tears in his eyes. As much as she wanted to hate him, she found it hard to hate someone who just saved her life. Subconsciously, she looked at the hands that had saved her. His leather gloves appeared spotless on the surface, but she was certain there was enough DNA on them to stretch for a thousand miles. And if she didn't get her pitch right, her DNA was going to be next on that long chain of human DNA.

"I always come out alive and I don't need a woman to protect me!" In a blur, he aimed his SIG P226 at her and with a barrel pointed at her nose, Slavena realized it was so quiet inside the car that she could hear her own breathing.

"I know you want to kill me," she said, and her voice was weak in her ear. "but you don't want to."

"What makes you think so?"

"Because you are afraid of what you don't know and afraid of being replaced by another actor who is more cooperative than you are."

He raised his eyebrows. "Replaced you say?"

"Oh. Did I say replaced? Sorry. I used the wrong adjective. Killed."

Orlovsky's eyes flashed with fury. He considered inflicting further pain on her but he knew pain was already throbbing in her body and there was no point to add more, so he carried on with his acidic tone. "And what is in it for you? I don't get it."

"Nothing. I'm just like you—a pawn on the board that can be removed with the snap of a finger." She snapped her fingers at him, but the clicking sound never came. She realized her hands were too weak to produce the crispy traction between her fingers. He watched her in silence with as much empathy in his eyes as a Venus flytrap. He was a coldblooded killer and the dried droplets of blood above his left eyebrow reminded her of what little patience he had.

"You're entertaining. I'll give you that, but your jester moves won't save you in the end. You know why? Because I can't stand arrogance and people like you, who think they are the king and everyone else are their pawns to be used and disposed of. Who think they know everything. But they know nothing! You hear me? Nothing!" He pressed the end of his SIG against her cheek and watched her eyes for signs of fright. She was terrified of him but too well trained to allow fear to enter her mind.

"You're right! I don't know everything, but I know something," she said cautiously. "I knew Bankov was on your list, didn't I? I also knew it rattled you to kill an old friend. I know how close you were with him."

"As I said you don't know anything. I don't have any friends in this life. Only enemies!"

"Perhaps I am your enemy too, but at least I can be useful to you."

"How?"

"You wouldn't be talking to me right now if you didn't kill Bankov. In a way, I know you think that you saved my life, but it's the other way around. You needed the motive to kill him and I gave you that motive."

"From where do you get all this information?" He scoffed.

Slavena's tired brain was working overtime. She couldn't

mess this one up. "From my job," she said. She knew Orlovsky would misunderstand her. She meant the CIA, but he would think it was from her work as a therapist.

Orlovsky raised his eyebrows. "Why would a therapist know this?"

Slavena kept silent. She didn't know how to respond without giving up information, she didn't want to share.

"You mean from your clients?" Orlovsky carried on incredulously. "Is the producer your client?"

Slavena shook her head. She sensed Orlovsky's brain was now working in her favor. She didn't want to interrupt it.

"Who is he then? Your lover?" He leaned forward and looked into her eyes.

His question, as bizarre as it was, gave her some relief. He still had no idea who the producer was, and more importantly, he was curious if there was another man in her life. There was still hope he would spare her life in the end.

"No! He is not! I thought we were discussing business, not our sex lives."

"The type of business I discuss with whores like you is negotiating how much I'm going to have to pay for a blowjob. So how about you get the fuck out of my car before I bash your head into the dashboard so hard you'll never draw another breath." Orlovsky grabbed the passenger door handle and pushed her out of the car.

She swallowed hard when she processed his last words. He could do all that and more. She knew how capable he was off killing people. But her life was no longer in his hands. He was letting her go.

As she slid down from the seat of his SUV, he tossed her shoes at her like she was a filthy prostitute that didn't do her job properly. Orlovsky certainly had a talent for humiliating her every single time. But that was precisely what narcissists enjoyed doing. Hook their victims in and then tear them down. Before she closed the door, Orlovsky was already in second gear.

The fresh air outside made her feel alive again and she knelt to pick her shoes from off the ground. Halfway up, she tossed one of her shoes at the moving car. "You're a disgrace to your father!" She yelled out and the thumping sound of her shoe hitting the back windshield echoed in the darkness.

The car stopped.

Her heart raced when she saw Orlovsky slowly backing up. If she had any strength, she would be running, but she stood like a blinded deer on the highway, this time certain he was coming back to finish her off. She heard the rolling of his window as his outstretched hand appeared with a cell phone. It was hers, and she wanted it, but she hesitated to move towards him. For a moment, she felt like she was in a horror movie, where the killer baited her with mercy right before he killed her.

"You need to call yourself a taxi! "He said nicely, confirming her suspicions.

Orlovsky was never nice.

"Drop it," Slavena said. "I don't want to touch your filthy hands."

"If it wasn't for my filthy hands, your body would be cold in the dirt right now," he said, tossing the phone into the darkness. He then rolled up his window and sped off, his break lights disappearing in the distance.

"And how is this any different?" She mumbled in the dark as she got on all fours to look for her cell phone. The ground was freezing cold. Regardless, she began groping through dry pieces of branches, gravel, and weeds. It was pitch dark. After ten minutes of fruitless searching, she collapsed on the ground and cried until a memory of her sister flashed into her subconscious mind. This is how her sister had died. In a forest just like this. All broken and humiliated.

Shaken by the memory, she got back on her knees and continued to crawl in the dirt, desperately reaching in the dark until she felt the plastic box in her hands. She pressed a button and the screen lit up her smile. Her fingers played with the light of her phone until she found the GPS coordinates of her location. She put on her shoes and dialed a number.

Inside Konstantin's car, she felt the comfort of the heated seat. It was a pleasure to be alive.

"This country is going to hell!" Konstantin complained as he stared at her bruised face. She'd explained to him she had been assaulted while jogging. "Should I drive you to the hospital?"

"I'm fine. Really. I just need to get some sleep."

"You should move to America. I hear it's much safer there for women."

"Perhaps I should," Slavena said as she discreetly pulled out her secret key to her building from underneath her seat. She had planted it in a hidden pocket some time ago and she had forgotten about it.

She thanked Konstantin for the ride before closing the door on him. The key to her apartment was inside the building, planted inside a wall. Relieved to be back in her apartment, she drank as much water as her body could take, collapsed on the sofa and fell asleep.

In the morning she was awoken by the noise of sirens. She had become numb to these sounds, but somehow her senses started to work against her.

She turned on the TV and listened to the news while taking a shower. It was a daily habit of hers. The warm water always soothed her. No matter how bad her day was. No matter how bad the news was.

"Five people were brutally murdered in their sleep last night in a house in Sofia. Among them Anton Bankov, the owner of BAM and his wife. The latest in a wave of killings of prominent Bulgarians with suspected ties to organized crime. The Police allege the murders were carried out by a trained professional. However, they do not rule out..."

Her Blackberry chimed and she turned off the water. She stepped out of the shower cabin to read a text message that consisted of only a phone number. She quickly dialed the number and listened to a recorded message that gave her another number that was randomized as if a code. She knew the cipher so she memorized it, dialed the new number, and waited for the secure line to be confirmed. A male's voice told her she was needed elsewhere and directed her to go to a known dead-drop location later that morning. Before Slavena could ask a question, the line went dead. Slavena suspected it was a burner number that would never work again.

"My God," she noticed the cuts on her wrists. She assumed she was getting called up for another mission but she wasn't operational in any shape or form. It was part of her job: to assess her condition after action and decide whether she was fit enough to continue the mission. Her body and mind were not ready for anything. She also feared that by the time she got back from wherever she was going next, Orlovsky would go cold and she would never hear from him again. But that's what the CIA was all about. You had to know how to continue playing chess even when the house was burning in flames.

MARINES

She woke up from the harsh rubbing of the tires on the airstrip and was surprised she'd fallen asleep on the plane. Her exhaustion had something to do with it, but also her relief to be getting away from Bulgaria for a while. Orlovsky's presence was wearing her thin.

She looked out of the window towards the Kiev airport. A typical glass and steel structure, illuminated by lights in the overcast afternoon. She could have been anywhere in the world—Helsinki, Cape Town, San Francisco—and it wouldn't have made a difference.

The aircraft came to a stop and people started getting up from their seats and collecting their stuff for disembarking the plane. Slavena remained seated and used the time to study the faces of the people around her. Happy with her accidental upgrade to First Class, she was sitting alongside a handful of other lucky people, who could afford to pay First Class prices. Those were mostly overweight, middle-aged men and the young, undernourished women at their sides.

In that respect, post-communist countries were catching up fast with the capitalist world. The idea of a new age hero was transforming from a prince on a white horse into a well-to-do man with glasses and a propensity for gaining weight and wealth. The idea of a beautiful woman, however, was stuck in a timeless, changeless zone. It was still expected of women to have long hair, lean bodies, and thin waists.

Slavena remembered that she'd had gotten her live drop for this mission from such a young woman, whom Slavena recognized from one of the Force Protection briefings months ago. She was the new Foreign Service Officer at the Embassy, working in the Economics section.

The pick-up was arranged at a busy farmer's market on the north side of Sofia. The documents were handed over in a plastic bag alongside a kilogram of tomatoes and five green peppers. The woman quickly disappeared in the crowd. Slavena suspected she had no idea who she was, or what she was handing her over in the bag.

Slavena'd walked to a coffee shop alone, sat in the back-corner seat, and looked through the papers she had been given inside the envelope. New personal identity documents, travel papers, and a note explaining her current mission. She quickly noticed that she was going on a black op in Ukraine. The timing couldn't be worse, but at least she was in the mood for some action. Anything to get her mind off Orlovsky and that night at Bankov's house.

She'd been briefed about the ongoing CIA operation in Ukraine back in Sofia but had lost track of developments in the past few months. Whatever had happened in the meantime, she couldn't wait to get back behind a rifle again. To her, the sniper's art was like a game of chess, where strategy and planning were essential. It was above all, a fight that was played with the mind and not the hands. *That* was why she needed to concentrate and keep Orlovsky in the far distance of her mind.

Before leaving Bulgaria, Slavena had tidied up her apartment until there were no traces left of her in it. She took all the hard drives and media from her communications room and passed it to Travis. The possibility that she might never return was always there. All her real and cover identity paperwork was hidden in safety deposit boxes at the Bulgarian Post Bank with instructions to Gavin on how to retrieve them if she didn't make it back. She hoped he wouldn't have to use the instruction she'd given him.

A Marine was waiting for her at the arrivals terminal and he approached her with his code-intro. "Spell Kiev in reverse."

"London!" she responded and he nodded. He was tall, energetic, and walked in silence until they were outside the terminal.

"Are you military?" he finally asked, assuming her military credentials would explain her bruised face and broken nose.

"No," she replied. "Civilian."

In a moment he said. "Then I'm lost because our support request was for an experienced MOS 0317."

MOS 0317 was a military occupational specialty qualifying you as a Marine Corps Scout Sniper and he was implying that she didn't belong there. One, she was a woman; two, she was expected to be a sniper and he didn't deem her capable.

"I may not be in uniform," she snapped, "but clearly I've met the standards to be here."

The Marine thought for a second. "The nuke scientist has already arrived—"

Slavena blocked her little-wheeled suitcase with a determined foot and turned to face the Marine. "Let me stop you right there. What rank are you?" She asked while taking her sunglasses off and revealing the shiner on her left eye.

"Master Sergeant Johnson."

"A small piece of advice, Master Sergeant Johnson. If you stick to discussing details of TOP SECRET operations only in authorized storage facilities and ditch your bias towards women, you might get lucky and be promoted to Sergeant Major. Heck, you might even retire honorably with some self-dignity still intact."

Johnson said nothing to that, so Slavena turned on her heels and continued towards the exit. He was not impressed with her, but she could care less.

During their short journey to the hotel, both Johnson and Slavena were silent. Johnson was clearly uncomfortable by the fact they had gotten off on the wrong foot. Slavena didn't care. She just wanted to get to the hotel. Without further chatter, he dropped her at the Radisson Blu Hotel, where she presumed the rest of the Marines were staying.

"Our team is meeting at a bar tonight. Care to join us?" He was trying to get back on her good side.

"Thanks, but I'll pass. I'll see everyone at the briefing tomorrow."

"Hope you're in a better mood tomorrow," Slavena heard him mumble before she closed the door of the car. She hoped so too, but she'd had a couple of rough weeks and was not at all convinced a single good night's sleep could fix things.

In her hotel room, Slavena had a quick hot shower before closing the curtains and going to bed. She turned off the air-conditioner to allow her body to get used to the natural temperature outside and fell down onto the bed with a sigh of relief.

She tossed and turned for hours and her much-needed sleep eluded her. Ever since her last encounter with Orlovsky, she couldn't forgive herself for the mistakes she'd made. She wondered how many more mistakes there were waiting to be made.

She got up, opened a bottle of water from the mini-fridge, and guzzled it. She learned back at the Farm, that prior to any mission, hydration was essential. She would never know to which hole they would send her and for how long she would be waiting there to complete her mission. So, she reached for the second bottle, emptied it, and went back to bed.

The pulsing glow of the city lights kept her awake even through her closed eyelids. She was never debriefed about Bankov or Orlovsky, and Gavin would not be pleased. That was all that was on her mind.

That and the future of her career.

She kicked off the comforter and jumped out of bed, but had to sit on the edge for a moment. The dizzy spells and the black eye she'd acquired in Orlovsky's car insisted on lingering. Her bruised body ached all over and her joints pulsed in pain with every step. On top of that, her nose kept bleeding randomly. It was almost as if her body was desperately trying to keep the memory of the ordeal. A subliminal warning for her to be more careful.

Five minutes later, Slavena was in the elevator, going to the bar downstairs. The elevator plunged to the first floor and when it stopped, Slavena pushed the door open. The first thing that assaulted her senses was cigarette smoke. It crawled up the walls and swirled around lampshades, thick as beer foam. The second was the voices of Marines echoing from inside the bar. Like most Americans when they had a few drinks inside them, the Marines' voices grew in volume and traveled through the air with the intensity of a supersonic fighter jet. The light at the bar's foyer was dimmed and Slavena paused by the door to allow her eyes to get used to the dark. She could just make out the Marines through the frosted glass door. Half a dozen men were playing darts with local women on their laps.

They were the only people in the bar.

Slavena cursed her luck and hid in a corner so the Marines wouldn't spot her. She had no idea that was the bar they chose to hang out at. All she wanted was a bottle of water and didn't feel like socializing right now. She watched the Marines lift their shot glasses and drink them in one gulp. Then they shook their heads and slammed the glasses down on the bar-top.

"This vodka is so fucking smooth!" one of the Marines shouted and grabbed the boob of the woman sitting next to him. She shrieked in mock horror and then proceeded to giggle.

Slavena watched them from afar. She had witnessed this before outside Camp Lejeune many times. She knew what was happening. The Marines didn't have officers with them and didn't have to be on their best behavior. Far away from the flagpole, as they called the headquarters, they'd let their hair down, happy to finally drink vodka shots unchaperoned in a country where drinking vodka was as common as drinking water.

"Dude, get another round!" the Marine who had his hand down the woman's blouse shouted.

"Vodka shots again? Or do you want a mixer?"

"Can't have a Bloody Mary," Johnson said. "It reminds me of the PMS sniper-bitch I had to pick up from the airport today."

Slavena froze in her spot. He was talking about her.

"Can't believe they sent us a woman for overwatch. I just hope you are wrong that she is on the rag or she will kill us all!" another Marine said. Rowdy laughter immediately followed

"Was she at least good to look at?" a dark-skinned Marine sitting at the head of the table and opposite the frosted glass door asked.

"Bellinger, you are married, man. You shouldn't be looking at her anyway. But to answer your question, I couldn't tell. Her face was all messed up."

"What do you mean?"

"Somebody didn't take her shit and used her as a punching bag," Johnson clarified.

"No fucking way! They sent us an abused woman?"

"You will see her tomorrow at the briefing. No makeup can hide that shit."

"Your lucky day, Puerto Rico! Didn't you say you liked them vulnerable? Besides, it has been at least six months since you haven't paid for sex."

"Shit man! That time in Bootyfest doesn't count!" Puerto Rico, protested, referring to Budapest. "I didn't pay her anything."

"A hundred dollars for dinner and drinks don't count as payment? In my book, that is considered prostitution."

"So that dinner you had with your mother three weeks ago? Was that prostitution?"

The Marine, whose mother's pride had been assaulted, took his hand out of the woman's cleavage and threw a dart at Puerto Rico. The targeted Marine shielded himself by turning as the dart hit him on the shoulder and hung there, buried in his flesh.

"What the fuck was that asshole? This is a brand-new shirt." He snapped as he pulled the dart out of his skin, causing the wound to open and pour blood rapidly.

Still unnoticed, Slavena could see from a distance the bloodstain spread to the size of a golf ball. Judging by their behavior, at first Slavena got worried that their mission was already doomed, but then on second thought, she knew that they were just putting on a show for the women. When it comes to the mission, these guys were professionals and Marines always excelled.

"Are you as deadly with your rifle as you are with darts?" Johnson's voice again. Slavena recognized it easily by now.

"My trigger finger is my second most talented appendage, isn't that right, baby?" he asked the woman next to him as he pulled her close to his body, not giving her a chance to object.

"Yes," the woman answered rather confused with her thick Slavic accent, clearly using the total of her English vocabulary.

"Come on guys! OPSEC. You shouldn't talk shop in front of civilians." Johnson intervened, clearly learning from his mistake at the airport earlier in the day.

"Don't worry Bellinger, she speaks as much English as a Coke bottle. Isn't that right baby?"

"Yes, yes," the woman said again, confirming that was the only word of English she knew.

"It's better that way," Johnson said. "No need for women to talk. The sniper-bitch already gave me hell today because of some OPSEC bullshit."

"Get over it, man!"

"Speaking of her, where is the fabled goddess with a

gun?" asked one of the quieter one.

"Powdering her nose."

"Dude, she will need to powder all night to hide that shit in the morning" Johnson chuckled and Slavena rolled her eyes. Clearly, the guy had a chip on his shoulder.

"Hey Bellinger, what do you say to a woman with two black eyes?" The quietest Marine finally spoke.

"Nothing. You already told her twice." Bellinger responded.

"I got a name for her. How about Bruiser"

"Fuck that. It rhymes with loser and we can't have a loser on our team!"

"Did you look at her knuckles? "

"Why would I do that, dickhead?

Slavena looked at her knuckles and they were bruised up and swollen.

"I don't know. Maybe the bitch put up a fight."

"Yeah! We will see tomorrow if Bruiser is a loser or a winner! Question is, who among us is gonna win her first? Oorah!!!"

"Oorah!!!" They cheered and clinked shot glasses again.

Slavena had heard enough. She turned around and walked back to the elevator, pressing the button so hard it got stuck in the socket. She didn't have to listen to what a bunch of cock swinging assholes had to say about her. What did they know about her anyway? They didn't deserve her acknowledgment or her anger. Since when did she pay attention to what people were saying behind her back?

By the time she was back in her room, she'd calmed down. Who was she kidding? Boys will be boys. She shouldn't take things to heart. It wasn't personal. She needed a good night's sleep and in the morning things would be different.

The briefing was at the US Embassy in Kiev, located in the former office of the Communist Party of Ukraine. The building looked more like an Italian villa by Lake Como, rather than a US Embassy in a former Soviet Union country. Apart from being pleasant to look at, it was unsuitable for the embassy's needs. Millions were being poured into building a new compound on the outskirts of Kiev, but that project was long in coming. For the time being, the United States had to make do with the vast offices of ex-communist party officials that were built to intimidate visitors, ignore practicalities, and basic human needs. On some floors, there was only one bathroom. On others, the bathroom facilities were bigger than the offices. Luckily for Slavena, she was to spend little time here.

That morning, she employed the evasive tactics she learned at the Farm and took a taxi to Melnykova Street where she got out, entered a café, and waited to identify a potential tail. After ensuring no one had followed her, she walked for a mile before she hopped into another taxi that took her a few blocks away from the Embassy. Once through the Embassy gates, she walked up the stairs towards the fortified front door, surveying the building and lush gardens around it. A plaster coat of arms of the Communist Party of Ukraine adorned the wall above the door. Slavena found it commendable that in order to preserve the façade the Embassy officials had not removed the crest but also ironic that Cold War enemies were now sharing a roof.

Inside, she was instructed to wait at guard post one — an American manned security point — for the Marine attaché who would escort her through the building. While Slavena waited by the bulletproof glass door, a group of toddlers passed by on the other side, each of them holding a walking rope and following one another like a row of ducklings. Suddenly the door opened and a man approached her hurriedly.

"Lieutenant Colonel Michael Davidson" the Marine Attaché put his hand forward and Slavena shook it.

"Jessica Honn," Slavena said and walked through the door he held open for her.

"There are children at the embassy?" Slavena asked the Attaché pointing at the little group.

"The day-care center for the children of the Embassy staff is in the basement." He carefully examined the sign-in papers before scribbling his signature and handing them back to the Marine guard.

So, diplomats can reproduce, Slavena thought. She pondered over the mental image of "diplomatic" sex. The man saying the nastiest things to his wife in the nicest possible way. Her insightful joke took her back to Orlovsky. He had a lot to learn from the good old diplomats.

The Lieutenant Colonel took her to the fifth floor where the briefing for the new mission was to be held. Before entering the conference room, he asked her to leave her cell phone and any other electronic devices in a small safe outside the room. He waved his ID in front of a scrambled keypad and entered an eight-digit security code. The door clicked open.

Slavena stepped in and was confronted by the faces of six men sitting around an oval table, staring up at her. She felt like a nun who stumbled upon a monks' party. Judging by their uniforms they were all Marines from Rota, Spain, where they were stationed with the Marine Air-Ground Task Force.

"Morning all," Slavena took the empty seat right next to Johnson, and one by one, each man introduced himself. There were seven Marines, and two intelligence officers from the Defense Intelligence Agency. When the Military Liaison Officer and the Chief of Station for Ukraine walked in, everyone fell silent. They were both middle-aged men, one thin and toothy, the other sporting perfectly white hair and heavy-rimmed glasses.

"Good morning and welcome to Kiev. Everyone, please get enough of what you're drinking. More coffee? Water?" The MLO, the thin one with overlapping front teeth, looked around the table. "Jesus, what happened to your face?" He said impulsively when he saw her.

"Sparred with a psychopath," she said, telling the truth. "You should see the other guy."

Everybody in the room laughed.

"Well, it's great to have you on our team! Let's begin," the MLO said with a serious face.

He cleared his throat and rocked on his heels to collect his thoughts. The PowerPoint presentation with its bright colored charts, graphs, and bullet points looked more like a bowl of spaghetti than a real attempt at conveying information. He let the image sink in as he looked into the eyes of his audience and then he started.

"You are here to neutralize key players in a Ukrainian criminal network that consists of among other things a group of Army officers who specialize in the sale of military weaponry. They recently got their hands on a miniaturized 6-kiloton Russian suitcase nuke and decided to sell it to the highest bidder. Luckily, we were tipped off by a local Lebanese contact that runs in the wrong circles. Thanks to our friends at the NSA, we ensured our two covert operatives posing as Syrian businessmen, became the highest bidder."

The MLO paused and looked around the table to make sure he had everyone's undivided attention. "To call the device a suitcase bomb is a misnomer. A bit of history. Fifteen of these backpack bombs were developed by the Soviet Union in the '80s for clandestine attacks, but all accountability was lost during the early '90s when Russian General Ledbed brought the existence of these nasty creations to international light. Since then intelligence services worldwide have accounted for twelve of the fifteen. This is number thirteen and we intend to neutralize it. While a six-kilotons device has a relatively small detonation radius, about one third the size of the bomb that leveled Hiroshima, it could still send Manhattan back to the Stone Age."

The MLO took a sip of water before continuing.

"Your job is to provide overwatch as our guys successfully 'purchase' the device in good condition then ensure our new Ukrainian friends do not live to sell another bullet or bomb."

The Chief of Station took it from here. He pushed his reading glasses up his nose, before saying, "The sale is set to occur four days from now near Yalta, in the Crimea, at an abandoned holiday resort. You will leave tonight to arrive in time to establish a sniper nest and ambush plan. Since we expect two to four sellers plus security detail, the element of surprise is essential to ensure no loose ends, which is why we specifically asked for the Marine Corps Forces Special Operations Command."

He paused to make a point.

"Our 'Syrians' will arrive on the scene with a former Russian nuclear engineer at approximately the same time as the sellers to avoid suspicion that they are being targeted. This will leave them at your mercy to conduct proper recon and planning. Once the Russian confirms the device is real and operational, our Syrians will transfer ten million dollars to the Ukrainian gangsters. Their likely intent is to transfer the money across the globe in a series of untraceable wire transactions."

Everybody at the table, including Slavena, nodded to the words of the Chief of Station. They were already planning the operation in their heads.

"When the money hits the holding account and our Ukrainian friends celebrate their newfound wealth, our pals back at Fort Meade will quietly repatriate Uncle Sam's money back to the good old United States. There will be a window of approximately five minutes before the Ukrainians realize they have been duped. That is when your team must eliminate all targets. I will let you be creative on how to keep anyone from escaping. I will have a mop-up team on standby to collect cell phones, pocket litter and dispose of the bodies while your team EXFILS."

"Any questions?" The Chief of Station asked.

"So, we are using a Russian mad scientist to help a group of Ragheads to buy a pocket nuke from a group of Ukrainian thugs for the CIA while the NSA plays money shell games? So long as I get to kill someone, and get back without getting my nuts shot off, I am happy," Johnson said looking around. Nobody nodded to that.

Slavena was glad Johnson embarrassed himself in front of his senior officers. He wasn't getting Sergeant Major anytime soon.

"Remember, we're dealing with trained Army personnel and ruthless street criminals. They're not people afraid of starting a firefight next to a nuclear weapon. So make sure your plan is decisive and eliminate the possibility of failure. All right? You got three days of recon and planning," The MLO said. "Briefing adjourned."

PLAN B

Slavena's motto, when it came to working with the military, was "Don't be first, don't be last, and don't volunteer to do anything." When she walked out of the hotel at 3:48 am with her backpack, the Marines were waiting in the parking lot with the equipment already loaded in the three SUVs. Johnson and Puerto Rico were milling around. Sergeant Bellinger, the married Marine from the bar, was smoking a cigarette. The other two, hands in the pockets, shoulders hunched over, quietly talked. The three drivers, who Slavena assumed were also Marines, were sitting behind the wheels with the engines on.

"Who are we waiting for?" Slavena asked.

Bellinger chucked the half-finished cigarette to the floor and stepped on it with his polished business shoe. "The officers," he said. "If you need an officer in a hurry, take a nap." He yawned and stretched up.

A Marine, Slavena had not met yet and introduced himself as Sergeant Patch, came out of one of the cars.

"Our fearless leaders are on their way," he said and the two officers walked out of the hotel. Once everybody was inside the cars, the three rentals slowly drove off the parking lot and gained speed on the highway outside Kiev. At this time of night, early morning, the streets of Kiev were deserted. Slavena looked at the angular concrete buildings along the road, with gray facades and ragged windows, and concluded that Ukraine wasn't that much different from Bulgaria to look at. If you'd seen one post-communist country, you'd seen them all. She wondered if that applied also to people.

Eight hours later, they arrived at the final point which was at a half-built, abandoned hotel complex by the beach, located twelve miles west of Yalta. They parked their cars a mile away from their destination and once every single piece of luggage—gear, rifles, food, and water—was unloaded, the three vehicles disappeared with a dusty cloud. The team cleaned up all traces and headed towards the building on foot. They didn't want to give any indication to their prey that they were lying in wait.

They had a whole day to recon the site, set up the sniper sites and spring the trap.

The complex, where the nuclear exchange was to occur, was surrounded by barren hills. The tallest building among the concrete rubble was five-stories high with no roof. It stuck out like a decaying tooth on the jaw of the seashore. The hotel was clearly intended to be a large-scale beach resort with hundreds of rooms. Instead, it was never completed and appeared someone had attempted to tear it down at some point but had given up. Thus, the compound resembled the set of a post-apocalyptic zombie movie. Nature had started taking over the site. Ivy and weeds hugged the walls, slowly covering what traces of humanity remained.

The perfect place for an ambush, she thought feeling the tension building up inside her.

On the brighter side, the compound offered endless places to hide and position a high caliber rifle, without being seen. Near the entrance of the concrete building, a grubby bathtub, filled with insects swimming in an inch of rainwater, laid on the ground.

"How about a warm relaxing bath?" Puerto Rico nudged Slavena in the ribs.

"Ask me again when I don't have eighty pounds of kit to strip off and I might say yes." She winked at him and an excited whistling came from the other Marines.

"It's alright. I only have one love in this world. Jessica Alba," he said and kissed his rifle.

Slavena broke a smile and met Puerto Rico's raised eyebrows. There was very little to smile about around here. The only pleasant thing was the breeze coming from the Crimean coastline.

From seemingly nowhere, a stray dog appeared, growling and bearing canines.

"Good doggy, nice doggy," Patch said and opened an MRE, offering it to the dog. It was a beef brisket packet.

"Dude, don't give the dog the best ones!" Johnson protested and everybody grinned knowingly.

The dog sniffed the food, immediately turned and walked away, swaying a bonny backside at the humans.

"Shit! Even a starved dog won't eat that stuff! What does it say about us? We're lower down the food chain than stray dogs?" Patch looked genuinely affronted.

"Teufel Hunde, dude! We are hell's dogs."

They entered the building and looked around. There was nothing inside to attract attention, but yards of cold concrete, rebar, and rubble, sprawling in all directions. The Marines dropped the equipment on the floor to catch their breath.

"I was gonna have a snack," Patch said, still sulking "but after the dog didn't eat it... I don't know."

A wave of laughter rippled through the group.

"Once, back in Camp Schwab, I dated the daughter of the Commanding General. She'd been all around the world." Johnson sat on top of a box. "How was I supposed to cook for somebody that's, like, eaten everything out there already? I ain't no cook!"

"What did you do?" Patch was all ears.

"I took three MRE ham slices and three pork chops and cooked them in a pan. In another pot, I blended three chicken-a-la-kings and eight packets of dehydrated butter noodles and some dehydrated rice. It made sort of mush that looked like succotash."

"Shit, man."

"I added some spices and baked it in the oven for about half an hour. When I took it out it looked like, well, meat on a bed of shit." Patch barked with laughter. Bellinger joined the circle around Johnson. "I covered the top of the meat with MRE cheese and added some green sprinkly thingys on top. Fancy right?"

"You bet!" Bellinger lapped up every word of the story. Slavena was surprised he didn't pen the recipe down. He looked like the kind of guy to cook stuff like this for his poor wife.

"For dessert, I took four MRE pound cakes, mashed them up. Added five packets of cocoa powder, powdered coffee cream, and water. Sprinkled powdered sugar on top. Voila! Jarhead Pudding!"

"You joking, right?"

"No. For drinks, I took a bottle of Military Special Vodka, you know the one that comes in the plastic bottle and mixed it with four packets of cherry flavored electrolytes. It looked like an eerie Kool-Aid with sparkles in it."

"Did she really eat that shit?"

"Hell yeah! She loved it. She balked at the makeshift 'wine', but she drank four glasses of it. Later on, as we were watching a movie, she went to the restroom and I heard farts louder than my .50 cal machine gun."

Everyone was laughing by now.

"That went on all night. She sprayed, like, half a can of air freshener in that bathroom. Eventually, she had to go home. Next time I saw her, I told her she had eaten up roughly 9,000 calories of 'Marine Chow.' She turned stark white."

"Did she kick your ass for that? I know I would've done it," Patch said.

"No. She was sweet about it. Said she didn't go to the bathroom for something like three days after that dinner. Had to work out for days to burn the calories. Said, she never wanted me to cook dinner for her again. Ever. We laughed about it, eventually."

"Oh, boy!" Bellinger was wiping tears from his eyes. "So you're cooking breakfast for all of us right?"

"Hell no!"

"Once I ate chow that expired before I was born—"

"All right, everyone. Enough chit chat and let's talk business now." Captain Kingsley called out. That was the first time Slavena heard his voice. She guessed he wasn't the talkative type and wasn't into storytelling. In a way she was glad. She couldn't stomach hearing more about MRE food when she was already starving.

Everyone from the group turned to face the captain.

"We set up four separate firing positions. The meeting is supposed to take place in the reception area. He pointed towards a niche in one of the corners of the ground floor. "Primary team will be on the third floor, left side. That will be myself and Patch."

He pointed up at the skeletal construction above their heads and Slavena followed the tip of his finger. There was nothing there but rubble. Since the plan was for the exchange to take place on the ground floor in 48 hours, it was safe to assume that they'd have to lay in that rubble for twenty plus hours flat. She wasn't looking forward to this.

Kingsley carried on. "Second team, Shields and Johnson, second floor right in front of reception. Both teams will form an L-Shape ambush lane of fire. The security teams will be outside. One in front of the building near the road. That'd be Patch and Bellinger. The fourth team, Honn and Recendez, will play clean up in the back of the hotel, beachside. The only communication between us will be radios."

Slavena and Puerto Rico were dispatched towards the beach, to set up their sniper nests in the rocks by the water. It was perched on top of a hill, among low bushes. As the most inexperienced sniper in the group, Slavena was given the nest with the smallest likelihood of firing a shot.

The four teams split up and walked in the directions of their appointed firing positions. Slavena walked behind Puerto Rico's rigid back. She could sense his reluctance to perform the task because he was teamed up with her. She wasn't sure if he minded her being a woman or that she was a newcomer and he didn't trust her. She turned her head and followed the other guys with her eyes spreading out in the nooks and crannies of the construction. In a few seconds, they had vanished from sight. She hurried behind

Puerto Rico and was glad when they were out in the open. The sun was setting and the shadowy building was giving her the creeps.

They climbed up the hill and Slavena paused at the top. The view of the Black Sea was breath-taking, but they weren't here for the scenery. Once they agreed on the final firing position, Slavena set up her rifle under Puerto Rico's watchful eye. She zeroed her rifle, the term snipers used when they set all their adjustments for their rifle, ammunition and a given range.

"You gonna mount that thing with a strap hold?" Puerto Rico asked and Slavena looked up at him with raised eyebrows. He looked away and said. "Just in case there is too much action or something."

"You know, Rico we're going be here for forty-eight hours. Just the two of us. Laying ass to ass in the sand." Puerto Rico nodded. "We better find a way to get along, or those will be the longest forty-eight hours of our lives."

Puerto Rico was silent for a moment. "How did you know I was from Puerto Rico?"

"Your accent and…" Slavena hesitated whether she should tell him the truth. She'd been lying for so long that confessing human stuff seemed awkward, but sometimes it was necessary. "When I came to the bar two nights ago, I overheard you guys talking about me."

"Oh." He cleared his throat. "Were you inside the bar?"

"No. I didn't have the guts to come inside after what I heard, so I just left."

"Ouch. I'm sorry you had to hear that."

"Don't worry about it."

"If I remember correctly, there were some embarrassing things about me in that conversation, right?"

"Hmm."

"Can we not talk about that ever again."

Slavena nodded and got back to work. She pulled out a few plants from around her and stuck them into the rubber bands that covered her bipod. She vegged up her gun until it was turned into a giant coastal dune plant, and put on her ghillie suit for beach-land environment. Then she pulled out her range finder and began scanning the engagement area. Together with Puerto Rico, they sketched the beach and its surroundings and methodically identified every significant visual element of the beach until all their ranges were worked out in their heads.

"Big cliff, 400 meters at twelve o'clock," Slavena called out the last element.

Puerto Rico nodded. "I think, we're all set now."

For the next couple of hours, Slavena performed all check-ups and drills on the weapons and the nest, exactly as they'd taught her at Camp Lejeune.

She was equipped with a long-range M40 and although its bolt action couldn't provide the rapid-fire performance of a semi-auto, it was extremely accurate. Puerto Rico, who was going to be the spotter, was armed with his beloved Jessica Alba or SR-25, which used a high-power spotting scope for targets and follow-up shots. It was a smaller and lighter rifle, with semi-automatic action which complemented Slavena's M40 perfectly. Together they were well equipped and prepared to operate in complete darkness with night vision scopes and infrared laser equipment. They went through a range of potential scenarios they might face in the next 24 hours and rehearsed the shooter/spotter relationship. It was already established depending on the number of targets. If the targets exceeded four counts, Puerto Rico was supposed to eliminate the additional targets in synchronization with the shooter. By the time they were done, it was past 11 pm. Slavena was exhausted and the temperature had dropped a few degrees.

"We don't expect action tonight so let's both get some sleep, all right?" Slavena said.

They'd just settled down for the night when the radio cracked. "How are our newlyweds doing on the beach, huh? Having fun?" A voice came from one of the other nests.

"Johnson," Puerto Rico whispered in the dark. "Don't you ever get tired from the crappy old jokes?"

"Don't mind him, Rico." Slavena turned to face the boy. Illuminated by the moon, his face looked young. "He'll cut it off eventually."

"What was that?" Johnson's voice sounded on the radio again. "Did I hear hard breathing?"

"Shut the hell up, Johnson and go to sleep!" The captain's voice in the radio stopped the exchange short.

"Yessir," Johnson said.

After some silence, Slavena realized she wasn't ready to go to sleep quite yet and slipped the microphone away from her throat.

"You probably miss your partner very much," she said. "What was his name?"

"Brown." Puerto Rico wasn't asleep either. "He is one of the best snipers out there. God of our craft."

"What happened to him?" She asked.

"He got on profile. *Somehow*."

"What do you mean?"

"We did a night jump in Zaragoza, right before this mission, and we made it home. Next morning, I found out at the debrief that Brown was hospitalized for a severe concussion."

"So, it happened during the jump?"

"That's what they told me but I'm not convinced. I saw him landing just fine."

Slavena was silent. Her brain was trained to spot random coincidences and do the analysis on the spot. From what Puerto Rico was telling her, there was some sort of outside interference of placing teams together and she was certain the CIA had a part in it. They wanted her to be there. That was her conclusion. But why? Different possible scenarios rushed through her mind, but Puerto Rico interrupted her thoughts.

"Where did you learn to shoot?" Rico asked.

"I did shooting sports for eight years," Slavena said. "But mostly I learned the craft at Camp Lejeune. I took the Scout Sniper Basic Course for twelve weeks."

"Did you ever get used to the fuck-fuck games?"

She laughed. He was referring to the constant push-ups, PTs, shouting, and harassment the Marines loved to use during training. "No! And you?"

"Sure I did. Something about our DNA. We, the Marines, love punishment. The more we get kicked in the ass, the more we are like, "Yessir, absolutely sir, may I have another one sir," He laughed and then asked, "How many were left at graduation?"

"Of the original fifty-eight who started the class, just twelve were left in the end."

"Good job!" He seemed genuinely impressed. "At what point did you know you'd pass?"

"It was probably one specific morning, deep into the training, during a seven-mile run when I saw something reflecting in the distance. When we got closer to it, I noticed that it was a bullet taped to the pole of a STOP sign, so I figured it was some kind of test. Immediately I started to observe and single out things that just didn't fit into the larger picture. When we got back from the run, we did our push-ups, sit-ups until our muscles screamed from the pain. And instead of giving us a break, the instructors gave us a pen and a piece of paper and asked us to list the twenty military items that were on our running route while they played loud heavy metal music, flashing lights on and off in our faces and banging on our desks to distract us."

"I know the drill. Were you able to list all of the items?"

"Just about."

"Let me guess, you were the only woman in that class?"

"Yes. Why?"

"Something about women, always paying attention to the tiniest details." They both chuckled. "Speaking of which, my favorite sniper joke is about women. What do women snipers in the French Army use as camouflage?"

Slavena shrugged.

"Their armpits."

"Gross!" Slavena elbowed Puerto Rico in the ribs and he pretended to roll around in pain. She laughed feeling good. She had been mission-focused and serious for so long that she had nearly forgotten what genuine camaraderie and friendship was.

About 4 am, the temperature dropped so much that Slavena woke up frozen to the bone. A cold wind blew in from the sea.

"You awake?" Puerto Rico asked in the dark.

"Yeah. I'm freezing."

"Same here. You wanna come closer?"

"If I do, there'll be no funny business, right?"

"Roger, but I wanna apologize for little Rico in the morning. I can't do anything about him."

"Yeah, right. Must be your hot Latino blood."

"You said it." She couldn't see Puerto Rico's face in the dark, but she knew he was smiling.

She never realized how close you become to the people you go on a mission with. They don't tell you that at the Farm. You spent days on end in each other's company. Cooped up in small, cold, nasty places. You put your life in their hands. No wonder Puerto Rico was cranky. His partner had been injured on a jump and Slavena had been called on the mission urgently. She could do the job, but she knew she could not replace him. He must be like family for Puerto Rico.

In the morning, they woke up with the sunrise. They watched the sun come up from behind the sea in silence. Slavena couldn't remember the last time she'd felt so at peace with her surroundings. She had slept well during the night and despite waking up at the crack of dawn, she felt refreshed and ready for anything. She was looking forward to the day ahead.

The quiet time gave her the opportunity to think about what happened back in Sofia. She'd told Orlovsky she needed him and by doing so, she placed herself in the center of his web. Orlovsky was going to feed on her until her wings stopped buzzing. It was a mistake that would be burning through her nerves for days to come, but she knew now was not the time to waste her mental energy on anything else but her current mission.

By lunchtime, the sun got baking hot and Slavena

remembered the cold morning breeze with nostalgia. They'd had early lunch and by 7 pm, she was positively famished again. They'd bantered with the other guys until they'd gotten tired of it and now, they were sitting in a comfortable silence that only came with time. Puerto Rico was chewing tobacco and spitting on the ground. Slavena was sitting by his side, watching the waves crash on the sandy beach, hypnotized.

The radio crackled and Bellinger's voice whispered in her ear.

"All elements! Car approaching!"

Slavena kicked Puerto Rico awake. "Come on, Rico, look alive. We have visitors."

"All teams," Kingsley said in the radio. "Secure lanes of fire and remain camouflaged."

An Audi Q7 came up the road and sped towards the building, stopping right by the main entrance, now engulfed in a cloud of dust. Four men jumped out of the car and headed towards the designated location of the meeting. They were dressed in black bomber jackets and jeans. From an audio transmitter Johnson had concealed in the lobby the day prior, they could hear their visitors spoke Russian. Slavena picked up a few words about them getting some food after they finished. They walked about the ground floor kicking rubble and peering behind corners.

They passed directly below Johnson and Shield's nest when Kingsley whispered through his throat microphone, "Call your shots."

"Brown hair, sunglasses," Bellinger immediately responded, followed by Johnson claiming his target.

"Shaved head, neck tattoo."

"I got the smoker," Patch hissed, leaving his captain to claim the "Tall one walking back to the car."

From their position, near the beach, they only saw the car and the driver who never stayed more than a few steps from his vehicle. Slavena held her breath in anticipation of an eruption of violence.

To all their relief, the group of thugs saw nothing that raised their suspicion they got back in the car and drove off.

Slavena couldn't relax again after that. It was the day of the meeting and she felt the pressure mounting. There were twelve more hours to go to show time.

Time passed slower and it was almost dark when they heard the first vehicles arriving for the rendezvous. It was their Syrian undercover team, here to do the exchange and the nuke inspection. They wore business suits and kufiyahs except for the Russian scientist, whose skin was much paler than his companions. Three armed guards wearing baseball caps and body armor stood on opposite sides of the main group that congregated near the former hotel front desk.

Slavena's heart skipped a beat at the sight of one guard wandering into the overgrown parking lot and better into her field of view. She recognized him immediately. It was Allan Hall or whatever name he was calling himself today. People in the Agency shifted names as often as a newly married couple moved furniture around. But she always called him Navy.

She and Navy had gone through training at the Farm together and she was relieved to see he hadn't flunked the final test as he'd told her. He lied to her, but she wasn't too surprised. She knew Navy wasn't the kind of man the CIA would let go easily. He was a Navy S.E.A.L, and among other Junior Officers in the CIA, he was the cream of the crop.

He also used to be her Navy. They were intimate during the last days of the training on the Farm and they continued to see much of each other during their sniper training at Camp Lejeune. Somehow, they managed to hide their dirty secret from everybody, including the CIA. But then came his good-bye letter and he disappeared, just like she did. She never thought their lives would collide again until now when he was standing 6'3 feet tall in front of her, sniffing out the environment with confidence.

He moved a pace here or there, a pace back again, getting himself familiar with the area. When he looked in her direction and his glare lingered a few seconds longer than it should, she became convinced he was aware of their exact location of her fire position. With that, many other questions rolled in. Why wasn't she told another CIA officer was working this operation in the field? Why him? And why is he the bait, in such an exposed role? When the firing began, he would be among the first targets.

There were too many questions and no time to register them because at 7:55 pm another two black Audis, bulletproof and with darkened windows, approached the complex of buildings. The cars stopped but nobody got out. There was no way of telling how many men were inside those cars or what weapons they had with them. The teams waited in their positions with nerves stretched to tearing.

Eventually, one man exited the car and began walking slowly toward the reception area. He wasn't a tall man but seemed to command respect with his slow, deliberate stride and apparent control over the situation.

"He's mine," Johnson squawked into the team's ear.

The man stopped a few feet away from Navy and offered a look inside his coat as he half raised his hands above his head. Without blinking, the man glared at the group of men and finally spoke.

"We decide not to exchange inside the building," he said

in English with a strong Russian accent.

"Where do you propose we do it then?" One of the Syrians asked.

"Outside," the messenger said. "On the beach."

Slavena's brain went in overdrive. Why would they choose the beach? In a way, it made sense. That's what she would do. Change the plan last minute to avoid a possible double-cross. Suddenly her stomach twisted into a ball of nerves.

"Nest Four, switch from sniper-spotter to sniper-sniper," Kingsley directed softly into his throat mic. Both Slavena and Puerto Rico were now to directly engage targets rather than he spotting targets for Slavena to eliminate.

"Roger," Slavena and Puerto Rico replied.

Over the headphones, she heard the Marines exchanging AFI bombs, which in military slang, meant "another fucking inconvenience". There was tension in their voices. It was clear in their radio chatter, things weren't going as to plan, but if there was one thing, she learned from her training at Camp Lejeune, it was that nothing ever went according to plan. *Ever.* So, they had to be creative with their experience and execute outside the box.

The cars circled around the building and appeared in Slavena's sniper scope. Johnson advised the team in a calm voice of experience, "Darkness is our friend right now. Switch scopes to night vision. Team Four spread out for a better field of fire. Don't offer them a single target. Team 1 and team 2 need to operate on your own. All other teams, start moving to alternative firing points once you break visual with targets."

Shields, the pointman added, "Unable to identify number of targets. Two cars approaching Nest Four. Once I give you word, start putting heavy rounds down there until we get in positions to support you. Neutralize targets before they know what's hit them."

So, the action was about to start. Slavena put both hands to the ground and closed her eyes for a second to collect her thoughts. She felt acid in the mouth and she knew what that meant. Adrenaline.

Bring it on, Slavena whispered in the dark and snapped her eyes open.

EXPOSED

Orlovsky slammed the car door and searched the crowd for Archie's face. Nearly everyone sitting outside Amnesia was looking up at him. Like human sunflowers upturned towards the bright sun. Orlovsky was pleased with the attention. He was feeling particularly good today. He'd just done a double hit and the adrenaline rush hadn't left his system yet. He felt half-human, half-God just like in Afghanistan when he was doing the proper fighting. The sensation of hunting insurgents couldn't compare to anything else. As Hemingway said: "There is no hunting like the hunting of man, and those who have hunted armed men long enough and liked it, never care for anything else thereafter."

At the sight of the skinny computer geek, Orlovsky smiled ear to ear. In recent years, he'd hardly ever seen Archie out of his mom's apartment. The nerd looked comical amongst the high-maintenance, sleekly groomed clientele of Amnesia.

Orlovsky pulled a chair and motioned at the people around them. "You don't have to look so scared."

"I'm not scared," Archie stretched the neckline of his T-shirt away from his throat as if it was choking him. "I just don't like the outdoors. Too… airy or something. Can't be good for you."

Orlovsky sat and noticed that Archie's T-shirt said EAT SLEEP **HACK** REPEAT in faded big black letters.

"Your shirt has a typo." He pointed at Archie's chest. "The highlighted word should be **FUCK**."

"What?" Archie said struggling to read the washed-out words from upside down. It was typical of him not to know what was written on his own T-shirt.

"Never mind," Orlovsky's said. The kill's high had started ebbing away and the fatigue from the past few weeks started to settle in. He was becoming irritable. "What do you have for me?"

Archie leaned forward, wiggling in his seat. "This was a tough one, but once I found her name, it became a joke." He was finally in familiar waters. He pulled out a piece of paper folded enough times to fit in his jeans pocket.

Orlovsky unfolded the piece of paper and browsed through it. Alena had lied about her name. That didn't shock him. Her real name was Slavena Ivanova. Both of her parents and her sister were dead. Slavena immigrated to the USA shortly after the death of her sister. She held a Bachelor's in Psychology and a Master's in Foreign Service at Georgetown University. At least she didn't lie about that part. She had a real Psychology degree, but not from the university she claimed.

Orlovsky looked at the man sitting to his right, reading a book and a memory of Alena's textbook library flashed into his mind. Most of her textbooks displayed on her bookshelf were in English and now he knew why. She'd never graduated the University of Sofia and her Ph. D. degree in Clinical Psychology that was hanging on the wall was forged with such precision that only an intelligence agency with resources could make it so real it fooled him.

Orlovsky looked back at the piece of paper and read the rest. Slavena was a participant in semi-professional shooting sporting events during middle and high school. She had no employment history and died about two years ago.

"Can this be right?" Orlovsky asked, already knowing the answer.

"Yes. According to her Social Security number, she died. The cleanup team did its job well, but forgot to erase her academic records from Georgetown University."

"And they made it so convenient for us!" Orlovsky sported a smile that was erased in seconds. He knew there was something shady about Alena, but the possibility of her being CIA hadn't crossed his mind. After he realized it, Orlovsky gritted his teeth. He didn't feel powerful and mighty anymore. He felt deflated and pissed off, for being played by a CIA officer.

"So, you finally hooked your mermaid?" The geek arched his brow, amused.

"Deeper than you think."

"What does she look like?" Archie was so eager to know more, he'd leaned across the table full-length and had his face as close to Orlovsky's as humanly possible.

"Jeez, Archie, back off. People will think we're smooching."

Archie leaned back in his chair with a wounded expression on his face. He knew he'd hit a nerve, but he wasn't worried. Orlovsky seemed overly satisfied with his product.

"Here's your money," Orlovsky handed him a thick wad of notes. This time Archie had asked for a lot more than the hacking of the website but the money was worth it. "Did you put fillers on the Google search?"

"Yup. If someone checks it out I'd know." Archie pocketed the money, looking around for people watching them. If Amnesia visitors hadn't suspected that shady information was exchanged for money under the table, they did now. Orlovsky mentally slapped Archie behind the neck. He was possibly the worst street criminal ever.

"If anyone checks out the profile, call me." He stood up and walked off, taking the folded paper with him.

Back home, sitting in his dark apartment, he studied the report Archie had given him one last time. He couldn't believe CIA had sent an amateur after him. Slavena was 28, practically just out of training. With his eighteen years on the job, he could eat her for breakfast. They were insulting his ego. He was tempted to cut their spring chicken open and send her back in a box with a note saying *"I am a sick man... I am a spiteful man. Next time send somebody who knows it."*

Then he remembered Slavena did know he was a sick man. She had told him the half-truth about her psychology degree. And, despite being so young, she had managed to make contact with him, latch onto him and suck all the information she could. She'd established stronger rapport than any others in her place could have. His father had taught him to respect professionalism, especially his enemies. Slavena might be a newbie, but she had a talent for the job.

The signs of her tailing him since day one had been in the air the whole time and he totally missed them. Realizing it, he stormed to his equipment closet and pulled out his bug detector. She had planted three bugs on him and the fact that they were all made in China didn't make him feel any better.

He was very much turned on by her performance just as an actor gets turned on by another actor's performance. But he was also avidly envious of how well she had deceived him. Her lack of accent, despite being in America for a decade fooled him completely. He rubbed his temple, feeling the strain of her deceit.

There was no more doubt that his back was scratched by a woman who worked for the CIA. They were interested in him because, as Alena had said, they had to protect some kind of an asset. That was always the case. Now he needed to find who that asset was and kill him. He liked shoving CIA's asses back down the hole of disinformation and this was a golden chance to do it. All he needed to do was trick Alena into believing that he was going to dance to the sound of her music and thus misinforming her so completely that she would mistakenly claim victory.

It was a genius idea. His father would have been proud of him and his newly conceived plan of handcuffing Slavena to her own lies.

Instantly he felt on top of his game again. He looked at the report one last time before he trashed it. The only other thing that jumped at him from the page was the death of her sister. What had she told him about Jaro? "He hurt somebody I loved." He put two and two together. She was using her job for personal revenge. He was willing to help her with that. If Jaro was responsible for her sister's death, then he was scum and had to die. Besides, Jaro was next on his list and had to get snuffed out sooner or later. Orlovsky was happy to oblige.

With that last thought, he sparked his Zippo and watched the flames turning the letters into ashes. He smiled. He couldn't wait for Slavena to resurface. He was going to have so much fun with her.

NAVY

Slavena looked through the scope of her rifle. There was a total of ten men standing by a group of cars parked near what was once a beachside pool and bar. Seven of them were hostiles. Four of them were her targets to engage. Puerto Rico had three. The rest were friendlies. The drivers stayed inside their cars, away from the beach, but she didn't need to worry about them for now.

"I got both men in bomber jackets with the Kalashnikovs, far left," she whispered in the now complete darkness. Her targets were the security detail and therefore the largest threat, but they were also the greatest immediate danger to Navy. She was determined to protect him.

"Roger." Puerto Rico responded. "I got the business suit on the right and his partner with the scarf."

The rest of the team was still repositioning and unable to call targets, leaving the responsibility of overwatch to just Slavena and Puerto Rico. At their distance, they could hear nothing but the crash of the waves. They would have to rely on visual cues. They stared unblinkingly into their Armasight night vision scopes as the man wearing the scarf removed a large backpack-sized hard, plastic case from the trunk of the sedan and placed it before the Russian.

He opened the case in the glow of headlights and began what appeared to be heart surgery through the lenses of the sniper scopes. Sea waves rhythmically crashed against the rocks below their sniper nest as the scientist operated on the device and the remaining bystanders scanned each other apprehensively. Under these watchful eyes, the Russian continued his work, every so often checking a stack of papers he held in his hands as if a store clerk checking inventory. After what seemed like an eternity, his arms stopped, his head lifted to the Syrians and gave a nod.

The nuclear device was real.

The man in the business suit handed a piece of paper to a Syrian, who pulled a cell phone from his pocket, dialed a number, and put the phone to his ear. After another eternity of uneasy glances, the Syrian nodded his head to the businessman who initiated his own phone call.

The salty humidity and tension of the exchange made Slavena's index finger sticky against the trigger of her M40. Despite the cold, sweat dripped down her eyelids, slightly blurring her vision as she focused her crosshairs from one gunman to the other. Then to Navy's unshaven face, and then back to the first gunman.

Just as the businessman lowered his phone from his ear, Johnson broke the silence. "I've got the engine block of the lead car," Johnson announced. He carried an M107 rifle that could disable a V6 engine if shot with precision.

Slavena exhaled, knowing the rest of the team was getting into position.

Without so much as a handshake, the businessman

turned his back to the Syrians and began to return to his car along with the man in the scarf. As he passed the driver's door, it opened and the driver stood, revealing a low profile QBZ-95 assault rifle as the men in the bomber jackets raised their Kalashnikovs. It was a double-cross.

Without hesitation, Slavena's M40 rifle released a thunderous boom and one of the bomber jackets delivered a burst of blood across a headlight beam. The driver could not unleash a single round from his QBZ-95 before his body was slammed against the sedan by the force of Puerto Rico's shot. Three loud booms erupted from the dilapidated hotel as the businessman's head exploded and one car's hood discharged a sudden gust of steam. As planned, with Johnson's second shot, he destroyed the engine's ability to function and had left them with no evacuation plan. The only option was for their targets to fight it out.

Before Slavena could manipulate the bolt of her rifle, the second bomber jacket was able to squeeze his trigger. The yellow-orange bursts from his muzzle made contact with the shoulder of one of the Syrians and at least two rounds impacted the abdomen of the body-armored gunman. Navy instinctively unloaded three rounds into the chest of the bomber jacket. Slavena added another through his throat before he fell lifelessly to the ground.

Another boom from the hotel threw the man with the scarf into the open car door just as a sudden snap of a bullet made Slavena realize she was now being shot at. The rate of fire and the snap-crack sound made it clear the Ukrainians had brought their own sniper. They had planned their own ambush. That's why they wanted to do the exchange at the beach instead of inside the hotel.

Slavena could hear Shields, Kingsley, and Patch shouting in her earpiece, but she understood nothing. Her face was pressed to the ground so hard, she breathed in dust and coughed.

For fuck's sake, she told herself, *I'm not dead yet to be breathing dirt.* There was still time for that. Until then, she ought to be shooting Ukrainian thugs.

"I got his location!" Puerto Rico screamed over the snap of another nearby round. "Past the pool on the hilltop!"

She lifted her head, testing the level of exposure she had. She was acting on instincts now rather than planning because it was pitch black and without looking through her night scope, she couldn't see much more than a blur in front of her.

She could taste the adrenaline in her mouth. It tasted bitter, but it was serving its purpose to fire her muscles for the next action. She adjusted her scope to thermal, raised it to her eye, and followed the pack of Puerto Rico's shot group. On a sand dune two hundred yards away, she saw a small red blob with a yellow corona among the sea of cold blue.

"Gotcha," she said as she inhaled and squeezed the trigger of her M40 and experienced an unexpected slow-motion effect. The recoil sank deep into her shoulder as the force of the bullet impact made the red blob in her scope jerk violently. She felt no pain or emotion as her shot silenced the distant sniper.

She adjusted her aim back onto Navy in time to see his infrared outline peppering the windows of the untouched sedan with automatic fire surely killing any surviving driver or gunman remaining inside. He then grabbed the Russian scientist by the collar and forcibly guided him safely to the steps of the long empty swimming pool.

Slavena scanned the area methodically to ensure there was no hidden threat to Navy or the scientists. Silence filled the dark beach that still remained partially illuminated by car headlights.

"Teams check-in!" Kingsley commanded. "Puerto Rico, go check on our Syrian and security detail. Jessica sit tight and provide cover while I confirm evac and a mop-up team. Well done, Marines."

In the silence that followed, Slavena heard the thump of the rotors of a helicopter. Tentatively, she stood up. In a few minutes, she would be airborne and away from here. Later they would do a debrief and AAR, but now she didn't want to think about anything.

All she wanted was to go home.

The helicopter was an MH-47-G, straight out of the Boeing lot. At the Farm, she heard about the new versions coming to the market, but she never thought she'd have the opportunity to fly in one. Her eyes lightened with joy when the twin engines blasted hot air in her face. As she walked to the ramp, the jet almost knocked her backward. It was like walking towards a giant hairdryer.

She sat inside and put headphones on. For the first few minutes of the flight, she looked out over the Black Sea waters. They were shimmering scintillatingly in the moonlight, in deep contrast to the conversation around her that turned to bar chatter. Over the sound of the rotors and the engine, she could hear the Marines bragging about their NFL Fantasy League picks. For them, the mission was over and they'd switched back to ordinary life as if nothing talk-worthy had happened.

Puerto Rico was the only one still paying attention to his

rifle. He gave his Jessica Alba a smacking kiss after examining it carefully for ding, dents or dirt. Everybody laughed.

Slavena's open-mouthed laughter spilled like sea waves on the shore. An immense feeling of satisfaction rippled through her body for her first successful operation. Like the salty air whipping her face through the open helicopter's door, her laughter cleaned away the anxieties of the last few days. She felt relaxed and grateful for the many little, unmentionable things, but mostly, she was relieved she hadn't seen the face of her first victim. She'd been dreading the thought of killing someone, anyone, for months. She'd imagined that taking a human life would torment her for days. But she felt nothing.

Or was this the fatigue of the last few days still talking inside her?

She closed her eyes and felt the muscles of her face relax. Then she thought of Navy and the corners of her mouth curled up in a smile. She couldn't believe their paths crossed on their first kinetic operation. What were the chances of that happening? Or was this a set-up, cooked up by Langley a long time ago? They'd teamed her up with Navy during her final days of CIA training, not knowing they were lovers. She saved Navy in the end, only to receive his "thank you for saving my life, baby, but you got me kicked out of the CIA" letter later on. That was his good bye.

All lies.

At that last thought, she opened her eyes to look at the man she could never trust again. Navy who was sitting opposite her, three seats down, glanced at her. Exchanging glances with him always felt like skidding off the road on an icy day, leaving her in a daze, but this time he gave her the clarity she needed. His nostrils reeked of guilt, leaving her to a conclusion: it was Navy who requested for her support. That's why he went out to the beach to surveil the area. To make sure she saw him on time to prepare herself mentally before the guts of the mission spilled out. It made sense. Him involving her in such an important mission was his way of apologizing for breaking up with her on a notion of lies.

She pondered another possibility. Maybe it was all the CIA's doing. Somehow, they found out about her secret liaison with Navy, they made him write the break-up letter to keep both of them safe. She would never know. In her line of work, there were always many scenarios, all with different flavors, and she was getting used to living in a world of secrets. A world where she fought a silent war against herself, always doubting her level of competence.

Including her dealings with Orlovsky.

After their last encounter, she had hated his guts, but he always seemed to come out on top of things, including her. She'd feared him but had also begun to admire him. He had crept up on her like frost over the glass on a cold winter day. She felt challenged and alive next to him. She craved that feeling, but she had no idea where they stood after their last encounter and her subsequent disappearance for the mission.

Despite losing control of her own feelings, she felt accomplished. She completed her last mission in Ukraine and was on her way to report back to base. This alone was enough to close her eyes with the comforting thought that this was exactly how she envisioned her life as a CIA officer. A life filled with danger, lots of questions, no answers, and a thumb up in the air after each successful mission.

Better than being dead, she thought and fell asleep.

The Middle Game

QUEEN SACRIFICE

The sound of the helicopter's rotors became distant, as she walked towards her boss. Gavin was waiting for her at the air hanger in Novo Selo, Bulgaria. He had his hair cut short, which made him look significantly younger. His warm smile made her feel accomplished.

He approached her and gave her a bear hug. "I knew you would do great out there."

"Thanks," she said pleased that she'd finally done something right by him but was aware that there was always an agenda behind everything Gavin did.

"You look tired," he peered at her face. "What happened to your eye?"

She touched her fading bruise with her fingers. She'd forgotten all about it in the past few days. "Orlovsky."

"Son of a bitch. Do you need a PSD team?"

He meant personal security detachment team and Slavena imagined a couple of men sitting in a car all day, right outside her window. Following her around. Poking their noses in her stuff. She felt claustrophobic just thinking about it.

"No. I'll be fine."

Gavin nodded while punching a badge activated Cipher keypad on the wall of the air hanger. Then he walked inside the secured office, went behind a monstrosity of a desk and sat. The semi-intimate moment was over. They were back to being case officer and Chief of Station once again.

Slavena didn't know who the desk belonged to—Gavin had borrowed an office for the day from some military officer—but the size of it was compensating for something.

Gavin looked at her seriously. "As much as I want to give you some time off, now is not the time,"

"What's happening?" Slavena asked.

"Have a seat." She sat in the visitor's chair that was intentionally uncomfortable so a person sat at attention and avoided lingering and wasting the officer's precious time. She had never met the man but already had an idea what he was like.

"There were two more hits while you were gone." Gavin leaned back and caught the light of a nearby window. Slavena saw extra lines on his face, around his mouth and eyes, that hadn't been there a month ago.

"Two?" She didn't have to fake disbelief. Two in one week was fast work even by Orlovsky's standards. "Why is he in such a hurry?"

"That's for you to find out. *Choong Sim* returned from his international trip yesterday," he paused and Slavena nodded in understanding. *Choong Sim* was the code name for Dragan Boychev and it translated as center gravity in Korean. Thanks to Gavin's obsession with Taekwondo, Slavena had no doubts she would speak Korean by the time she left Bulgaria. "And your Eagle is about to make his next hit."

"Do we have the name?"

"No."

"Then, how do you know he's already working on his next hit?"

"I sent someone to tail him while you were gone. According to her reports, he gave every indication that he had another name on the list and was preparing for his next hit. But he left town and she lost him."

And here it was: the reason Gavin was nice to her. He needed her to hunt Orlovsky down and serve him on a plate. Little did he know she was part of Orlovsky's diet and she gave him indigestion the last time they discussed the CLEANSING. She was suddenly reminded she never gave Gavin a debrief on the night at the Admiral's house.

"We don't know who Orlovsky's next hit is," Gavin carried on, "but there are only a few people left to kill and Choong Sim is one of them."

Slavena looked down. For all she knew, Orlovsky's trail had gone cold. By now, he probably knew he was being watched and would never make the same mistakes twice. Then Slavena looked out of the window, gathering the courage to broach the subject about skipping her debrief.

"Keep safe, Alena," Gavin said. "It's almost over. Let me know if things get out of control."

"I will. Thanks." She stood to leave.

She couldn't do it. She couldn't tell Gavin that she screwed up her pitch with Orlovsky and that he was a lost cause now. Gavin had just told her he was pleased with her performance. She could do with him thinking positive about her for longer than a day.

She had no idea how to reverse what had happened with Orlovsky to reach the objective of the CLEANSING, but when it came to chess, being defeated was just a short-term state. Giving-up was what made it permanent and she wasn't ready to give up on it.

Not just yet.

Slavena unlocked the door of the apartment and stood at the threshold. The air inside hadn't gone stale. Instead, it was rather fresh. For some reason that put her on guard. She was reluctant to walk in. It had been seven days since she was last here. In an old building like this one, the air went musty as soon as you closed the door behind you. Why hadn't it gone sour this time?

Her eyes widened at the sight of her chess board atop her coffee table. It was a habit of hers to glance at the chess board to ensure all the chess pieces were lined perfectly. But now she noticed the white queen was off the board and her breath was in her throat. Someone had been in her apartment to deliver a message.

She listened to sounds from within but heard nothing. She took a step forward, still dragging her bag on the floor. Was she imagining things? Perhaps the stress hadn't limited itself to her muscles but had gone into her head too. She kicked the door closed and froze. There was somebody sitting on the couch behind her. This time she wasn't imagining anything. She was certain.

She let go of the bag and quickly examined her options. Before she'd gone to the mission, she'd cleared the flat out. No incriminating materials, technology or anything else that connected her to the CIA. But this also meant no guns around or any other weapons. If there was a trap, she was in bad shape to fight or flee.

Slowly, she turned to face the intruder.

"Orlovsky?" She drew her first breath after the shock. "How did you get in?"

Orlovsky didn't look like he was about to attack her. He was sitting on the couch with his arms spread over the backrest, relaxed, almost happy given the expression on his face.

"You can't possibly think the locks on your front door would be a problem for me," Orlovsky said with a faint smile. "You know what I'm capable of, Alena."

"I guess it is pointless then to ask how you knew I'd be back tonight." Slavena wanted to return Orlovsky's easy smile, but she couldn't muster the expression. "So why are you here?"

"You know exactly why."

She studied his face, but it was impassive and difficult to read.

"I do, but I want to hear it from you," she bluffed.

"You have no idea, do you?"

"You are here to apologize."

Orlovsky wrinkled his brow with amusement. "Apologize? If anybody should apologize, it's you for risking my life to save you and then making me listen to your lies."

Another ping-pong match Orlovsky style. She thought to herself, remembering the humiliating consequences of their last conversation. This time, she was not going to give him a chance.

"Listen, this is not a good time for me to have visitors."

"But I'm not just a visitor. Isn't that so?" His smile broadened and sent chills down her back. It made her wonder if he knew something she didn't. Orlovsky carried on, "We've been through a lot together. We are partners now."

"Partners?" Slavena's eyes narrowed and subconsciously she looked at the fallen white queen on the chess board. "That is not the impression I got from the latest news reports."

Orlovsky noticed Slavena's focus on the white queen and leaned forward to return the piece back onto the board. "I know neither of those two hits interested you!"

"And how are you so sure?"

"Because you were out of the country. Do I need to explain?"

She shook her head, giving a thought. Orlovsky presumed since she was out of the country, Boychev must be safe for the time being. Not bad. Orlovsky was a smart operative. And well informed.

"No, you don't, but you need to explain what our partnership entails."

"I'll inform you about my hits from now on, so you can have these pieces of junk back," he said, throwing the three listening devices on her chessboard. The fingernail size bugs she had planted in his apartment clinked on the board, knocking the white queen back down. She had to agree they were pieces of junk that never really worked properly.

"That's... wonderful," Slavena pivoted on her heels and went to the fridge with her mind racing. What other surprises did he have for her? His sudden change of heart was disturbing. Her instincts told her to be watchful. Orlovsky always had an agenda. By the relaxed pose he'd adopted on her couch she guessed he wasn't going away any time soon. She might get to find out what he had in mind. And what the consecutive removal of the white queen really meant.

She pulled a bottle of wine out of the fridge. "We need to celebrate then."

"Not so fast," Orlovsky said and she stopped on her way to fetching glasses.

"All right," she turned to face him. She never thought it was going to be easy. "What's the catch?"

"No catch. Just a simple question. Why is the CIA interested in Bulgarian mafia affairs?"

Slavena laughed easily. "How would I know? The CIA?" She shook her head, as if she couldn't believe his silliness and carried on towards the glass cabinet. She forced herself to drop her shoulders down and act as if he hadn't just freaked her out. "You totally overrated me."

"Well, that's disappointing," he said without emotion. Somehow the calm Orlovsky managed to be scarier than the angry one. "I've always wanted to fuck an FSB officer. I wanted to see for myself if they teach them how to screw properly. I figured CIA was the next best thing. You disappoint me, Alena."

Slavena poured white wine into two glasses, watching her hand tremble as she lowered the bottle.

"Yeah," she said lifting the glass, feeling Orlovsky's eyes burning a hole in her. "That's too bad. But you're a big boy. I'm sure you'll manage to live with the disappointment."

She took a sip, watching Orlovsky watch her. He stood up from the couch so fast, her head spun. He snatched the glass from her hand, slammed it on the counter top, then squeezed her shoulders between his palms until she was shrugging from the pain.

"Now listen to me carefully," his spicy breath evoked unwanted longing at the pit of her stomach. She felt threatened and aroused at the same time. What was wrong with her? "If any of my information gets leaked, I'll kill you. If I ask you to come with me, you'll do it. You'll do everything I say. You'll follow my lead, understood?"

"Come with you?" her eyes widened. "That's a sure way for both of us to get killed."

"I don't think so," he leaned forward and whispered in her ear. "You are a big girl too. Something tells me you'll do just fine."

He let her go and she lost her balance, stumbling forward. He caught her in the crook of his left arm, putting his right hand inside his jacket pocket.

"One last thing," he smiled.

Slavena could do without more surprises but she didn't see a way of putting a stop to them. Orlovsky was on a roll. He pulled a dildo out of his pocket, smiled mischievously and switched it to vibrate. "Look what I found in your apartment among other things."

"Is that it?" she snapped. "You can borrow it if you like?"

Slavena's eyes wandered around the room. She was more concerned about the *among other things* part.

Orlovsky gave her a crooked smile. "Relax, I'm not going to take your precious toy."

He picked her up by the waist and placed her on the kitchen counter.

"I only pointed it out because I have a better toy for you."

He put his lips on hers, parting them with his tongue and reaching deep inside. Slavena did not resist. She had been craving exactly this for the last two days while lying in the cold ground in Ukraine. He bit her lower lip and she pulled out of the kiss. She pushed him back.

"I need a shower. I've had an awful few days."

"Shower, it is then." He lifted her from the bar counter and led her to the shower cabin near her bedroom. She was not surprised he was already perfectly familiar with the floor plan of her apartment.

His palms felt warm on her waist. She welcomed the warmness of his tight embrace, but she knew it wouldn't last. Judging by the glee on his face, she knew he was about to play with her like a cat with its kill.

Still, Slavena was relieved to see the return of his former self. The cooperative, agreeable Orlovsky gave her the creeps.

He turned on the cold water and twisted to face her with a wicked smile. Slavena felt like a lifeless puppet in his hands, but then again that was his intention: to show her who was in charge.

He tossed her under the running water with her clothes on, like a dirty rag doll. The freezing cold water gave her an adrenaline rush. She was instantly alert. The shock woke up all her senses. Orlovsky held her still underneath the whipping shower. She gasped for breath and fought back. Fully clothed, Orlovsky joined her, pinning her to the wall.

The warmth and strength of his body aroused her.

"What is it with you and cold water?" she finally caught her breath.

"It makes me feel alive," he said, ripping her shirt off, "and makes your nipples hard…"

He leaned to drink the dripping water from her nipples and she felt the pleasure of being exposed. Nothing more underlies a man's dominance than a woman's naked, wet body next to the man's fully clothed, muscular one. Underneath his wet clothes, Slavena could see the contours of his body, resembling a statue made out of flesh. His body was a hot and pulsing masterpiece. The Marines from Ukraine would kill for a body like his.

She felt his nails dragging against her thighs while peeling her pants off along with her panties. Her nerves ignited when he buried his face between her thighs. She was shivering and her skin was covered with goose bumps until the water turned warm and then pleasantly hot as he stood up. She melted into the heat of the moment, inside his arms, surrendering to all his wishes. He kissed her and fingered her until she didn't know where she was anymore. The thought of his fingers, inside her and of what they were capable of, brought her to a climax.

He took her breath away as if she was one of his victims.

He dug his fingers into her body and lifted her up like a new rifle he couldn't wait to use for the first time. He held her and thrusted inside her as if he could somehow absorb her into his body. He dug into her flesh deeper with the rage of orgasm.

When it was over, he whispered in her ear: "Knight takes queen!"

An hour later, the memory of the freezing shower was long gone. They were in bed. Her body warm next to Orlovsky's. He was fast asleep. She was still awake, thinking of their conversation and his suspicion that she was a CIA officer. The more details he'd uncovered about her, the more ammunition he had to use against her. But what triggered the land mine in her psyche was his last words in the shower.

Knight takes queen.

Orlovsky, like her, was a chess player at heart and in the face of a threat, his defenses would take over and counterattack. Hence the queen sacrifice move. But what did that mean in a real kill-or-be-killed world? What was Orlovsky up to? She had to find out before it was too late.

VELINA

Velina walked into Slavena's office with an air of importance.

"The storm is coming," she said, handing Slavena a piece of paper. She unbuttoned her trench coat and sat on the couch.

Slavena did not move behind her desk. It was a rare courtesy for Velina to come to the office unannounced and the curiosity inside Slavena was taking on a life of its own. Armed with a constant stream of Velina's information, Slavena knew who and what was a threat to Boychev's campaign. Thanks to Velina who was now promoted to the head editor for Vestnik, she knew who to libel, when to tip off Interpol and what political themes the official campaign manager of Boychev should focus on. So far it all had worked nicely. Her little team had Boychev up 20 points in the polls and steadily headed toward victory. But something big was about to be revealed, something that could annihilate her mission to get him elected and the unknown put her on edge.

"Do you want some coffee?" Slavena asked calmly from her desk.

Velina smiled faintly. "I do, but I'll make it myself. You need to read my summary. It's important."

Velina got up from the couch and Slavena watched her as she paced the length of her office. Velina was an exquisite beauty with luminous blonde hair that waved softly over her delicate shoulders. A straight nose, full lips, foxy green eyes, and flawless complexion—one of the most beautiful women Slavena had ever seen.

But Velina was more than just a beauty. She was her most reliable propaganda mouthpiece. She had the experience and spirit of a street journalist who socialized in high society. She knew every rumor and piece of gossip. What politician was aligned with what mafia group? Who was sleeping with whom? And what secret political or business deals were occurring? The information and influence she provided Slavena was invaluable.

She also had an infectious personality that made people gravitate towards her. But the best part about Velina was that she always got her information before anyone else could. In the CIA world, that was crucial.

Slavena looked back at the piece of paper and read it with narrowed eyes. "What am I reading?"

"It's a summary of a book that's going to be published just before Christmas. It's called *The Reins of Power*," Velina's voice came across the room.

Slavena continued to read steadily. The summary accurately described what Slavena already knew about Boychev's father. His dark past was not a secret to her. But she was relieved the report said nothing about Boychev working with the USA to host CIA black sites. She'd stumbled upon a secret interrogation facility for terrorists during her recent trip to Novo Selo Army Base and she knew it was a CNN time-bomb that would eventually explode. But thankfully not today.

"And who is Stefka Kaneva?"

"A hot-shot investigative reporter who chases after corrupted politicians, but nobody takes her seriously."

"Why?"

"Because there is not a single politician in Bulgaria who is not corrupt," Velina said, taking a sip of her creamy espresso. "Anyway, her book is about the link between Dragan Boychev's rise to power and the mafia."

"Do we know her source?" Slavena asked.

"No. Someone anonymous who claims to have worked for Boychev's father back in the '90s. According to him, Boychev Senior was the architect of the modern Bulgarian mafia."

"How so?" Slavena asked, already knowing the answer. It was her way of testing Velina's knowledge.

"Kaneva's book claims that as the Director of the National Police, Boychev's father only arrested petty criminals while the big Mafioso and the real criminals, prospered."

"How did they prosper?"

"The protection Boychev Senior provided to the mafia allowed their racketeering and other criminal activities to flourish. He targeted any competitors to his friends in BAM and SIN thus allowing those empires to grow. This gained him influence and power that could be bought and sold."

"But isn't that always the case in Bulgaria?"

"Sure, but nobody until now dared to put it in a book."

Slavena remained immersed in her thoughts for a moment. Until today, Slavena was the only one who knew about Boychev Senior's alleged associations with the mafia and its deadly potential to hurt their campaign. She was the one who destroyed all the government records and all evidence that could hurt Boychev's campaign. But apparently, that wasn't enough. There was always somebody out there who remembered and was willing to talk for some extra cash and there were plenty of journalists who wanted to jump on the bandwagon of fame by publishing the story.

"Would she take hush money?" Slavena finally asked.

"And take the book off the market?"

"Yes."

"No, she would cut someone's throat to make sure her book sees daylight. "

"Then what else is on the table?"

"If anybody knows, it's *you*, Alena. It's your campaign." Velina looked at Slavena with her mischievous foxy eyes. She looked beautiful with her little espresso cup in her fragile hands. Subconsciously, Slavena thought of Orlovsky and his strong hands.

The things Alexander Orlovsky could to do to help her.

"Thanks, Velina! I'll take care of it," Slavena said, dropping the piece of paper into her drawer.

Velina stood up to leave right as Orlovsky walked inside the office with a puzzled look on his face. Unlike Velina, it had become a habit of his to always come unannounced, but it never bothered Slavena until now. Without saying anything, he scanned Velina's body and made a quizzical but friendly expression.

Slavena looked away from Orlovsky and turned back to Velina. "Call me later to set up your next appointment."

"Will do," Velina replied with a much softer and intimate voice than Slavena remembered. Apparently, the appearance of an attractive stranger never failed to trigger the tick-tucking mechanism of her flirtatious nature. Sensing she got the man's attention, Velina picked her red purse from the glass table and walked towards the door with the neat precision of a confident woman who was desired by many men. Orlovsky included.

Her heels clicked with a loud echo before she stopped at the door where she and Orlovsky exchanged a discreet gaze that was a pretext for something more exciting to come later on. The sign of chemistry between them gave Slavena a jolt of concern. His body language — the raised eyebrows, his posture standing tall and his parted lips — was enough to convince Slavena that her best agent, Velina, was suddenly a threat.

Narcissists like Orlovsky always enjoyed the chase, the hunt, and the prospect of a new unsuspecting supply of adoration. And Velina, her beautiful agent, was turning herself into his new supply right in front of her eyes. Slavena knew from his profile that Orlovsky grew easily bored with every woman he encountered, but she didn't expect herself to become a drag for him so soon.

For a moment, Slavena imagined Velina and Orlovsky together. As two primal forces fighting each other for dominance. Velina slapping his face and Orlovsky ripping her clothes. Slavena glared at Velina's delicate body like a horse buyer at the thoroughbred yearling auction in Churchill Downs and wondered if Orlovsky found her as fascinating. The muscles on her arms were delicate and smooth, but too weak to handle a man like Orlovsky. He enjoyed the fight too much. Like a real chess player, his mind was a battlefield. Especially when it came to sex. With that last thought, her certainty of Velina's feminine supremacy had worn thin.

At the sound of the door closing, Slavena came back to reality only to find Orlovsky's eyes glaring at an object on her desk. She looked down at the object and her heart skipped a beat. It was her listening device jammer he was interested in and she regretted instantly for not placing her trade tool in a less visible location. Now it was too late because Orlovsky's hands were already on the device. He took the jammer with him and sat on the sofa to take a better look at it. He patiently peeled the wrapper of chocolate while glaring at the gadget.

"Didn't know therapists use jammers during sessions."

"It's for high-profile clients."

"The man you're trying to protect?"

Slavena didn't respond.

Unimpressed with the device, Orlovsky placed it back on the table and swung around to face her. "I have a tennis match this week and you're going to play doubles with me."

"Doubles?"

"Yes. Canadian doubles, two on one."

He meant doubles versus single and that was his cryptic way of reminding her about their agreement. What was it with men in the clandestine world using sports metaphors as cover talk? Gavin with Taekwondo, now Orlovsky with tennis. Luckily for her, she played tennis and she knew her terminology well. Canadian doubles-two on one was similar to cutthroat tennis, and it was a method of playing tennis with three players. Two players against one player on the court at the same time. Which could mean one thing only: Orlovsky had received a new name on the CLEANSING list and he was asking her to join him on the kill.

"Who is the opponent?" she asked conforming to his cryptic talk.

"He was seeded as number four in the last tournament."

It alarmed her. Jaro was the fourth richest man in Bulgaria.

"He knows how to insult a good backhand and has excellent spins," Orlovsky carried on, "but *we* can take him by surprise with one deadly serve right in the heart."

"Shouldn't be that hard since *you* are serving," she said, still in disbelief that they were discussing the killing of a man.

"When was the last time you practiced on your serve?"

"Practice?" Orlovsky meant guns. "I don't have a racket to practice with."

"You can borrow one of mine and we can practice tomorrow night."

"I can't tomorrow," she said. "Something urgent came up and I have to work."

That surprised him. "Blow it off. We had an agreement!"

"I can't blow off clients when they need me."

Orlovsky raised up sharply from the sofa and headed her way in the same threatening posture as the day he slapped her. "Are you telling me that you're seeing a patient tomorrow?"

Slavena nodded, feeling like a matador, waving her red cape and waiting for the charging bull to crush her down.

"Your session can wait till later."

"Can't. My client was blackmailed."

Orlovsky raised his eyebrow. "Blackmailed by whom?"

"You know I can't tell you that. It's confidential."

He snatched her purse and emptied its contents on the desk with a crash. Condoms, pens, notebook, wallet, loose change, and her five cell phones spilled across her desk.

He observed the contents with a smirk on his face. "You can open a cell phone store with all your phones."

Swift anger came into her voice. "What are you looking for?"

"This!" he waved her notebook in her face and ripped a blank page with rage. "Write the name of the person who blackmailed your client and I'll take care of it!" he laid out the piece of paper in front of her along with a pen. His request gave her a déjà vu. If she didn't write the journalist name, he would hurt her again. If she wrote it, the journalist would get hurt instead. It didn't feel right either way, but the part of her brain that could register pain reigned her decision to write *Stefka Kaneva*, realizing that by doing so, she signed the death sentence for somebody who was as young and ambitious as herself.

Orlovsky folded the piece of paper with his fingers, put it inside his pocket, and walked towards the door.

Slavena was distressed by what just happened. Playing footsie with a professional killer was quickly turning her ethical ceiling into a floor. And a slippery one too, because Orlovsky was not the kind of man who negotiated for peace. His mind was stuck in a war zone and he just needed breathing space to find a new way to kill more people and kill the journalist.

Realizing her mistake, she ran towards the door and closed in on him. "Promise me that you won't kill her."

"I don't make promises I can't keep!" He cracked an evil smile and pushed her out of his way.

One of the hardest things about her job was to continue liking herself, regardless of the dirty work she had to do. What she did, as calloused as it was, served the national interest. It was as simple as that.

"So goodbye conscience!" she mumbled and went for a run.

It was the longest run that she ever did—almost two hours. Fueled by guilt, she ran like a machine. Was Boychev worth a life? She wasn't convinced, but if she wanted her mission to survive, Kaneva had to die. There was no other way.

Exhausted, she ran back home. She walked inside her apartment, turned on the TV and went straight to her shower. The warm droplets of water were soothing to her muscles until she was stopped cold by the murmurs of the news. She turned off the water and listened.

"Stefka Kaneva, a prominent investigative journalist who regularly reported on the mafia in Bulgaria, was severely injured in a mysterious accident in the capital, Sofia. According to sources, the 28-year-old reporter plunged five floors down from the balcony of her apartment but miraculously survived the fall, sustaining severe skull fractures. Her doctors confirmed she is in a coma and uncertain if she would ever be able to fully recover. Unnamed sources allege she recently completed a book manuscript describing her three-year investigation into the corrupt linkages between Bulgarian organized crime and national political leaders. Authorities have —"

Her phone chimed.

"The word is already out," Slavena mumbled as she reached for a towel. She quickly wrapped herself in it and answered the phone.

"Did you hear the news?" Velina was ecstatic.

"Yes," Slavena said sullenly. "We got lucky, but at what price?"

Velina, being the astute reporter, picked-up quickly on Slavena's tone. "But it was none of our doing, so don't bring the Karma out of the drawer now."

"You're right," Slavena said with a shiver.

"By the way, I meant to ask you, who was that hottie I saw in your office the other day?"

"A client of mine," Slavena replied hastily. The last

person she wanted on her mind was Orlovsky.

"Mmm. I would love to get inside his head."

"Trust me, you wouldn't," Slavena said. "Speaking of the devil, I promised to call him."

"I'll let you go then," Velina said and hung up.

Slavena looked at the clock with a cold knot in her stomach. It was 6 pm. She knew Orlovsky would come looking for his reward for doing her dirty work and the longer she waited to contact him, the more opportunity he had to plot a wicked surprise. To keep some semblance of control, she typed a message on her phone: *Still practicing tennis tonight?* She typed, holding her breath, her text, her fear. She held the phone for a moment longer before she hit Send.

Her phone chimed soon after.

No time for practice. Tonight is the big game. 1900. My place. Our team wears black.

After reading it, Slavena exhaled a wave of relief, mixed with anxiety. Relief, because of the discreet nature of his message. Everything Orlovsky sent her was being read by the CIA and she didn't want to get caught, doing precisely what CIA trained her to do.

And anxiety, because she had only one hour to get to Orlovsky's place. One hour of waiting before discovering what kind of tennis bluff Orlovsky was running.

Orlovsky opened the door with scrutinizing eyes. Slavena had chosen—in her hurried twenty minutes—the same black assassin's dress she wore on the evening she surveilled Orlovsky at the night club. She wore a black leather jacket on top that made Orlovsky pause with admiration in his eyes. Knowing that Orlovsky was not the kind of man who knew how to compliment a woman, Slavena waited for his insult.

"If all tennis players looked like sluts, I would have to chop my own dick off to win a game," he said with a big grin, pleased he'd thought of it.

"Do I need to reply to this?"

"No, but you probably will."

Her eyes narrowed against his challenge that was burning hot inside her like a fever. Her muscles itched to strike back and forgetting to be cautious, she launched her right arm towards his jaw, realizing she started a battle that was already lost. When he blocked her flying fist with his hand, she tried again with her left arm. This time, she aimed for his stomach, but Orlovsky skillfully hooked both of her arms with his own, pinned them behind her back, and leaned over her body with a conceited look on his face. He moved so damn fast that she missed seeing it at all.

For an instant, their bodies stood locked, face-to-face. She stood silently looking at him. There was no use fighting him.

"Is this how you thank me?"

"Thank you?" she said, raising her eyebrow. "For what?"

He released her from the lock. "For helping you out."

"I told you *not* to kill her!"

"But you wanted her dead, didn't you? I could still see it in your eyes." He hissed. "Anyway, the bitch is still alive, so what's the big deal?"

"The big deal is that you tried to kill her."

"And you're surprised? You know who I am, Alena, don't you? I'm a fucking killer with no conscience, no compassion, and no capacity for guilt or remorse. I perceive people as objects that I destroy because they are inferior. What does that make me *Doctor*?"

"Let's see." She played along. "If I throw your cruelty into the mix, add your constant need to control and pair that with your chronic boredom, and a complete lack of fear, I think I have a textbook case of Antisocial Personality Disorder. In other words, you are a sociopath, Alexander."

"And what are you, Alena?" He punched a passcode on the wall. "A therapist who teams up with an assassin, so she can pick and choose which patient of hers gets to live or die. I think you are a textbook case of an evil hypocrite. Do you still think that I'm the crazy one?"

A big vault opened and her eyes narrowed at the sight. "Yes, I do," she said. "Only a crazy man would have enough firearms in his closet to fill a gallery in a museum."

"Pick one."

"I don't know anything about guns."

"You don't?" His eyes hung on her for longer than she cared.

"Why should I? I am a therapist, not a killer."

"Just. Fucking. Pick. One!"

Hearing his bark, she wrinkled her brow slightly amused and walked to the Remington on the second shelf. She touched the weapon—with the same amount of care and curiosity as on the day when she touched her first Remington 700 M24 when she was only ten.

"So, is this what you used at the Farm?" He screwed up his eyes at her.

"Not even close," she said, realizing she'd been waiting to say exactly this for a longtime.

"Sure about that? I have an SR-25. On the third row far left. Not a favorite of mine. It is a jamming disaster. The .300 Win Mag on the second row is a fine weapon too." He walked to it and pulled out the rifle to demonstrate. "It uses a manual bolt action, but it's way too heavy for you *Princess*." He smirked over his shoulder and placed the rifle back on the rack. "Or how about the .50 Cal Machine Gun?" He pointed to the big black monster in the far corner.

"I don't know what any of this really means." She suppressed her smile to keep the match away from the powder keg that was Orlovsky.

"If you don't, then pay attention to what I'm saying and stop standing there like some Prima Donna!" He tossed a duffle bag on the floor. "Get busy and put your rifle inside!" The menace in his voice made her kneel down like a dog who sensed the threat in its master's tone. Orlovsky turned his back on her, selected his weapon—Anschutz Rx22 MSR—and placed it carefully in a plastic case.

"So, where are we going?"

He came slowly towards her and gazed at her. "I already told you. You're insulting my intelligence."

"We're going to a tennis game?"

"Yeah." He gave her a thin smile. "The bloodiest tennis game in Plovdiv."

She was lightheaded by the surprise. Plovdiv was her hometown. The same as Boychev and the same as Jaro. Could Orlovsky be targeting one of them? It was simply a thought, but she became prey to it because Boychev could be dead in an hour and her mission to make him Prime Minister along with him. The unknown began to suck up all the oxygen from her air.

As soon as the wheels of his Range Rover licked the pavement on the road, Orlovsky turned on his CD player. The beats of the bass instantly pulsated throughout her body, piercing her internal organs. If there was a genre of music that accurately described his state of mind, it was precisely this psychedelic trance.

She turned to observe his profile. As disorienting as the music was for her, it seemed to calm him down. All the visible signs of his tension — the rocking of his feet and the drumming of his fingers on the steering wheel — were gone. He was a different man now. His expression was calm. His mind was at peace.

Slavena leaned her head back against the seat and listened to the menacing lyrics of the song about a rabbit: *"skin him down to the bone, and at the Farm, they skin them really nice..."*

Hearing this line, her mind raced along with the car like a bullet in the night.

Who was the rabbit?

BULLET CHESS

Jaro was edgy and scared tonight. The rumor that he was next on the CLEANSING list had gone off with a bang and he prepared for the recoil by increasing his security to the highest possible level. He traveled to the stadium in the back of an old Audi, covered by a blanket on the floorboard of the back seat. During the soccer match, he refused to sit in his VIP room. Instead, he sat among hundreds less prominent guests, in the trophy room. It was a spacious hall with big windows, where biggest fans watched the match in the stadium and then celebrated if their team won. He was well protected there by the moving bodies of innocent bystanders. He looked across the stadium to see the VIP area was empty with the exception of one room.

Inside it, Nikolov was standing up with six of his meaty bodyguards, who were watching the crowd with the eyes of a cat. Only Nikolov got to watch the game.

Plovdiv strikers, which was Jaro's team, scored their first goal and the crowd roared. Nikolov eyed the cheering crowd with fury.

"Boss, Jaro is here," his bodyguard said while looking through his binoculars.

"Where is he?" Nikolov asked and the bodyguard handed him the binoculars.

"Hiding in the trophy room with the rest of his pussies," the guard said and everybody in the room laughed but Nikolov.

In the past few months, three of his biggest competitors were killed and Jaro was the only one left. The thought of Jaro still breathing and cheering for his team angered him. But Nikolov knew it was only a matter of time before Jaro joined his best friend, Little Christ, and the others for an everlasting sleep in his gold-plated coffin with a bouquet of flowers. Everybody was already talking about it.

The problem was Nikolov was on the CLEANSING list too.

Jaro's team scored another goal and Nikolov looked through his binoculars. It took him two minutes to spot him. The son of a bitch looked as elegant as always even in a pair of jeans. Nikolov pulled out his mobile phone and dialed Jaro's number.

"Why are you hiding in the trophy room like a mouse?" Nikolov asked with his eyes fixed on Jaro.

"And why are you so placid in your VIP room after all the news?"

"Forewarned is forearmed!"

"Did you read that phrase somewhere or you made that up yourself?"

"Does it matter? It got your attention!" Nikolov said, pleased.

"What do you know?"

"That you're next on the list"

Jaro exploded with laughter, but Nikolov knew that it wasn't meant as an insult. It was rather Jaro's fragile psyche and nerves taking the form of verbal false confidence, so Nikolov waited patiently for him to calm down.

"And since when are you so concerned about my life, Sinner?" Jaro said at last. "Since you killed my brother or is this your conscience speaking on your behalf?"

"If I ever had a conscience, it has long been covered by spider webs. "

"So insightful suddenly! Did you start reading poetry?"

"Yeah, poetry about a woman who does all the CLEANSING in the house."

"A woman?" Jaro's voice softened suddenly.

"Yes, a woman. The Admiral called me the night he got slaughtered to tell me he caught a woman snooping around his house. A dangerously skilled woman."

"A woman can't pull this off unless she is working with someone."

"And that someone is capable of killing the Admiral and all his guards with a knife," Nikolov said and all his bodyguards became perfectly still. His last words got their full attention.

"Orlovsky?" Jaro's voice cracked. "I thought the son of a bitch was in Russia."

"He was until recently. Coincidence or what?"

"Maybe, but if there is a woman involved, there is no way Orlovsky is in on it too. He would never trust someone else to do his work for him, much less a woman."

"Or work with him. Either way, how do we know for sure that it's him?"

"We don't. I say we just kill the son of a bitch. Him and any woman who gets near him. Just to be on the safe side."

"Now, we're talking. I'll send my hounds after him and work out where his hole is. I hope you do the same. Until he dies, we are partners in this."

"Deal. Oh, one last thing, I hope your team loses tonight."

"Fuck off!"

The line went dead.

As they entered her hometown, Plovdiv, Slavena felt on her home turf at last. She looked at the clock on the dashboard. It showed 21:04. Orlovsky turned off his music with a sudden jerk of his hand and Slavena took note of his hands. The veins on his hands protruded like electric wires ready to execute. The man who was about to be executed had no chance against the high-voltage energy that was Orlovsky.

At the sight of a tall building, Orlovsky made a sharp turn and entered its garage, making the tires screech on the smooth surface of the concrete like rubber-soled shoes on a polished floor. The screeching of the tires died away and the car stopped.

For a moment, he watched her eyes, as she watched his. He said nothing, but her question had been answered. She was going with him. Orlovsky put on his leather gloves and jumped from the driver's seat. His shadow was on the move, unloading equipment from the trunk and vanishing in the dark. For a moment, Slavena waited inside the car. It was pitch black outside and she was terrified of seeing Orlovsky in action.

By the time Slavena slammed her passenger door, Orlovsky was already by the exit staircase with both bags in his hands. If his idea of working in a team was carrying everything for her and not saying a single word, then she was fine with it.

At the sound of the door crushing near the staircase, she hurried up. An elevator stood invitingly on the side, but for some reason, Orlovsky preferred the stairs. Once inside, she became disoriented from the darkness until she saw the distinct shadow of Orlovsky standing over her. He was waiting. Although she couldn't see his face, the angle of his head told her a great deal. He was growing impatient with her.

"If you were a fucking slug, you will be crawling faster than this!" he finally spat the venom he had been holding for an hour and leaped up the stairs like a panther. Now that she was warned, she tried to match his pace, but no matter how physically fit she was, she remained many steps behind him until he once again disappeared in the dark.

At least now, she knew where he was going — to the roof.

By the time she reached the top, Orlovsky was already on the freezing tarred roof, constructing the two rifles.

"So, what's the plan?" she asked, shivering. She had never been so cold.

"The plan is that you shut the fuck up and let me do my work."

"Then why did you bring me here?"

"Isn't that what you wanted? Or do you suddenly have amnesia?"

"What I wanted was to be informed about your hits so we can negotiate. Instead, you choose to keep me in the dark until it's too late," she said with a touch of anger in her voice.

He didn't say anything. He checked the wind, calculated the range, and mounted both rifles with the precision of a

Swiss watch. With his electronic wind gauges, he measured the direction and speed of the wind and reevaluated his estimates. Slavena observed his methods carefully, matching every step he made to what she already knew. What would probably take her thirty minutes to do, took him less than five minutes.

So far, she was impressed.

He positioned himself behind her M40A3, observed the target area through his night-vision scope, then he laid behind his Anschutz Rx22 MSR and did the same. After some readjustments, he looked at her. Her hands were deep in her pockets as she was desperate to stop shivering. She had been cold before. But never quite like this.

"Are you going to just stand there?"

Jaro hung up and exploded with rage. "Fucking Sinner! Doesn't he know that I'm a lucky son of a bitch?"

"Yes, boss. You are one hell of a lucky man!" His bodyguard chimed in.

Jaro's racy thoughts took him back to the night when Lozanov, his former boss and the President of BNB, got assassinated a few months ago, possibly by the same woman who was now after him. That night, all of Lozanov's most trusted partners had gathered to mourn their beloved boss and friend, with the exception of Jaro, who was not invited to the secret gathering. Jaro grew suspicious and feared they were discussing the future leadership without including him. Feeling hurt, he ended up drinking all night and was hospitalized for alcohol intoxication. On the next morning, a phone call brought him back to life. He was informed all four of his former partners were killed in a head-on automobile accident. With all the BNB leadership instantly wiped out, Jaro — the sole remaining BNB Olympic medalist — took over the business the very next day as the President. That's how he became one of the richest men in Bulgaria. Luck was always by his side. With that last thought, his team scored another goal.

"We won!" Jaro cheered. "It's time to celebrate boys! We're done hiding."

At 10 pm, Jaro's team — Plovdiv Strikers — won the match. Slavena and Orlovsky glanced at each other when the drunken euphoria spilled into the air. Despite his calm demeanor, Slavena noticed Orlovsky could hardly contain his eagerness. He knew Jaro would come to celebrate the victory of his team at his favorite night club where there would be plenty of alcohol, drugs, and women to go around.

For twenty minutes, Slavena and Orlovsky laid side by side in total silence looking at the club in the distance, waiting for Jaro's appearance. A crowd began to form outside the club entrance, as the wind on the roof grew stronger. Her body shivered and she could no longer tell if it was from anxiety or coldness.

"Here, take my gloves!" Orlovsky said while leaning so close to her that she could feel the warmth of his breath down her neck. His body felt feverish, but she knew it wasn't from illness. It was from the excitement that boiled inside his veins.

She put on the gloves and looked at him. "This isn't about the money, is it?"

"Nope. It's always been about survival of the fittest." Orlovsky's teeth flashed in the dark.

For a moment, Slavena remembered the lyrics of the rabbit song. "*Skin him down to the bone, and at the farm, they skin them really nice…*"

"What if I'm the rabbit and not the predator?" she said carefully.

Orlovsky's nostrils flared. "Then you'll never have this opportunity to kill him."

"So *I* am killing Jaro?" She saw this coming but was still surprised. "That was not what we agreed!"

"Either you do it or let the bastard walk."

He knew how to play her. She looked again through the scope and paused, trying to calm herself. Her target wasn't there and she almost hoped Jaro changed his mind.

He didn't.

Right at midnight, Jaro arrived at the club with his five-car entourage. Men with thick necks dismounted the cars and rushed to the entrance, shielding their boss.

Twenty minutes later, Jaro reappeared on a balcony. He was on his phone, walking back and forth, appearing and disappearing from her vision, making it impossible for her to aim. It was strange to her that he walked so recklessly on the balcony when minutes ago he arrived with so much security. Then she remembered from one of her psychology lectures what social scientists refer to as *deindividuation* or the inability of sports fans to let go of the euphoria they experienced after winning a game. The sense of goodwill, bonding and shared victory was too difficult to contain and it was nearly impossible for Jaro to feel lonely and alienated. His team had won and he wanted to high-five anyone in his surroundings. Even when his life was in danger.

"He keeps on moving," Slavena whispered.

"Wait for it." Orlovsky's voice was calm, almost playful. It was as if they weren't waiting for a victim to appear in the scope but looking through a peephole in the girls' bathroom. "Ok, wait...Now! Aim for his chest!" Orlovsky ordered.

Indeed, Jaro appeared in the scope. He was on his cell phone, talking and laughing. He was pacing back and forth, appearing and disappearing from her scope's reticle. Slavena's heart was pounding so hard that for a second she hesitated, but she wasn't letting Jaro get away. Not now when she was so close.

"Hit now! NOW is your chance to avenge your sister!"

He didn't need to say anything more. Slavena squeezed the trigger. The bullet went through Jaro's chest and made him lurch into the air before violently slumping onto the ground. Mayhem and screams of the people in the club immediately followed the delayed crack of the rifle.

"We're out of here," Orlovsky said and pulled her up by her jacket. He disassembled his rifles in less than a minute and they both ran down the stairs towards the car. Orlovsky calmly placed his equipment in a hidden double bottom of his trunk and jumped inside with a big, bright smile.

"You got him!" he said, but she didn't hear a word. Her thoughts were somewhere else.

Not only did she violate the provision in the Directorate of the CIA to take human life without authority, but her mounting suspicion that Orlovsky compromised her identity was finally confirmed.

The car zipped through the deserted Bulgarian highways. Cities, petrol stations, and the total darkness of farm fields took turns appearing outside Slavena's window. Orlovsky's words, right before she'd pulled the rifle's trigger, played in her head on a loop *avenge your*

sister...avenge your sister...avenge your sister. How did he know she had a sister?

"I don't have a sister," she finally said.

"What?" Orlovsky was miles away.

"I don't have a sister," Slavena repeated.

"All right. Cool." He didn't seem bothered, but Slavena's anxiety was rolling like a disco ball. What did he know? How much did he know? How did he find out?

"But back there you said, 'This is your chance to avenge your sister'."

"Yeah, I know." He shrugged. "It was a guess."

Orlovsky was a good liar, but he didn't look like a lucky-guess-kind-of-guy to her. He was a professional. He knew something.

"What do you mean it was a guess?" She insisted.

"You told me Jaro had hurt someone you loved. That's why you wanted him dead. I put two and two together and since he had a few rape charges under his belt, I figured that ought to be it. He raped your sister, cousin, mother, granny, who gives a shit? The guy was a scumbag and now he's dead."

"How do you know for sure that I killed him? I don't even know how to shoot."

"I saw you fucking nailed that jerk right in the heart." He smiled. "Despite the high winds and his constant moving."

"If Jaro is dead, it's pure luck."

"Maybe, but aren't you glad you saved yourself fifty grand?"

"What are you saying? You don't want me to pay you?" Slavena's brain was racing ahead. It was her turn to put two and two together. "Was Jaro next on your list?"

"He'd been on my list for a while." Orlovsky looked at her with a confident smile. "Remember, you ordered him?"

"And I said I'd pay you. Why wouldn't you take the money?"

"Because you pulled the trigger. In my book that counts as a kill, for you, not me."

It sounded right, but Slavena did not feel reassured one bit. She needed to think this over. It was just one shot from a rooftop, but enough to make her soul-searching for the rest of her life. If CIA found out that she used her job for personal revenge, she would be fired on the spot. She felt a cold knot in her stomach.

Behind the wheel, Orlovsky whistled tunelessly to the song that was playing on the stereo. His feelings of the situation were the opposite of Slavena's. When he finally pulled over in front of her building, he handed her a bottle of sleeping pills.

"You may consider taking one. It helps me sleep on a night like this."

"I'll think about it."

She stuffed the pills into her jacket pocket and closed the door. His kindness worried her, but she also knew her exhaustion made her extra paranoid.

As his taillights faded in the darkness, anxiety weighed heavy on her chest. Jaro was dead at last, but now there was something more ominous that was crawling all over her. Her cover was blown for real and it was no longer an inside joke between her and Orlovsky. The evidence of her blown cover was enough to keep her awake all night. She pulled out the bottle of pills from her pocket and read the label. Orlovsky knew exactly what she needed. Sleeping pills.

The End Game…

BLOWN

Slavena didn't remember the last time she was so eager to meet with Gavin. She woke up at 1 pm the day after she killed Jaro and she felt groggy from the second she got up from her bed. At first, she blamed the sleeping pills Orlovsky gave her the night before. Then came the recollection of the heart-to-heart chat she had with Orlovsky in her bed. She had told him details about her mission in Ukraine. But why were they discussing Ukraine in the first place? And what was Orlovsky doing in her place? She certainly never invited him over. She looked at the date on the clock and her nerves vibrated like harp's strings. She discovered she'd been sleeping for two days straight.

"Damn Orlovsky and his sleeping pills!" She mumbled. She had been drugged by a truth serum and Orlovsky possibly got enough information to shove her mission deep into the ground. This was a huge screw up on her part that she had to report to Gavin. Only she didn't know how to. Or whether she had the guts to tell him the whole truth.

Two hours later, she walked inside Gavin's office while he was having an afternoon coffee in a fine Dutch porcelain cup with a blue-flower design and a saucer underneath it. Slavena eyed the cup with more astonishment than she'd looked at the M40 in Ukraine.

"What's up?" Gavin looked up from his post. His expression was "You better make this quick."

Slavena took a deep breath. "My cover was blown and my identity potentially exposed!"

"What?" Gavin dropped the papers in a pile in front of him and almost spilled coffee on his shirt. "How do you know?"

Slavena was taken back for a second. There was no way she could tell Gavin that she'd shot Jaro a few nights ago; or that Orlovsky had been there and supplied the gun; or about what he'd said about her sister.

"I think I may have been drugged," she said but even to her that didn't sound mission-abandoning worthy.

"When?"

"Two nights ago. I'll do a test to confirm it, but I'm pretty sure. I can feel the drugs still inside me."

"How did that happen?" Gavin finally showed some concern.

Slavena shrugged her shoulders. She didn't have the guts to tell him that she did it to herself by taking the sleeping pills Orlovsky gave her. He would never understand.

"Alena, you are under a lot of stress. It's normal to be paranoid." His patronizing voice sounded much worse than him not taking the situation seriously.

"I am not paranoid! Or stressed." She paused and retraced her thoughts. "All right, I am stressed, but that's not paranoia I'm feeling. Stuff has been happening—"

"But is it serious enough to leave the mission so close to the end?"

Seriously? Her voice echoed inside her head. *I just killed a man...that is serious enough.* But she couldn't tell him that and after a moment she said: "I don't know. You tell me. How does the Company proceed in such a case?"

"Honestly, I would need to call Devin Becker back at Langley. Most likely the Company will request a transfer. But in your case, I am not so sure."

"What makes you think my case is different?"

He leaned back in his chair. "Do you want my honest opinion?"

She nodded.

"Because it's your first assignment and everybody gets the shivers in the beginning. The Company knows it. I know it. That's why I am not letting you go Slavena and you'll thank me later for saving your career."

"What career if my life is at stake?"

"Is it?"

"No,' she said with an air of defeat. "But I'm terrified of what Orlovsky would do with the information."

"Ok, let's do this for now. I will request Becker for more support for your new cover. We'll close your studio, find you a new apartment, new safehouse, but you'll continue to monitor Orlovsky. We can't give up so easily now when we are so close to the finish line."

"I'm fine with that, but I'm telling you our mission is going belly up. The whole plan from the beginning was bad. Orlovsky is not after money. He is already loaded with money and is simply feeding his addiction to the taste of blood."

"Maybe he spent it all. Why else would he accept the job?'

"As I said, for the thrill of the kill. To him, this is all a game. And now that he knows I'm CIA, he will do everything possible to beat me to the punch. Because of his father, he hates the CIA and will do anything that his father would have done. Anything to see us on our knees."

"How do you know for sure he knows you're in the Company?"

"He has been hinting at it for a few weeks now."

"And this is the first time you're telling me about this?"

"I didn't take him seriously back then. Anybody can joke about the CIA. You know how boys like to tease."

"I see," he said. "So, you don't think he'll take our money?"

"Of course he will. He'll take the money, kill our asset, and do everything to have it his way and make us look like idiots. Trust me, I know this guy better than he knows himself and we went too far down the wrong path with him."

"So, what's keeping us from getting back on the right path?"

Slavena hesitated. She had found out Boychev helped the US build and operate a CIA black site prison, and because of it, the US was willing to go to great lengths to protect him. But what if he was feeding them with false information. She knew she had no other way but to question Gavin about Boychev and his source.

"Before I suggest anything I need an answer to a question." Slavena met Gavin's eyes to observe his reaction.

"I'll answer if I can."

"Did our analysts ever find out why Boychev was on the CLEANSING list? You told me in the past that it was Russia's way of securing the seat of the prime minister before Bulgaria enters the EU, but was this ever confirmed?"

Gavin didn't respond, so Slavena carried on. "How do we know for sure he is on the list anyway?"

"He has his own source."

Bullshit. CIA buys spies to tell them lies. Slavena wanted to say, but there was no room for personal attacks. "Have we corroborated his information with our own sources?"

Gavin paused for a moment and Slavena read his expression as "Even if I knew I wouldn't tell you." In the silence that followed she could hear the conversation that was going on inside his head. *NOC requires new cover, she is developing the need to know, how much can we tell her?*

I already know everything, she wanted to tell him. It was true. She'd worked on Boychev's platform since the day she arrived and she knew firsthand the intimate details of his pro-USA political campaign. The West Pointers at the Pentagon used him as a pawn. They had a plan for Boychev. Once he becomes the Prime Minister and king on the chessboard, he would modernize the Bulgarian military and open its bases to the US and NATO in exchange for billions of dollars of US weapons, planes and military technology. To them, Boychev was a gold mine, but could they trust him all the way? What if he was behind the CLEANSING? It certainly was possible. If he was able to convince the Bulgarian Government to build CIA prisons behind the EU's back, then why couldn't he fool the CIA that he was on the CLEANSING list as the victim and not the killer himself. Or maybe the CIA already knew all this and turned a blind eye to Boychev just to avoid a tough decision: get in bed with the devil in a part of the world Americans knew nothing about; or lose billions of dollars. She concluded Uncle Sam was sitting on it because the West Pointers wanted their dough.

A sudden thought interrupted her brainstorming. *That's why Langley assigned me to Boychev's campaign. They thought I was too green to ask questions and get so close to the fire that I would blow the whole CIA program through the roof.* The CIA was up to their old games of regime change through any means necessary and they were using her as an inexperienced pawn to do it.

"There are some things I can't tell you," Gavin said finally. "I can only say that you're reading too much into this."

"Maybe, but isn't that what they trained us to do? If we don't get answers, to take matters into our own hands?"

"And do what?"

"I'll find out who made that list. But first I need you to grant me full access to every SAP in Bulgaria." She requested, referring to special access programs, the CIA's most guarded secrets.

"You know the protocol. I'll have to arrange a conference call with the Langley brain."

"That'll be a great start. I'll speak to the analyst directly and make sure we're on the same page."

"What about Orlovsky?"

"I'll keep my eye on him, but I don't think he'll ever negotiate with us or do what we tell him."

Gavin sighed.

"One last thing! Please arrange a meeting with Boychev. It's about time I meet the creator of my 70-hour workweek."

"I don't think that's a good idea"

"I understand your concerns," she said carefully. "But since we're running out of time, isn't it wise to ask the only man who knows the source?"

"Perhaps. But before we do anything, please go to the lab and find out what cocktail of chemicals is boiling in your blood."

She got out of her chair with a dangling smile. "Whatever it is, it's making my head on fire."

As soon as she heard the door close behind her, she called her tech guy.

"Travis, I need a favor."

"What is it? Foot rub? You know I'd do anything for you!"

"Nothing as exotic as that, I'm afraid. Remember, you were able to trace a text message a month or so ago?"

"Oh, that one?"

His question disturbed her. There was nothing he could have said that would have triggered more anxiety than *oh, that one?*

"Yes, *that one*," she stressed on the last two words, hearing the anger in her tone. "Any updates on it?"

"I can follow up with my team at the headquarters, but I wouldn't get my hopes high if I were you."

She wanted to ask him what was taking so long for them to release the information, but what was the point? The CIA was either hiding something from her or their bureaucrats were sitting on it waiting for approvals. Or worse. It was a dead end.

"Hope is the only thing I have right now, Travis. Don't take it away from me."

"I'll see what they found and come back to you by the end of the day."

"Thanks."

"And if you rethink that foot rub, you should know I'm your guy. I could supply references from…"

"Bye, Travis," Slavena hung up.

Travis was the best there was. He was able to trace the text message that ordered Orlovsky to kill Bankov, but someone in the Company was holding onto the information not understanding the importance of the message. It was the only clue that could lead her to the man behind the CLEANSING. The "screenwriter".

She should have done the digging a long time ago. She'd trusted the CIA to keep her informed and protect her. But she was the NOC and for the first time, she understood the implications of it. She was playing off the chess board now and her time to develop a plan was limited. She was beginning to panic and in her line of work, there was no room for panic, because it was deadly. She couldn't be another pawn removed from the board. The CIA wanted their objective accomplished and if she happened to fall casualty, they would shrug and move on. She was on her own now and she hoped the text message would lead her somewhere.

Her phone chimed.

Choong Sim agreed to meet you tomorrow morning @ 0800 in his office

The message from Gavin cut into her like a stiletto. It was exactly what she asked for—a meeting with Dragan Boychev—but it gave her a good deal of anxiety because he was the king and she was just a pawn. But even the king could be used as a fighting piece that could win the game for her.

DRAGAN BOYCHEV

Sleek in his tailored silk suit, Dragan Boychev greeted Slavena halfway across his office.

"Sir, it's a pleasure to finally meet you."

"The pleasure is all mine, Alena!" the future Prime Minister said with an amiable smile. "Have we met before?"

She smiled. "Never. May I sit down?"

"Please." He pointed to the couch and sat behind his desk, watching her face with scrutinizing eyes. "I'm trying to decide where I had seen you before, of if I ever had," he said. "Where are you from originally?"

"Sofia," she lied.

"Really?" He narrowed his eyes. "For some reason, I thought you were from Plovdiv. Perhaps because of your accent."

"My accent?" she asked with a quizzical look, giving herself time to correct her mistake. "Oh!" she laughed, tossing her head back. "I used to spend my summers in Plovdiv with my grandparents."

"That can explain it, I guess." He wasn't convinced, always thinking with his gut. "And where in Plovdiv did your grandparents live?"

Slavena's heart raced. Boychev was smooth. Never to be

underestimated.

"Near the subway station on Velik Den street."

"I know that area well. I used to ride my bike there when I was a child."

Slavena chose to say nothing. She knew it was a trap and she didn't need to give him any more rope.

"What school did you go to in the US?"

"Georgetown."

"I was considering Georgetown, but my dad sent me to Stanford instead."

"I know." Slavena smiled. "I know your full biography."

"Of course you do, but not everything is written in a dossier," he said with a dark smile. "Besides, I wanted to test you. After all, you are pulling the strings of my campaign."

"Yes. I am"

"What did you graduate in at Georgetown?"

"Bachelors in Psychology," Slavena said, "and Masters in Foreign Service."

"What year did you graduate from your Masters?"

"2003." She sensed his rope around her neck, tightening by the second.

"How interesting." He shifted uncomfortably in his chair. "It's unusual to assign a brand-new recruit like you to an important election campaign unless your Company didn't think it was that important."

Slavena felt her cheeks burning and for the first time, she understood the true meaning of being under the heel of her master. Boychev could kick her anyway he wanted and she still had to keep her tongue behind her teeth.

"You must be smart enough to work for me," he continued, "but you are still a novice."

"With all due respect, sir, I may be a novice, but I do believe I have done an outstanding job for your campaign so far. Ms. Stefka Kaneva must ring a bell."

He looked at his work phone to mask his immense surprise that this young girl who stood in front of him so innocently was capable of pushing someone off a balcony. He was informed by his Secret Service agents that someone with exceptional skills attempted to silence Kaneva, but he had no idea it was the CIA. Suddenly he looked back at her with a higher mark of alertness inside his eyes.

"So, tell me why you're here. What is it that requires my immediate attention?"

"I'm concerned about your safety."

"Well, you shouldn't be. I have an outstanding security element."

"I'm aware of that, sir." Her voice was hard now. "But we are talking about two different things. The security I'm referring to requires refined negotiating skills."

"I thought it was a win-win negotiation and he decided to cooperate."

They were discussing Orlovsky now.

"It's true, but I suspect he's playing us and we can't afford to take the chance"

"What are you telling me?"

"That he'll take the money and finish his deal without our consent."

"Then finish him off!"

What? Her inside voice raged, but she managed to keep it in control. Was he telling her to dig a grave for Orlovsky?

"Sir, isn't that a bit rushed—"

"I don't have time for this." He stood up from his chair. "You asked for my guidance and I gave it to you."

"But then we are back to square one."

"Not my problem."

"Assassination orders take a long time for Langley to approve and we may run out of time—"

"I'll get your approval by the end of this week. That should stop the clock from ticking." Boychev started to walk towards the door. "Now, I have to attend another urgent meeting."

"Sir, I have one last question."

Boychev turned back to face her glaring from a distance. In reality, she had many questions. The most important of which was concerning his source and how he knew so much about the CLEANSING. But sensing he didn't trust her enough to tell her anything of value, she decided to proceed with her personal agenda instead to suit the scene.

"What happened to the person that I reminded you of?"

"Do I have to answer that?"

"I just want to understand why you have so little trust in me." She managed to say.

He stared at her for a moment, and she caught a glimpse of hesitation in his eyes.

"The person you remind me of died a long time ago because she was a careless girl who liked to play with fire."

"What are you implying?"

"That I have nothing to do with the death of your sister, Slavena!" he said as he showed her the door.

COUNTER ATTACK

Orlovsky was at Caffeinated, having an afternoon coffee and enjoying the scenery when his phone rang. He was tempted to ignore the call. Instead, he picked it up absentmindedly, eyeing the caller ID.

"Archie? What's up?" he said after he'd pressed the green button.

"I've got news for you."

"You're finally getting married and moving out of your mom's place?"

"Bite me, Eagle. Do you want me to tell you why I'm calling, or are you going to be an asshole and make me feel sorry I did?"

Orlovsky laughed. It was so easy to tease Archie and get him riled up. It was like taking away a Pop-Tart from a premenstrual woman. "I'm all ears, Archie."

"Somebody checked out that profile you told me to keep an eye on."

"No fucking way."

"Computers don't lie. You set a proxy chain and install a meterpreter and sooner or later you'll record something of interest."

"You lost me at 'computers don't lie'. Who's been spying on our girl?"

"I don't exactly know that—"

"Then what do you know?" Talking to Archie was like trying to hold down a fish. You never knew which way it would twist and jump.

"She'd been searched for by her real name Slavena Ivanova. And the searcher downloaded only one thing—a picture of her from her prom. She's wearing a pretty sexy dress."

Orlovsky gave a short laugh. Archie thought every woman was sexy.

"Is that it?" Orlovsky asked.

"Pretty much."

"Alright," Orlovsky started thinking. Checking people online was common these days and if the picture was really sexy, this could be a random thing. "I don't think—"

"One more thing," Archie interrupted. "The computer's IP that had searched her and downloaded the picture, came from inside the Ministry of Interior."

Orlovsky held his breath for a moment. "You sure about that?"

"Yeah, I'm sure."

"That could become useful, I guess." Orlovsky still wasn't sure what he had on his hands. "I'll give you the money when I see you." Orlovsky disconnected.

He'd just walked outside the cafe when his phone vibrated in his pocket. He'd received an email. It was from an unknown address. Orlovsky clicked on it. It was a picture of Slavena in a short green dress and black high-heels. She had a wide, brown-lipsticked grin on her face and a raised champagne glass in her hand. She looked young and vulnerable.

Was this the picture Archie was talking about? He had to agree with the geek: she did look sexy. He scrolled down and read the email. It was only one sentence, but enough to stop him in his tracks. *Make sure no one finds her.*

His eyes darkened. Questions started to roll around his head like dice: Why did his employer want Slavena dead? Did he know Slavena was now his CLEANSING partner? Was his life in danger?

Only one thing was for certain. The man Slavena was protecting was the Holy Grail to all these questions. Unfortunately, he wasn't able to extract as much information as he was hoping to when he drugged Slavena. The CIA trained them well nowadays. But there were still two people who could clue him in. The first one, the journalist Stefka Kaneva, was in a coma—all thanks to him—and the second one was a woman he had been craving since he set his eyes on her.

Velina Mentova.

It was 5 pm and the sky was bright red, illuminating the first snow on the mountaintops. Orlovsky noticed it as he touched the control system on the wall. The floor-to-ceiling windows opened with a soft hiss, then silence, save for the millions of sounds coming from the city. The cold air stormed in passing through his naked body as he continued to watch the mountains. The Russian blood in him loved the cold, but hated the color red, because that was the color of the sky on the night his father died.

Bloody red.

He stepped away from the windows and leaned to pick up the scattered clothes on the floor. He'd just finished having sex with Velina—a very difficult woman to please. A real nympho. She squeezed him like a sponge, and he didn't disappoint. He fucked her like a bull in the peak of breeding season, but it was time to put a price on his performance. He needed the information from her about Alena and he needed it now.

He turned and looked at Velina's naked back as she walked toward the bar. *Her ass looked like a million dollars*, he thought as she approached his bottle of scotch. Oblivious to his reptile stare, Velina poured herself three fingers of his Macallan 18 year old scotch, opened the freezer, pulled out an ice tray, and slammed it on the bar top. The cracking sound of the ice cubes, entering the crystal highball, violated his very soul. To him, the act was like smearing BBQ sauce on a $100 dry-aged porterhouse steak. An unforgiveable crime.

Oblivious to his frowns, Velina drank from the glass, exposing her perky breast. The hard as rock nipples filled him with lust. He knew he wanted her again and cursed himself for having no self-control at the sight of a nice pair of tits.

In a blur, he slammed her naked body against the cold surface of the bar and even though she knew it was pointless to fight him back, she fought him like an animal. Thrilled to see her enthusiasm, he decided to be creative. With a wicked smile, he pulled an ice cube from her glass and made her swallow it.

She spat it out with vengeance.

He laughed and took another ice cube. Then he melted it on her back, leaving traces of water. He took another, and another, melting them slowly and watching her body twitch. He felt intense pleasure in watching her fight. She had no chance with her wrists trapped in his unbreakable grip.

"I have no pity for nymphos like you!" his aroused voice came out like a dictator. He drank from the lines of water streaming down her skin and Velina grinded her back into him, giving him access. He stopped in the middle of tasting the diluted scotch and released her wrists from his hold.

Velina spun around with disappointment on her face.

"What was *that* for?" she asked with acidity in her voice.

He took a sip of his highball with leveled satisfaction and then walked away.

"*That*, my dear, was me teaching you a lesson!" his voice echoed in the distance.

"A lesson?" she frowned.

"Yes. A lesson on how to drink single malt scotch. Never with ice!" He said, belting his jeans. Then he turned back to look at her. In his mind, what was five-minutes-earlier perfectly charred, tender, juicy, Velina steak was now a leftover that needed to be discarded. At the thought of it, he realized that his eyes were no longer fixed on her, but on the painting on the wall that hung right above her. A black and white print of the London Bridge with a man carrying a red umbrella. It was a good-bye gift, mailed from Alena right before she disappeared three weeks ago. It was her way of reminding him that she knew about his father.

"Don't tell me you're looking at the painting and not this body," Velina said right as a bullet whistled above her head, dislodging the painting from the wall.

He looked her squarely in the eyes. "I'm looking at you now."

"Good, you should feel goddamn guilty for leaving me

starving all day."

"Want to go eat?" He asked, knowing he still needed to pry information from out of her.

"Yes. Take me somewhere fancy," she pressed her phone with her thumb to open the screen. "How about Revolver? I haven't eaten there yet."

"Sounds like my kind of place. I'll get my kids ready."

"No guns!" She said sternly as she collected her clothes and disappeared in the bedroom.

"Whatever you say," Orlovsky smiled as he cocked his Sig and confirmed a round was in the chamber.

Slavena's Blackberry vibrated in her purse just as she unlocked the door. She didn't answer right away. Instead, she entered her apartment and hung her damp coat on the hanger. It was pouring rain. She figured if it was important enough, it could wait, but whoever was trying to get through was persistent.

"You had me worried for a moment." It was Gavin. The clock on the wall showed half past 10 pm and Slavena took note of it simply because Gavin never called her that late.

"Sorry. Just got home all soaked from the rain," she said as she put the keys on the kitchen counter.

"I know what you mean. When it rains it pours."

Hearing this, Slavena's body froze and her eyes widened. Sure, it was raining outside, but Gavin was talking about something else. *When it rains it pours* was an established code phrase for an agent down and her first guess was Orlovsky. She had a mental image of a hail of bullets ripping through his body; his blood flying in all directions;

the sarcastic smile disappearing from his face, and the life going out of his eyes. She was dying to know if it was Orlovsky, but questions like that were not allowed over an unsecured line.

"I didn't know it was raining that bad," was all she could say.

"Raining?" Gavin said. "We're talking about a monsoon here, not just rain. Did you know that *they* were together on a date?"

The word *they* echoed in Slavena's mind as loud as M2 .50 caliber machine gun. Was he talking about Orlovsky and Velina? The last image of their bodies turned into a bloody, crumpled mess was more than she could handle. She ran to the bathroom with her phone in her hand and threw up.

"Are you all right?" she could hear Gavin's voice faintly from her phone.

"I'll call you back," she managed to say before the spasms engulfed her once again.

 hours earlier...

Velina and Orlovsky walked inside Revolver. The newest fine dining restaurant and by virtue of its name, the only place in town that was frequented by the mafia.

"I have the perfect table for you." The hostess took them to a table with a radiating smile that failed to warm the coldness in Orlovsky's eyes. The table was by the window. He preferred tables in back corners, away from outside doors and near emergency exits and kitchens. It gave him a better vantage point to see everyone who came in. This was not a habit due to vanity, but rather a survival instinct. When it came to his safety, he was meticulous to death.

He pointed to a table that better met his preferences. "How about that one?"

"It's already reserved."

Ignoring her, Orlovsky walked towards the table, moved its aluminum sign *Reserved* to the next table and looked at the waitress with a light of joy. "It's not anymore."

The hostess had a moment of quietness. She was conditioned to appraise men from head to toe and in her expert opinion, Orlovsky wasn't worth half his attitude. Sure, he wore a shiny Rolex, but its bulkiness was a giveaway it was fake.

"This table remains reserved whether it has a sign on it or not," she said firmly.

"Then you have two choices. To give me this table or give me this table." Orlovsky barked at her with such an evil undertone that a chill ran down her spine. Even she—the expert of assessing net worth—recognized in the tone of his voice that in her presence stood a man high on the food chain. She placed the menus on the table with an air of defeat and retreated to the safety of the front door.

Delighted by the scene, Velina sat at the table with a gleam of arousal. She had a thing for men who showed their dominance in public and she decided right then that she would be having Orlovsky for dessert.

Already warned by the hostess, the server flew to their table with a basket full of warm bread.

"A bottle of Chateau Haut-Brion and a liter of Evian," Orlovsky ordered without looking at either of them.

"What year is the wine?" Velina asked with her eyes cruising the wine list.

"The year of your birth—1976," he said still looking at the waiter, "and we'll start with black caviar."

Velina's eyes stopped searching the menu after she discovered the wine Orlovsky had just ordered was the most expensive bottle on the wine list. Relieved that Orlovsky wasn't cheap, she went back to the dessert section with a tiny smile dangling on the corner of her lips.

The waiter swiftly disappeared to carry out their order with a grin from ear to ear. When he saw the 750 levs at the bottom of his computer screen, he looked back at Orlovsky with deep respect as if he had a halo glowing above his head. The man was filthy rich.

The only two customers in the restaurant both buttered their bread and fell into silence while browsing the menu. Orlovsky could bet his newest SIG SSG 3000 that Velina didn't recognize half the words on the menu and he couldn't blame her. If he had a choice, he would get out of this pretentious place and eat pizza somewhere else, but the type of conversation they were about to have required the right atmosphere. A candlelit dinner with not too many people around.

Orlovsky closed the menu and scanned the room for security cameras. His inquisitive eyes moved slowly from corner to corner and then returned back to Velina. He realized Velina was much better to stare at than talk to, but if she was in touch with Alena, his efforts were well worth it.

The server brought a plate with a minuscule amount of black caviar surrounded by toasted triangles of rye bread. Orlovsky ignored the fancy plate and looked directly at the bottle of wine that was being opened. The cork popping and the pouring that followed put him instantly in a good mood.

Orlovsky swirled the dark red liquid in his glass, sniffed it before he took a mouthful, let it linger on his tongue and after a half minute he nodded with approval. The server proceeded to fill their glasses and when he finally set the bottle down, he asked if they were ready to order. Orlovsky nodded while Velina continued to leaf through the menu undisturbed.

"He's waiting for you, darling." He drummed his fingers on the table.

"I'll take the lobster with rock salad and papaya."

"You should order white wine with it." He eyed the server. "What is the best Prosecco you have?"

"Nino Franco."

"She'll have a glass of that." Orlovsky winked at her with fondness while eyeing the bottle of red. He hated sharing.

"And what would you like, sir?"

"The triple-seared Japanese Kobe steak, medium rare."

"About that steak, the price on the menu is per ounce," the waiter said as he looked at Orlovsky with an affable smile.

"Are you saying I'm an idiot who can't read the menu?"

The waiter's jaw tightened with fear. "No, sir! I am not implying that it's just that we've had a few customers who—"

"I'll tell you what." Orlovsky contained his anger. "If you get me the steak, the way I want it cooked—*medium rare*—I'll leave you enough tip for you to try it yourself, deal? And bring another bottle of red when I'm finished with this one."

"Umm? The same?"

Orlovsky slowly turned his head towards the waiter robotically. "What do you think?"

The waiter nodded quickly and left almost springing in the air. He didn't remember ever getting a 300 lev tip.

Once the waiter disappeared, Velina tilted her head to one side and rested her chin in her palm.

"So, how did you meet Alena?"

"Same way you did," Orlovsky winked at her. "I'm her patient."

"What's your diagnosis then?"

"A malignant narcissist with a special gift of making people talk."

Velina chuckled. "And what happens if *they* choose not to talk?"

"Then *they* may accidentally fall off their balcony."

Velina's face suddenly lost its color, knowing he was talking about Stefka Kaneva. "Did you—"

"Did I what?" Orlovsky cupped his wine glass, looking into it patiently. He took a morbid pleasure in making people wait. "Of course not," he finally said. "Don't be so hasty. The journalist's fall was really an accident."

Velina gave him a long stare. She was finally beginning to understand that Orlovsky was a killer and not the sweet talker he claimed to be.

"Did Alena ask you to kill her?"

"Let's not mention names here," Orlovsky said, motioning with his hand, "or they may ricochet back at you."

Velina took his reaction as a *Yes* and plunged into silence, leaving Orlovsky to enjoy every bit of it drinking his wine.

"Did she ask you to kill me as well?" She finally said.

"If I wanted to kill you, sweetheart, you wouldn't be having caviar with me right now."

The waiter reproached the table and despite the tension that was thickening the air, he served the entrees with a poker face. He returned with the bottle of Prosecco and uncorked it while watching Orlovsky slice his steak. At the sight of the red meat inside, Orlovsky nodded with approval, and the server popped the cork with relief. Then he filled Velina's glass with the sparkling wine and floated away as light as a butterfly.

Orlovsky sipped his wine, gazing the black eyes of the lobster.

"It's Velina that killed you buddy, not me!" he said, wondering what it was like to be a lobster in a steamer. He'd heard lobsters didn't feel any pain, but judging by its bright red color, and God he hated that color, it must have hurt like hell. He got sick of looking at it.

"Are you going to demolish that communist or what?"

"I've lost my appetite," Velina said.

Orlovsky shrugged with a degree of indifference and continued eating until the silence at the table became too oppressive to ignore.

"So, tell me. What's boiling in that pretty head of yours?"

Velina tipped her head. "For somebody who prides himself at making people talk, you're not doing a good job here."

"Perhaps because you don't have anything that interests me."

"Really? What if I told you I'm still in touch with Alena?"

Her sudden willingness to talk was refreshing, but he didn't need to clue her in that he was interested, so he shrugged.

"Or what if I told you," she carried on, "that I know you killed the Admiral and all the rest."

Orlovsky snickered. "I see! You've watched the news, connected the dots, and discovered it was me behind the killings of those bastards. And now you think you know everything. As I said, Velina, you don't have anything that interests me. All you know is gossip. That's it."

"Where there is smoke there is fire. Do you know that old saying? You are certainly the killer, but you didn't kill them for the money. Did you? The CLEANSING was your idea to wipe out the most powerful men in Bulgaria, so you can take over their firms and unite them into one. That's the smoke I'm talking about."

"And what's the fire?"

"That Dragan Boychev is pulling your strings and when he becomes the Prime Minister, he will legalize your empire."

Orlovsky's heart skipped a beat at her accusation, but he remained cool and watched her steadily with his poker-face. "You should be more wary of using names in public."

"It's him, isn't it?" she persisted. "You thought I was too dumb to see the big picture."

Orlovsky's nerves had reached a boiling point and he needed something to cool him off. He reached for her chilled glass of Prosecco.

"What kind of drugs did they put in your wine?" He said before he sipped from her glass. He swallowed the frizzy liquid hard as he noticed a group of stout men entering the restaurant. Their attitude, posture, and bulging muscles told Orlovsky they were here for business. They assessed the empty dining room and when their eyes stopped on him, Orlovsky's fingers curled in a little quiver. He was their target. He was certain of that. They were here for him. He slid his hand to his SIG P226 that was snuggly tucked away in his DeSantis SOB holster and waited for the right moment.

The men continued to chat with the hostess as their restless eyes worked out the angle of their attack. With the edge of his peripheral vision, Orlovsky waited for them to make their first move. He knew it was a matter of seconds before they fired and with only one handgun, he felt like a defenseless baby in a lion cage.

"Get under the table. *Now!*" he ordered Velina.

"I am not into public sex—" was all she could say as a spray of bullets plunged into her back. Everything that followed happened in a blur. Orlovsky managed to flip the table and duck behind the solid wood frame, but he knew his life was hanging like a fly in a spider's web. Seeing the table get shredded to pieces urged him to make his move. With his right hand, he shot at the large front window that stood directly behind the group of hitmen. It shattered, showering the restaurant with a thousand shards of glass.

Distracted by the noise, the assassins reflexively looked at the window. Taking advantage of their distraction, Orlovsky pulled a pin from out his oversized Rolex watch that he inherited from his father and threw it with his left hand in the direction of the five men. Within milliseconds of landing, it exploded, killing two of them instantly in a gust of flame and shrapnel. He followed up with a volley of five rounds at the two men who remained standing, half emptying his SIG magazine.

"Amateurs!" Orlovsky mumbled.

The only man who survived the onslaught laid in a wasteland of smashed glass with one arm missing and the other hand holding a gun tightly as if his last breath depended on it.

Orlovsky kicked his gun clear and the man whimpered. "This," he said as center-knuckled him in the mouth, "is for ruining my nice dinner. Now tell me, who sent you?"

"Fuck you!" the man replied with his teeth coming out of his mouth.

Orlovsky center-knuckled him again and the man curled his body with his eyes flooding with pain. "It was the Sinner," he spat at Orlovsky, staining his white shirt with blood.

"Thank you! And this," Orlovsky shot the man in the head, "is my dentist referral!"

He returned to Velina's lifeless body. He amputated her thumb with his knife and bent down to rummage inside her purse until he found her phone. The sound of the police sirens jerked his attention away and he jumped to his feet. He raced towards the back of the restaurant where the manager cowered in his office. He retrieved the security camera film, slipped out the back door and on his way out, he ran into the hostess, who blinked at him beyond terrified.

"If you sing a word to the cops, I'll find you and kill you with my bare hands, do you understand?"

She nodded with tears in her eyes.

Inside his car, Orlovsky waited for a moment, listening, watching every movement on the street. Relieved that he wasn't being followed, he looked in the mirror. The blood on his face made his features exceptionally cruel and godlike. He reached for the glove compartment where he kept wipes for days like these and cleaned up his face. He put on a new shirt, looked back in the mirror with approval.

"It's time to go to war," he mumbled as he turned on the engine.

As soon as he sped off, he dialed a number and put the call on speaker. The ringing tone stopped when someone picked up. There was no voice. Just the sound of heavy breathing.

"I got some bad news for you, Sinner," Orlovsky said. "Your boys are waiting for the tooth fairy at the morgue."

"At least they have your beautiful woman as company."

So the Sinner was already informed. The bastard was good.

"You got the wrong bitch."

"Speaking of bitches, I got one sitting on my cock right now and I would hate to disappoint her. You wouldn't do that to your woman, would you, Eagle? "

"I don't have a woman!" Orlovsky snapped.

"Oh, that's right. I forgot you prefer cocks in your ass,

just like your dad."

Orlovsky's eyes clouded. Nobody ever talked to him like this and it infuriated him. He had to get the rage out of his system. "When I send you to hell, my father will show you who the real faggot is,"

Orlovsky hung up and pressed the gas pedal down to the floor. Furious of what the Sinner had said about his father, he drove like a maniac for another ten minutes until he found a discreet place to stop. He parked and after the sound of the engine died away, he realized it was the same place he dropped off Slavena half dead after he had rescued her from the Admiral.

"It's a sign," he mumbled at the irony as he pulled out Velina's phone from his pocket. He pressed Velina's thumb to open the screen. Once it lit up, he quickly scrolled through all the texts and it didn't take long to find what he was looking for: *Meet me at the gala party in the Sheraton for some girls time – A*

Orlovsky smiled. The message was from Slavena.

INVITATION

The gala evening was a black-tie event for five hundred people. The sheer number of people made security tight, but Orlovsky found a way to get in. He bought his invitation from a psychiatrist, who was delighted to part with it for $500 in cash.

Orlovsky bought a new tuxedo, a white, pleated shirt and fixed a bow tie on it, just before getting out of the car. He caught a glimpse of himself in the glass façade of the hotel building and shook his head disapprovingly. He looked like Daniel Craig from the new Casino Royale trailer. *Fucking James Bond*, he thought. The clothes were so restricting, no way could he do any proper fighting in them. The whole James Bond lifestyle was a lie.

The party was jam-packed and he managed to blend in with ease. He picked up a glass of scotch and stood in a corner studying the room. There were more men than women, which made his job easier, but still, sifting through five hundred people's faces, coming and going, wasn't easy.

Finally, he spotted Slavena. She'd put on a little weight. Her figure looked curvier, her breast fuller. It suited her. She was radiant in her black dress. Her hair was held up by a jeweled clasp. He imagined the shock on her face to see him here, and that gave him a buzz. Finally, the power he needed to break her.

He waited patiently for the right time to approach her. She was talking to a tall, skinny man with an empty glass. Orlovsky ambled around until the man excused himself to go to the bar.

"Sure you don't want anything to drink?" The man asked, pointing at her glass.

She smiled. "I am sure, nothing for me. Thanks."

As soon as the man left, Orlovsky approached Slavena swiftly like a ghost.

"Hello, stranger. Long time no see."

"What are you doing here?" Her eyes ran over his tuxedo, then narrowed. "I know you weren't invited."

"But I belong here among all the Freudians talking about crazy people—"

"Little do they know, the craziest man of all is standing right in the middle of the flock like a wolf in sheep's clothing, blending in and planning its attack."

"A wolf doesn't lose sleep over the opinion of sheep."

"Then what is the wolf here for? To negotiate a peace with the sheep?"

"Cut the small talk. I'm running out of time." He took a step back to see if her date had finished ordering his drink and she watched him with amusement.

"So you noticed I'm not alone?"

"Yes. I had!" He hissed. "Don't you get tired of using men?"

"At least I keep my dates alive. I should thank you by the way for never taking me out to dinner."

Orlovsky's jaw tightened. "Listen, sweetheart, I would love to chat with you all night with my tongue in your mouth and my dick inside you, but you already have someone else." His voice boomed with anger and she waited for the fallout to come down, but he contained it.

"Then why are you talking to me?"

Orlovsky noticed the man coming with the drink and lunged a step forward.

"I have the next name on the list." He whispered. "It'll interest you. Meet me in the parking lot in 20."

Then he was gone.

He knew Slavena was familiar with his car and would have no trouble spotting it in the parking lot. Still, he drove as close to the entrance as the valets would allow him and sat in silence, waiting. When half an hour passed and she still hadn't appeared, he was furious. Who did she think she was playing with? He'd never waited for a woman before. Perhaps, he should drive off and leave her in the mess. What did he care about her?

Yet, he sat and waited.

Forty minutes in, Slavena appeared at the door in a floor-length black coat. The moment Orlovsky saw her, his eyes lightened and he forgot the reasons behind his rage. Her presence had that effect on him. He unlocked the door to let her in, then pressed the master lock as soon as she was inside. He didn't want her fleeing before she'd heard what he had to say.

"Looking good, Slavena," he said. She blinked when he used her real name for the first time but she stayed put in her seat.

"You don't look too bad yourself," she said, leveled.

"You know, your disappearance has been a real turn on?"

Slavena didn't reply, just waited.

"What do you say about a session in my apartment later on? For old time's sake?"

"You have something for me, Orlovsky? Or am I wasting my time?" She watched him, unblinking.

"All right," he said, leaning closer to her. "It's you."

"It's me what?"

He looked at her lips briefly before glancing up at her. The softness in his eyes gave Slavena a jolt more than a slap across the face would have done. Orlovsky didn't do compassion.

"You are next on my list, Slavena," he said. "My employer wants you dead. Maybe something to do with you being C....I....A."

It was Slavena's turn to look away. She was stunned into silence.

"Why else would he want you dead, Slavena?"

"I don't know," she shook her head and the jeweled clasp at the nape of her head caught the lights outside. "Who is your employer?"

"I was hoping you'd know that."

"I don't."

"Perhaps, you do. Perhaps you have the last piece of the puzzle and you don't even know it."

Slavena remained silent and looked at him unconvinced.

"The man you are trying to protect?" He raised his eyebrows. "What's his name?"

"Nice try, Orlovsky!" Slavena chuckled, forgetting her controlled demeanor. "You nearly had me fooled."

Orlovsky suddenly snapped. "You know what, I don't have to give you a head start."

Slavena reached for the car handle. "Let me out."

"You walk out of that car, the order becomes active."

"I'll take my chances."

"What makes you think I'm not going to do my job?"

"And kill me?" Slavena gave him a quizzical look.

"Yes, Slavena. Kill you. That's what I do for a living."

"Because I'm pregnant," she said.

"I can just drive you to the woods right now and…" Orlovsky stopped. "You're what?"

Slavena studied him for a moment. She'd never seen that expression on his face before — confusion mixed with a stab of triumph.

"I'm pregnant," she repeated.

"Is it mine?" He asked, bringing her back to the night when Orlovsky had removed the white queen off the chess board in her apartment.

"Do you remember when you said 'knight takes queen'? What exactly did you mean by that?"

He looked suddenly surprised. "Nothing. It was just pillow talk."

She watched his eyes intently, not trusting what he was saying. He took it as an accusation. "Come on, you can't possibly think I planned to get you pregnant that night? Why can't it be just a coincidence?"

"That's one bizarre coincidence, don't you think? Your words precisely matching the conception date?"

"Yeah! The same time you were away for a week? What were you doing in Ukraine with all those young Marines?"

"You know exactly what I did that week. Remember, you drugged me?"

"Of course, I do," Orlovsky chuckled. "You told me a lot of good stories that night. There was some Navy guy you bragged about how great of an asset he was for your Company. And your boss.... What was his name? Gavin or Devin, can't remember. His midlife crisis and his affair with his analyst. Or how about that Rovish guy. The sexy professor. I could tell you're in love with him."

Her heart skipped a beat on the last accusation, but she didn't want to reflect on it right now and so she carried on. "Don't change the topic. Did you plan to get me pregnant that night or not? Answer my question!"

"How can I plan something like that when you told me you were on the pill?!" He touched the clasp of his Rolex and Slavena noticed. Orlovsky was lying.

For a moment, she tapped into her own memories from that night when she came back from Ukraine. "I know how you did it," she finally said. "When you searched through my apartment to plant your three cameras—"

"Three? That wasn't me!"

"Yes, it was and do not interrupt me," she said, raising her voice.

"I only planted one in your bathroom," he grinned wide. "But keep going."

"That's where you found my pills. You counted how many days I missed the pill, thus how many days I was gone. But then you also noticed that I was in my ovulation cycle and decided to use that against me. What better way to fuck with my mission than getting me pregnant at the wrong time. Right? But wait, that wasn't all. Was it?" Slavena's eyes opened wide in anger.

"Do you even hear yourself? This whole pregnancy is making you sound crazy."

"I know what I'm talking about Alexander. I know who you are, I know your kind and how your kind operates. You got me pregnant to reinforce your dominance over me." She smiled like a schoolgirl who just solved the hardest math problem of her life.

"What the fuck are you talking about?"

"I'm talking about something that only a narcissist like you is capable of doing since nothing is off limits to you. In your head, everything is a game, and what better way to underline your power than the act of entering my most private of places, deposit your essence deep inside me, conquering your desire to create a new life without including me in the decision. This is the supreme act of conquest. Deep in my sacred and intimate place, you have placed yourself. You narcissistic asshole!"

"Oh my God! You've gone insane! If you think that I tried to ensnare you to control you with little to no thought about the consequences of bringing another being into this world, then why don't you have an abortion?"

"Because if I have an abortion, I'll become a devalued property to you and you'll discard me the second I do it. In other words, you'll kill me. That's why."

"I'm starting to see why my employer wants you dead."

"Your employer wants me dead for the same reasons he wants you dead!"

"What?" he asked incredulously. "So you lied to me. You knew who—"

"No. I just figured it out all thanks to you."

"Tell me his fucking name!" he growled.

"I will when you admit your dickhead chess move."

"A queen sacrifice move!" he corrected her.

"I see your father was too busy drinking to teach you how to play chess like a man."

"I think we're done here!" He unlocked the car.

"Good luck winning your game!" Her hazel eyes gave him one final glance before she slammed the door and walked away.

Orlovsky lowered his car window. "I don't need luck," he yelled. "I have the Eagle's blood in me!"

"And so do I," she said without turning back.

This was the second time she walked away from him. The first time, he wanted to chase her down the street and slap her. Now he wanted to kill her and he had the order to do it, but she carried his blood inside her and even he drew the line of cruelty at such an act.

Orlovsky got home and turned on his gunfighter simulator as soon as he was through the door. He shed the tuxedo jacket eventually, but not before it was soaked through with sweat. He'd arrived home just after midnight but hadn't stopped shooting until the sun was up. He collapsed on the floor, shaking with exhaustion and stone-cold from the immense sweating. But his mind wouldn't shut down.

The word bitch was embossed on a roller stamp and was printing all over the curves of his brain. *Bitch bitch bitch bitch bitch bitch bitch bitch bitch bitch bitch bitch bitch bitch.* All he could think about was her accusation of using her as an incubator. She called it a dickhead move. And she had the right to call it that because his dick had a head of its own.

What was he thinking? He'd never wanted children. In fact, it was one of the few things he'd been certain about for as long as he could remember. No way was he helping the fucked up human race to proliferate. No way was he bringing a tiny, innocent mind into this blood-soaked, twisted, and corrupt world. He'd seen a thousand deaths and he didn't wish any of them on a child of his. But Slavena had taken away that choice by choosing not to have an abortion, and now he was having a child all because of his blunder.

He remembered exactly what happened. He could picture the pillbox she was talking about in her bathroom cabinet and she was right. He'd counted the six pills that were overdue for the days when she was gone and he'd had the headstrong urge to come inside her knowing that she was ovulating. The idea of his sperm advancing with blind passion to conquer her ripe egg deep inside her aroused him. It was like a whole other battleground for him with one target in sight. And now that he found his target, mixing his DNA with it, he felt like an idiot. Worse. An idiot who was about to have a child.

But who was she kidding? She could still remove it. In fact, she may have already removed it, but then realized without the baby, she knew her chance for survival was reduced, because he was unpredictable like that, and so she made up the lie.

"Fucking bitch." He was pacing in his living room like a madman.

He came to the decision to go ahead and kill her, but then he dismissed the idea. She did look pregnant for sure and by killing Slavena, he would kill the baby. He could never kill a child. Especially his own. He could find somebody else to do the job. What else could he do?

He had never been so confused. There was only one thing he was sure about. Slavena was the only woman fit to be the mother of his child. Perhaps his primitive instincts to impregnate a woman weren't that primitive after all. At that thought, he collapsed on his couch with a smile.

If it was a boy. His name would be Peter Orlovsky.

Another Eagle would be born.

By the time the sun had fully lit the room, he was still sprawled on the couch. It was clear what needed to be done. If that baby was his, he'd have to take care of it and make sure his son or daughter would live better than he had done. He'd broken a lot of rules, but he wasn't breaking this one.

He got up and switched on his computer. He opened a browser and searched for flights to Geneva, Switzerland. Like most Europeans with money to hide, all his funds were stored there, safe from any taxmen that became clever about looking into Orlovsky living above his means.

If Slavena could prove that the baby was his, by a DNA test, she could have some of his money. He would arrange it with his bankers and his lawyers.

BLACK KING

After she closed the secure line, she thought about the information Travis had just given her. The message she wanted to be traced was sent from the Ministry of Interior and Dragan Boychev working there as the Deputy Minister convinced her this wasn't a coincidence.

She had all the pieces of the puzzle in front of her and all she needed now was to connect them. One by one. She had the names of all Orlovsky's latest victims by now. She dug out all she could find on them: family history, business ventures, personal and professional ties. She created link diagrams from association matrixes, and time event charts in an effort to find patterns, intersections, and similarities. There had to be something that connected them, in order for them to be on Orlovsky's hit list. Something more than just being mobsters.

The now-dead mafia bosses had nothing in common besides their dealings with Boychev's father. All roads led to him. During his reign as the Director of the Bulgarian National Police, more than 40 killings were carried out but never investigated, all the while SIN, BAM, and Jaro's empire grew bigger and stronger. And Boychev's father grew wealthier than ever.

Of course, common people didn't know any of this. They never suspected Boychev's father was protecting all these firms and enabling them to become the future crème de la crème of Bulgarian criminal circles.

And now his only son, Dragan, was climbing the ladder of Bulgarian politics towards becoming the Prime Minister of Bulgaria. The elections were in less than a year and he was cleaning house. Every Mafioso Boychev Senior protected had to be assassinated.

Dead men didn't talk.

Slavena was one of those people. Not only was she a CIA officer poking around for more information, but she also held in her possession a piece of Dragan's dirty laundry. Dragan was in the club the night Boyana was approached by Jaro. Although he knew about Jaro's history of gang rapes, he did nothing to protect the girl he resented for rejecting him. He wanted her punished for spurning him. Even worse, he lied to prosecutors that he was never in the club and his father protected him by covering everything up and creating a fake alibi. Soon after, Dragan was coincidentally dispatched to Stanford University to study Political Economy.

Now years later, back in Bulgaria, Dragan was a changed man. He thought things couldn't be traced back to him until he met Slavena in his office and sensed that she knew more about his dirty past. He was willing to risk everything to cover his tracks and so he decided to eliminate her. Just to be on the safe side.

Slavena smiled. She'd solved it: Dragan Boychev was simultaneously the person she was protecting and the man behind the CLEANSING assassinations.

Orlovsky was working for Boychev.

Slavena had resumed running in the mornings a few weeks after the ordeal at Bankov's house. She was more careful now with the paths she ran, favoring busy pedestrian streets and well-lit public places. Changing her route every time and programming double backs to ensure she was never followed.

The first Monday of December was the start of the Christmas festivities in Bulgaria. Unlike their Christian counterparts in America, who decorated their houses as early as November, in Bulgaria, people waited until December. Slavena trotted by freshly hung Santas climbing through windows and blinking Christmas lights left on during the overcast winter days. Out of breath and distracted, she didn't spot the black Mercedes-Benz G-class driving slowly next to her until it was too late.

Slavena eyed the car's tinted windows, but couldn't see the man behind the wheel. When she recognized the B7 Level armoring of the car her instincts told her to run.

Slavena made a sudden turn away from the Mercedes and ran as fast as she could. The heavy SUV made the sharp turn as well and caught up with her. It stopped and the man behind the wheel buzzed the window down.

"Get in," he said. "We've got to talk."

It was Orlovsky. She'd expected him to show up; there was too much-unfinished business between them. Slavena circled the car and climbed into the passenger seat.

"Any developments?" Slavena asked sarcastically. Since she was the target, she'd be the first to know if there was a new development. She would be dead.

"The money for the hit was already wired to me."

"Hence the new car. A bit heavy on the armor, if you ask me."

"I need it. I've got a job to do."

Slavena chuckled.

"Not funny! Especially, if what you told me is true." He motioned with his hand towards her belly but averted his eyes away. He was in denial. Slavena couldn't blame him. She was pretty much there herself.

Orlovsky drove until they reached a mall a few blocks down the road and parked in a corner of the nearly empty parking lot.

After he turned off the engine, he faced her. "Why didn't you tell me," he said with a sullen voice. "That the person you've been trying to protect was you all along?"

So, that's what he'd made out of this. That the person she was trying to protect was herself and not Boychev. He'd got it all wrong, of course, but she didn't contradict him.

"I didn't know you'd care," she said. Orlovsky didn't deny that. He probably wouldn't have. "So, how much is my life worth?"

"Not much," he said.

She figured. For Boychev, she was a minor disturbance. A speck on his glittering future. She wondered why he'd bothered at all.

"You have to come with me," Orlovsky told her.

"Why?"

"Because I need some time to figure things out and I don't want anything to happen to you in the meantime."

She thought about it. Boychev directed her to get rid of Orlovsky, but she didn't work for him and Langley hadn't authorized it yet. Leaving with Orlovsky would be the true test if she was capable of killing the father of her child.

"All right," she conceded. "Where are you taking me?"

"To the mountains."

"To the mountains?" She gave a short laugh. "What a convenient location for a clean kill. I guess I should have drafted my will when I had the chance."

He didn't say anything, but there was something in his eyes that told her she was safe with him. And if there was one thing she was particularly good at, was reading men.

"I'll come, but it'll take me an hour to jog back home —"

"10 minutes!" he said sharply. "I know where you live!"

"Fine!" she wasn't surprised. "But I'll still need to take a shower, change and pack. You can come over if you would like."

"And take a shower with you?" He gave her a thin smile. "Tempted, but we need to get on the road. I'll give you thirty minutes tops and I'll wait for you here. Make sure nobody tails you." Orlovsky leaned and clasped a watch on her wrist. It was a platinum Rolex, encrusted with diamonds.

She took a deep breath to say something, but he stopped her. "You were right. Jaro was on my list and all the money I earned from the job is in this watch. You killed him, not me, so the money belongs to you."

Slavena stood quietly. She had no idea watches could cost so much.

"I can't wear it," was the only thing she could think of saying.

"And why not? Because it will make you look like a double agent and you're afraid of losing your job at the CIA? If I'm right and you're still working for those assholes when you have the baby, I promise you this: I will find you. I will kill you and I will put the baby up for adoption!"

"Finally, the sweetheart Orlovsky I know is back."

"You like him better, don't you?"

She smiled and opened the door. "Don't quack like a duck."

He smiled back. "And soar like an Eagle instead. I'll see you in thirty."

Exactly thirty minutes later Slavena was back by Orlovsky's side. Her hair still wet from the shower. The watch still on her wrist. Her eyes firmly fixed on a road that was taking them south of Sofia and towards Bulgaria's famous ski resort — Bansko.

DOUBLE GAMBIT

Bansko was only a couple of hours drive from Sofia, but as far as Slavena was concerned, it could have been on the other side of the planet. There were no tall buildings, wide roads, giant supermarket chains or malls. There were new hotels popping up here and there, but the place largely remained wild as a ski resort should be. It was the beginning of December — right before the peak season officially started — and the view was serene.

Orlovsky rented a log cabin, one of the few built in the wild pine forest closer to the base of the slope. It was all luxury — a double bedroom, enormous panoramic bathroom, spacious kitchen, fireplace, and a hot tub — built primarily for people who valued privacy above anything else.

During the first three days, Slavena and Orlovsky did nothing, but argue, have sex, and argue again. Tearing off clothing, slapping, fist fighting, scratching and biting became their daily routine. The king size bed turned into their battlefield for their primal fight for dominance.

Once the battle horn was blown — and always by Orlovsky, who loved to humiliate her at every chance he got — they attacked each like two opposing forces craving to be united into one. The professional hitman against the novice CIA officer, who fought hard, but she always let him win. If it wasn't her thirst to learn from his vast experience, she wouldn't have been as patient and submissive. She hoped it was only a matter of time before she would get to dominate him.

On the fourth day, they both agreed to take a break from each other.

At the end of the day, Slavena lined up for the chairlift back up one last time. She was skiing on her own. Orlovsky was a snowboarder and liked to go off-piste, just like with everything else in his life. She didn't see his face all day long, but in no way was she missing him.

Slavena observed the chaotic queue before her. Her eyes were drawn towards a tall, broad-shouldered man at the front of the queue. He was surrounded by a few thick-necked men, who followed him obediently. *Those are his guards*, she thought as she looked for their big bulges on their sides. The tall man had adopted a nonchalant stance while waiting in the queue. His companions were far more vigilant in surveilling their surroundings. Slavena allowed her eyes to drop towards the tall man's companion. The girl was probably twenty years younger than the man, slim, long-limbed and gracious. The one-piece snow-white ski suit she wore fit like second skin on her flawless figure.

Slavena's eyes were glued to the girl, not because of her beauty or that she was out of place in such a setting, but because she was a copy of her dead sister, Boyana. She had blond hair, tied in a high ponytail that swept her upper back as she moved. She even had the same posture as Boyana did when she was waiting bored in line at the ice cream parlor.

Slavena felt dizzy and disoriented. The cool air suddenly felt hot on her face. She was short of breath. She struggled to unzip the top of her coat that was covering her mouth and throat. When her sister was killed, all those years ago, she had many episodes like this one. With time their power had worn off. As a result, she'd lost her ability to cope with them and now felt overwhelmed by grief and longing. As she watched, the girl lifted her face up and laughed at something the man said. Slavena felt a stab of agonizing pain when she realized that the girl wasn't Boyana after all.

As the man twisted his face sideways, Slavena caught a glimpse of his profile. She had to do a double take to convince herself she wasn't hallucinating. The man was Dragan Boychev. The thick-necked, sully men surrounding him were his government-appointed bodyguards.

"Excuse me," someone tapped Slavena on the shoulder. She turned to see a red-cheeked woman in a brightly colored, 80s style ski outfit. "Are you even queueing at all?" She asked with a strong British accent.

Slavena looked forward and noticed the people in front of her had moved on. She tried to clear her dry throat in order to speak, but it was clamped tightly as if by an invisible hand. She only managed to nod. As she ambled on, she caught a glimpse of Boychev and the girl catching a double seat chairlift and vanishing among the tall mountain trees.

By the time she caught a seat herself, Boychev and the girl were long out of sight. Next to her sat the Englishwoman that had been queuing behind her.

"Bloody hell, look at that," the woman pointed at a tourist information board below their feet, carved of the trunks of whole trees. "It was there ten years ago when my husband and I first came to Bansko for our honeymoon. Some things have changed since, like the hotels for instance.

They're much better now, to tell you the truth, but many things are exactly the same. Nice to know you can go back to a place and find it as you left it, right love?"

Slavena was staring blankly ahead, nervous she would lose Boychev in the crowded slopes. She needed to follow him and find out where he was staying. She had a nagging suspicion that Orlovsky was in Bansko to kill Boychev and she wanted to confirm it.

Unfazed that Slavena wasn't listening, the English woman carried on. "We've been having some rough times recently, my husband and I. We needed some distraction if you know what I mean."

Further ahead Boychev and the girl jumped off their seats and sleekly disappeared down a slope. Slavena followed their bodyguards with her eyes. They jumped and followed their charge. Slavena thought she saw which way they went, but she wouldn't know for sure until she got to the top of the hill and followed them. The old, dated lift was taking ages. The British woman dragged on. "I thought a good ski trip and romantic chalet would be just the thing to spice things up. But you know how married men are. If you let them, they'll ignore you till it's too late."

Slavena nodded, relieved that they were about to reach the small plateau where they were to jump off their seat. The Englishwoman jumped off too early and was hit in the back by the lift. She fell, face down, on the icy path.

"Sorry, sorry, so sorry," she kept saying when everyone rushed to her aid. By the time Slavena disentangled herself from the mess another minute had passed.

Slavena stood at the top of the hill, undecided. On her left was a friendly blue-graded slope that she knew well. The path going to her right lead to the top of a black slope that Slavena had been avoiding all day. She didn't want to take any risks with her pregnancy.

Boychev would go right, she feared. He was exactly the kind of man to show off in front of a girl. Reluctantly, she pointed her skis to the right.

At first, the slope wasn't challenging. Slavena wondered what the big deal was all about. Why had she avoided it? The snow was better here than on the more popular blue slope which was eroded to ice and dirt by the end of the day.

Slavena picked up speed and focused on finding Boychev. She slid effortlessly from one side of the slope to the other, enjoying the ride. Until she got to a point that made her stomach contract. She stopped and looked down, discovering why the slope was marked black. It was a steep and icy piste, shaped like a half funnel that was wider at the top and narrow towards the end. The shape would make her speed up and lose control at the same time.

Slavena doubted any of the ski techniques she knew would help her here. She would be lucky if she didn't break a bone or worse. She disregarded the knot in her stomach and pushed on, using the snow plow at first to slow herself down. Halfway through it didn't work anymore. She slid sideways, but the width of the slope wasn't enough for her to turn on time. She risked skidding off the edge and bashing into a tree trunk at full speed. For a lack of knowing what else to do she carried on that way. Left, right, left, right.

Eventually, she couldn't control the skis any longer. Her weaker left foot gave out. She fell sideways and slid down on her right side until she reached the bottom. She was covered in frost and thoroughly humiliated. Worst of all, Boychev was nowhere to be seen. He'd vanished. Her efforts had been in vain.

Angry and boiling over with unanswered questions, she picked up her skis and went home.

"You lying bastard," Slavena said as soon as she was through the door. Orlovsky was freshly showered and wore only a towel around his midriff. The six-pack abs on his stomach were playing with the soft light of the fireplace, as he patted his hair dry.

"What now?" he said, unwelcoming the distraction.

"I know why you brought me here. And it's not about my protection at all."

"What are you talking about?"

He poured himself the usual dose of scotch.

"I saw him, Alexander. Your fucked up little game is over."

"You saw who? Calm down. You are not making any sense."

"He didn't order me, did he? You lied to me about that as well."

"Why would I do that?" Orlovsky looked up with his eyes as cold and intimidating as mountain glaciers. "I don't need to lie to you. I don't need to tell you shit unless I want to."

His calm manner enraged Slavena even further. She removed her ski boots and hurled them across the room. "The man I wanted to protect," she said, "the one we negotiated about. I saw him on the slopes today. Are you trying to tell me that's a coincidence?"

"Dragan Boychev? It's all right—you can admit it's him you were after."

Slavena was silent.

"If you had told me his name upfront," he added, "he

would be dead now and we wouldn't be having this problem, would we? See I think ahead of the game."

"Yes, you do. You think ahead of how to screw everybody for the fun of it."

"Have you ever asked yourself, Slavena, why Boychev signed your death warrant when the CIA wanted you to protect him?"

"No." She had asked herself that many times, but was afraid of the answer. It only brought more questions.

"He has the CIA wrapped around his little finger."

"I don't care about the logistics of all this," she countered. "I have a mission and you're not going to stop me from bringing it home!" Slavena mumbled while she put on her snow boots.

"Where are you going?"

"Out," she said. "I need to think."

"You are not going anywhere!" Orlovsky slammed his empty glass on the bar. "Yes, I knew he'd be here. As a matter of fact, he came today."

"How did you know?"

"Does it matter? He's here now and one of the three of us must die. It's a deadly triangle if you ask me. I don't want to die. And, convenient for you, I don't want to kill you. So that leaves only one option."

"So you're going to kill him?"

He nodded, confirming her suspicions.

"No!" she said. "I am not going to let you!"

"Fine. Then we go to plan B."

"Which is?"

"An old tested recipe of mine. We fake your death." Orlovsky smiled. He had a beautiful, disarming smile when he wanted to. Perfect white teeth. Smooth skin, spreading over high cheekbones.

Slavena smiled back right as the front door was violently kicked open and bullets flew towards Orlovsky's body. Hidden behind the door, Slavena instinctively pulled her Glock from its holster and unloaded it at the intruders assaulting Orlovsky with their Kalashnikovs. In a split second, both fell dead in a heap on the floor. Killing was becoming easier for her.

Slavena kicked the door closed and looked outside an adjacent window. There was only one black Audi parked in the far distance down the gravel driveway. It was the car of the intruders.

"Motherfuckers!" she heard Orlovsky yelling from behind the couch. She turned back to see his wounded body crawling out from what used to be a sofa, but was now a mutilated piece of wood, springs, and cushion. The sight of him, still breathing, gave her a jolt of relief as if his presence made the current situation somehow bearable.

He stood up, inspected his wounds on his left shoulder, and once he confirmed they weren't life-threatening, he started pacing around the living room like a caged animal. His silence baffled her. Knowing him, she was certain he blamed her for everything. Never mind she saved his life.

"Did Boychev see you?" he snarled at her finally like a pit bull about to attack.

"No," she said calmly. She didn't feel like arguing with him right now. Not when his body was bleeding with humiliation.

"You know, sometimes I wonder how you passed your fucking training at the CIA."

"I thought I did all right by saving your life."

"What?" he stopped abruptly and looked at her. "Don't fool yourself that you saved my life. I was just getting in position."

"And what do you call that position? *'Is this how it all ends?'*"

"Shut up and listen to me." He raised his voice. "You have to leave *now*! These guys weren't the killers. They were just the scouts. Do you understand?"

"Why can't we both leave?"

"Because I have some unfinished business!"

"Boychev?"

"No, obviously my priorities have shifted," he pointed to the dead bodies on the floor. "As you can see, I need to clean and mop this place and wait for the others to show up unless you wanna help me?"

She glanced at the dead men. The coppery smell of blood, mixed with the stench of bowel-loosening from the corpses made Slavena sick and she threw up on the floor.

"Didn't think so!" He shoved his car keys in her hand. "You need to get back to Sofia! Now!" His orders were coming faster than the bullets from the Kalashnikovs earlier.

She considered his last words. Running to her safehouse could mean the difference between life and death, but how could she trust the CIA when she was certain Boychev wanted her dead now?

She gave a sigh. "I prefer to take their Audi. It's much faster."

"Negative. My car is much safer for you," he said as he put his hands on her waist, pulling her closer. "You can trust me!" She trusted him as much as Russian roulette, but she nodded and he carried on. "If you pick up the slightest hint that my car is GPS tracked, park it far away, get a taxi and wait for me at this address." He scribbled an address on a piece of paper and gave it to her. "It's my safehouse. When I come back, I want to find you naked in my bed, reading your surveillance manual, understood?"

Her nerves tingled at the sight of the hungry look in his eyes.

"You'll need to see a doctor first."

"Yes. I do," he replied lightly, but Slavena didn't miss the dark shadows in his eyes. It was the first time she saw him scared and that concerned her.

That is how she knew it was time to run.

The moment she turned the ignition key, the speakers inside his G-Class exhaled waves of loud trance music. Slavena never understood Orlovsky's desire to listen to this kind of music in the confined space of a car. It ripped through your body and silenced your thoughts. What was the point?

She sped around the curvy, mountain road that led out of the village and onto the highway back to Sofia. As soon as she got to the highway, she pressed the gas pedal all the way down, but she couldn't reach higher than 80 miles per hour. The armored G-class, Orlovsky gave her, was too heavy to be used for a quick escape. Suddenly it struck her that Orlovsky may have deliberately made her take his car so they could follow her and not him. The sheer thought of his betrayal felt like a piece of glass stuck in her eye, but she couldn't think of that right now. Not when she had to keep one eye looking at her rearview mirror. She was safe for now. But with the speed she was going, and Orlovsky was aware of that, things could get ugly quick. They could finish her before she reached Sofia.

The more she analyzed his last words, the more calculated his plan sounded. He certainly knew his car was GPS tracked and she couldn't go far with it. Realizing it was a death trap, a sense of panic crept over her. *You can trust me*, he had said, but could she trust him with her life? Questions like these started to storm in like uninvited guests ready to make her night a living hell. The sky started to darken along with her mood, and she realized she was physically trembling with the blasts of music.

She turned off the CD player. Instantly, she was relieved the booms and the growls of the music that had been filling her mind with fear and paranoia were gone. In the silence that followed, she worked out the odds of her survival in case of a car chase. *My car is much safer for you,* Orlovsky's words echoed in her mind. Sure, his car was bullet-proof and could withstand a firefight, but what if they used armor-piercing rounds or a damned RPG? In that situation, her odds were slim. The plan had to change. That was her conclusion. Her new course of action was dangerous but was the only way to find out if she was being followed. Most importantly, the plan was hers and not Orlovsky's.

At the first sight of a dirt road, she steered away from the main road and entered a dark pine forest. She drove for ten minutes before she found the perfect place to stop — a well-lit clearing in the forest. She turned off the lights and got out of the vehicle. The cold air outside felt like a slap in the face for diverting from the original plan. But once she opened the trunk and saw Orlovsky's favorite toy — a customized FN P90 with thermal scope — laying on the floor, she warmed up to her new plan quickly.

Become a master of your fate! Her sniper instructor had told her that once and she was doing exactly that. She wasted no time and after fifteen minutes of preparation, including covering up her tracks with a fern tree branch, she laid prone on the frozen ground, one hundred feet from the car in a well-concealed position. After she carefully surveyed the area, she appreciated the excellent vantage point of her firing position. Reassured and warm in her blanket, she waited for the unknown.

She didn't wait long before the lights of cars approaching the area alerted her. She eyed the stopped vehicles behind her thermal scope for about two minutes, counting the number of red silhouettes hiding behind the tinted windows. The first movement was a rainbow-colored image exiting the lead car. She quickly picked up movement everywhere and her suspicions were confirmed. Orlovsky's car was GPS tagged. Her pulse quickened. Yet her head was clear.

She stalked the rainbow images of ten men approaching the parked G-Class in a loose "V" shape formation. She attuned her eyes to their images, her ears to the sound of their footsteps, and waited patiently for them to walk into her trap.

From the angle of their positions and the silence that followed, she could tell the men were plotting to initiate a surprise attack on her. They must have assumed Slavena was still inside the car waiting in the dark.

A deadly assumption, she suppressed a grin as she looked at their vigilant bodies circling the car she was supposed to be inside. Their images, one by one, came into full focus. They spread their formation into what appeared to be assault positions. The sequencing of their movements confirmed they were a well-trained, professional kill squad. The target was her or the woman inside the parked vehicle. Only it wasn't a woman but a decoy she made out of branches and a hoody she found in the trunk. Any second now, these guys were going to start playing checkers, shooting blindly and peeling off the armor plating of the vehicle, inch by inch, without realizing the woman they were after only knew how to play chess.

Hidden in the dark, like any chess player, she waited patiently to take them one by one like pawns off the board. She calmly adjusted her elevation and windage. She then placed her index finger on the trigger and paused.

The first gun shot from a gunman was followed by a violent volley from the kill squad at the vehicle. There was nothing quite like the sound of machinegun rounds going off in a forest. The echo was surreal, providing the perfect cover for Slavena to execute her hits.

"One pawn, one square inch at a time!" Slavena said as she squeezed off the first headshot.

CHECKMATE

Slavena had been on the run for 24 hours and she was beginning to feel the strain of it. From the moment she killed the two men at the log cabin to the moment she killed the rest in the failed ambush deep in the forest, she was leaving a trail of bodies everywhere. Bodies that were probably buried by now and rotting away in their final resting place. She would've been dead too if she wasn't properly trained by the CIA. The one rule she didn't follow per Company instructions was to go to her safe house and wait there for support. Instead, she boarded a plane to the one place that she knew for certain wasn't a death trap. Her only safe heaven.

The Statue of Liberty.

To most, the majestic lady was just another curious landmark to be checked off the tourist list of things to see. But to her, it was far more. It was her real safe house. It had been since the day she saw it from the plane window on her way to the United States when she immigrated. She was only 18 years old, running from her misfortunate past, hoping for a brighter future. And she'd found a better life until the CIA recruited her and showed her the real purpose of life — to stay alive.

If only it was that easy when you were just a pawn in a ruthless game.

The doors opened abruptly and Slavena walked out of the train. As she made her way out of South Ferry subway station, she could see the Statue of Liberty in the distance. Every time she looked at it, she got goosebumps across her body. It was as magnificent as when she saw it for the first time. But most of all, it reminded her that she was safe and free. She'd gotten out of Bulgaria alive, and she was grateful to America for sheltering her once again. Her adopted country had become her home.

She walked into Battery Park and saw Rovish sitting on one of the benches, waiting for her. He was also looking at the Statue of Liberty. She wondered what it represented for him. As she approached, he stood up.

"Glad you are home safely!" he said and gave her a hug. She'd missed him, but she would never tell him. There were boundaries.

"It is good to be back," she said, returning the embrace.

They sat on the bench and remained silent, gazing at the giant statue.

"Here is your death certificate." Rovish handed her a piece of paper. "Alena is dead now, but Slavena is still alive."

She smiled. Finally, that chapter of her life was closed.

"I guess that concludes your mission."

Slavena never expected to hear those exact words. The Agency was releasing her of her duty as the NOC and she felt like a ship-wrecked sailor staring at the debris of her sunken ship. But she had no time to wander in the wastelands of her ruined career. She was more concerned about what happened back in Bulgaria. Her guess was that Boychev was still on the chessboard, writing death certificates. And his knight, Orlovsky, was carrying them out.

Rovish knew when to stay silent. He'd been on missions himself. He knew the feeling afterward of being fed up with mind games and keeping secrets. Not knowing what facts were real and where all the pieces laid on the board. Needing genuine, decent human interaction, so you could regain trust in humanity.

"I'm pregnant," Slavena said not looking at him this time.

Rovish was taken by surprise, but he was a seasoned spook and his face remained impassive, non-judgmental. "I see. You can still work for the Company. Headquarters is always in need of good analysts."

Slavena shook her head, still not looking at him. "I'm not sure I believe in the whole Company thing. There're too many unanswered questions. Questions no one seems willing to answer. That's why I want out."

"Can't say I blame you. I've been there myself."

"Have you?" Slavena glanced at him with hope. "But you always seem so sure about everything. So balanced."

"With experience, you learn how not to let these things get to you. Still, every decent officer knows that doubting authority and surroundings are a matter of survival. Sometimes you question your enemy; other times your allies."

"Did you ever get your answers?"

The answer was no, but Rovish didn't think telling her would be of any use. Slavena was too young to become a cynic.

"If I were you, I'd stay with the Company a little longer. It can give you a new identity and good protection."

"Protection from whom? I thought this was taken care of."

"You never know. It takes a while to get back to normal life after being a NOC. You need time for things to settle down."

Slavena pondered his words as she stood up. She squeezed his hand. It was warm and gentle.

"Thank you."

"For what?" Rovish asked.

"For taking care of me."

"Don't mention it. It's been a pleasure," he said with a layer of intimacy hidden deep in his eyes and Orlovsky's words echoed from the past— *"that Rovish guy. The sexy professor. I could tell you're in love with him."*

Slavena smiled at Rovish one last time before she turned back towards the Statue of Liberty in the distance, lost in thought. Rovish looked at her back with such longing that had Slavena faced him just then, he wouldn't have been able to hide it. He knew he had better chances with her now when she needed a man by her side to rake over the ashes of her burned career. Someone to help raise her children. He'd always known that he was going to settle down with her one day, but he never expected that day to be so close.

As soon as Rovish's shadow disappeared into the darkness, she discreetly slid her left hand into her jacket pocket and pulled out the platinum Rolex Lady Pearlmaster. Her fingers softly caressed the surface of the impressive watch. She felt the edges of the diamond-set bezel that illuminated the blue enamel Roman numerals. The watch was an extravagant present from Orlovsky. The one she had tried to refuse.

She glanced at it with disbelief. *Why give me this and then send me to die?* Her inside voice was tearing her up. As a CIA officer, she knew she was betrayed by him, but as a woman, she knew she couldn't have been. She felt anger at herself for the weakness of allowing this man, *this narcissistic bastard*, to mean so much to her.

She gazed at the face of the watch, following the movements of the second hand. It trembled on the number 6 for less than a milli second, getting her attention. She followed the smooth sweeping of the second hand until it reached the number 6 again. The stutter was no longer an illusion. There was a subtle magnetic pull behind the face of the watch. Orlovsky planted a GPS tracker inside. It enabled the killers to follow her into the forest when she left Bansko.

This confirmed he had betrayed her.

"What?" she mumbled as she noticed for the first time the engraving on the inside of the clutch. She read it with narrowed eyes: *Checkmate!* Slavena remembered the night when she told Orlovsky that he was a lousy chess player and a thin smile ran across her face. She'd been expecting this. Orlovsky was a narcissist with a mortal fear of losing all his life and he was never going to let her win. That was his plan from the beginning. To defeat her and he did. But that was just a game. Life continued even after checkmate.

She clasped the watch on her wrist.

She wasn't going to get rid of it quite yet. The engraving came with a long numeric combination that looked like a bank account number with a bar code. Perhaps Orlovsky didn't betray her after all. Perhaps she was wrong that Orlovsky worked with Boychev all along.

The men were dead. Every single one of them, laying cold on the snow. Orlovsky crouched to inspect the wounds on their bodies. It was precision work of a professional sniper with an FN P90. It was his rifle that he always kept in his trunk and Orlovsky concluded Slavena was the shooter behind the massacre.

It's my child inside her, he thought proudly, *that makes her so deadly*. But mostly, he was amused by his ability to read her so well. As if he was sitting inside her brain, maneuvering her every action to ensure her survival. He'd set her up and knew precisely the things she would do, like doubting him the second she got on the road and ignoring everything he told her to do. That was part of her trade. To mistrust everything and everyone. She was used to it and he took advantage of knowing it. She then was going to find out who was after her and look for a way to put him in the crosshairs. By predicting her strong intuition, he had pushed her in the right direction and this was the outcome. A victory march over a mass grave of enemies.

Peter Orlovsky would have admired his son's excellence.

But sometimes excellence came with a high price tag. He was badly injured and the pain burning inside him didn't give him peace. He pulled out his phone and dialed a number.

"I've got nothing to do with the attack!" The voice on the other end of the phone barked without preliminaries. Still, it felt good to hear a human voice in a place like this, where corpses laid quietly on the ground, their eyes staring at the only living being present.

"Then who?"

"The Sinner. It was your job to finish him."

"I was busy with another job you gave me, remember?"

"What's taking you so long?"

"It's done. She's dead."

"Prove it," Boychev said. "I want a picture this time."

Orlovsky's body stiffened unprepared. Never before had Boychev requested pictures. "I already buried her in the ground," Orlovsky said and waited for Boychev to answer, but he was silent. "If you don't trust my word, I can dig her out, but I'm injured."

"No need." The voice softened. "Keep your energy for your most important job."

"The Sinner?"

"Yes! Make him *the last* Sinner and your precious firm is as good as yours."

"BAM is already mine by law!" Orlovsky snapped.

"The law is not on your side yet. Not until I become the next Walt Disney!"

Bastard, Orlovsky thought. *I almost got killed and all Boychev cares about is his seat as prime minister.*

"What about *my* Disneyland? Remember what you promised?"

Boychev gave a short laugh and cleared his throat. "I've been working on it since the day we signed the contract."

"Doing what?"

"I've already hired a team of loyal bureaucrats and financial wizards to do their magic and blend the three business accounts into one big firm. Your Disneyland is ready for its grand opening, but are you ready for it? Becoming an oligarch overnight is a huge responsibility."

Orlovsky's muscles relaxed. The plan hadn't changed after all. Uniting BAM, SIN, and BNB into one was still in the making, but Boychev's questioning of his ability to manage the empire of firms was new and that concerned him.

"I've been ready for a long time!" Orlovsky tightened his grip on the phone.

"Then get it done!" Boychev barked and hung up.

Orlovsky was glad to be left alone again. Boychev was right. He was a lone wolf and managing a business empire was not something he was cut out for. But neither was Boychev fit to be prime minister. That man's mind was like the footprints of a hunted mouse, deviating in hundred directions.

Orlovsky laughed at the image of Boychev as a mouse. "Fucking Mickey Mouse!" Orlovsky continued laughing as a sharp pain stabbed him in his collarbone. The adrenaline was wearing off and he knew he had little time before the pain became unbearable. He lifted his sweater to inspect the bleeding and twisted his mouth into a grimace. He had a job to do and he was in no shape or form to do it.

He dialed another number.

"Boss?" The voice on the other end made Orlovsky realize how long it had been since the last time he was called that.

"Send me a mop-up team and have a doctor ready to stitch me up," Orlovsky ordered.

"Roger. I got your GPS coordinates. Give me an hour top."

"Hurry! And one last thing. Spread the news that I'm dead."

"Cause of death?"

"Mowed down by two Kalashnikovs. A surprise attack in my log cabin."

"Nobody would believe it. How about a kill squad?"

"Whatever, but don't be too creative."

"Roger."

Orlovsky hung up with a smirk on his face. No matter what Boychev said, BAM was always going to be his and all the BAMERS, his former battle buddies, already knew it.

Orlovsky was waiting in the dark with his eyes hooked to the entrance of the nightclub Sugalips. The club's cliché neon sign flickered bright pink on the damp sidewalk. He was sitting on his motorcycle in immense pain, but he had a job to do. All he had to do was wait, he hated waiting.

Luckily, he didn't have to wait long.

It was just after 2 am in the morning when the bodyguards came through the outside door. The Sinner, Stefan Nikolov, walked out last. Orlovsky watched him from a distance. He showed signs of fatigue in his walk and Orlovsky, feeling like a shark before a feeding frenzy, smiled at Nikolov's weakness. But it was the guards he had to worry about. They were in top shape and he could tell by the way they carried themselves that they were well trained and professional. He had contemplated a course of action that involved stealth, but every time he wargamed it in his mind, he was unable to get away, especially with his current injuries slowing him down. No, he was going to have to do this hit fast, deliberate, and loud.

He was half-dead, half-alive but still lethal.

Orlovsky continued to observe their bodies silhouetting against the bright neon lights of the club until his mind worked out all the moves and angles to kill them. One of the men adjusted the holster strap under his jacket as he called the driver by waving his hand as if hailing a taxi. He was the leader, the more experienced one, and Orlovsky mapped him out as the first target. The Sinner was going to be the last.

Orlovsky waited for the Bentley to pull away from its parking spot and once it was in motion, he closed the visor on his helmet and accelerated his motorcycle. The bright lights of the Bentley shined directly into the guards' eyes obscuring Orlovsky's approach from behind it. Knowing he had exactly five seconds before their nervous system reacted to the noise of a fast-approaching motorcycle, he opened the throttle wide open and shortened the distance by half.

It took them less than five seconds to reach into their jackets and pull out their weapons, confirming they were well trained. When the first burst of shots came his way, Orlovsky leaned forward and accelerated again. With his right hand grasping the handlebar, and the left on his MP5, he was still able to keep control of his direction thanks to the adrenaline that was running in his blood like strong scotch. Orlovsky was glad his body and mind were on the same page as there was no room for mistakes tonight.

He knew it was a matter of seconds before a bullet found its mark, so he turned his muzzle on them and fired back. The muzzle of Orlovsky's MP5 burst with a flash and echoed violently in the street. *Rat tat tat tat tat tat tat.*

Time slowed for Orlovsky as he saw each individual shell casing eject out of the top of the weapon. His hypersensitivity allowed him to compensate for the shifting center of gravity of the weapon's action as well as the rising muzzle.

He saw the men dropping like rag dolls one after another, with blood springing from their bodies. Once they were out of his sight, he turned his head back to see if he killed them all. There was no movement on the ground. Even the girl had to die. He had to protect himself from any risk of exposure. No witnesses. That's how he always did it. No questions. No conscience.

After a hundred yards, he stopped and waited in the dark with the engine silent. There wasn't much traffic at this hour, except for police. He waited for the sirens and once he picked up the direction of their sound, he turned the engine on and sped with the lights off.

A job is a job.

HEARTBEAT

Slavena dialed Orlovsky's number and waited in the darkness of her hotel room. The phone went on ringing. Thirteen rings and no answer. She hung up and laid on the bed with closed eyes. Sleep was out of reach once again: shadows lurking in the dark, footsteps crisp on the snow, voices haunting her now. All she wanted was to rest.

The phone chimed and she answered eagerly, "Hello?"

"How is the queen?"

The sound of Orlovsky's voice made her feel instantly alive.

"No longer on the chessboard."

"But neither is she in the *box*, is she?"

He was referring to a coffin and she didn't know what to make of his insensitive remark, but she didn't care. There was no point in drowning over the events that led her here. She was safe now. Slavena jumped off the bed and took a few steps towards the window with her phone to her ear. It was still raining outside. Her finger traced a raindrop on the glass, flowing down and merging into another raindrop until the two raindrops crashed further down and off the window, disappearing. The question that had been on her mind for the past week resembled that raindrop, first forming slowly, then gathering speed and finally crashing down. It was time to ask.

"You were with Boychev the whole time, weren't you?"

She'd asked him softly and it was a good question, but Orlovsky opted to remain silent.

"Why?" She persisted. "Why didn't you tell me?"

"Save me the melodrama," he said coldly. "I don't have time for this!"

"But you had time to destroy my career?"

"You were already walking on thin ice and I just made it crack."

"I nearly drowned!"

"And I knew you wouldn't."

She decided it was better not to say anything and instead looked out the window. The rain was heavy now. A young couple was running down the side walk, splashing through the deep puddles with laughter. It reminded her of the night she considered the most intimate moment in her life. Navy and she were also running in the rain, holding hands. Two brand-new recruits, excited to be there, at the Farm, wondering what their future in the CIA would be like. She certainly didn't picture it like this. Stranded in a hotel, exhausted from all the lies and desperate for a normal life where there were no strict rules and plenty of human warmth.

"Are you safe in New York?" Orlovsky asked at last.

His question rattled her. It was finally confirmed that the watch Orlovsky gave her had a GPS tracker. There was no hiding from him. Still, not wanting to admit it, she soaked deeper in the silence. For a full minute, there was total silence gathering tension until Orlovsky decided to break it.

"My dad used to say move in silence, only speak when it's time to say checkmate."

"And your point is?"

"That you're still playing chess, Slavena. So, let me help you make the right next move. He thinks you're dead for now. But he will figure it out eventually, mark my words, and when he does, you should be somewhere safer to hole up than New York."

He was talking about Boychev, but in her mind, Orlovsky was her only threat.

"The safest place for me would be the furthest away from the man who betrayed me!"

Orlovsky laughed. "Spoken like a sore loser, but you know you won in the end!"

"I did? How?"

"You managed to transform a lone wolf into a lapdog, get out of the country alive and with enough money to raise your children like the chess player *you* always wanted to be."

"Amen."

"Eight million dollars Amen in the Credit Suisse Bank. On that lapdog note, keep our communication open so I can see my kids one day."

"Your *kids*?"

"Yes, my *kids*. I know we're having twins, and I—" he went on saying, but the connection suddenly went dead.

Slavena waited in the dark, but she didn't expect him to call her back any time soon. After the silence settled back in, she pulled out the ultrasound from her OB/GYN appointment from that morning and looked at the two beating hearts. She shook her head with disbelief. Orlovsky never missed a beat. Especially a heart one.

CHECKMATE

Slavena Ivanova →	♙	♟	←Foreign Agents
Marines →	♘	♞	← Alexander Orlovsky
Professor Rovish →	♗	♝	← Little Christ
Langley →	♖	♜	← Mafia
U.S. Government →	♕	♛	← Dragan Boychev
Promoted Pawn →	♙	♟	← Promoted Pawn

ABOUT THE AUTHOR

Demi Bom is a former American intelligence professional who was injured at the height of her career yet continued to pursue her passion for spy craft through fiction writing. While recovering, she realized a rich world of characters and stories from her professional experience lived inside her mind. It took a battle with her severe spinal injury to give her the courage to write and share that amazing underworld of intrigue and spies. An imaginative writer with professional training in human intelligence and martial arts, Bom effortlessly transforms the bare bones of a historical event into a compelling story that captivates readers.

Her novels are a series of suspenseful spy thrillers with a distinctly dark edge premised on the famous quote by Oscar Wilde: "Everything in the world is about sex except sex. Sex is about power." Bom's writing focuses on the complexity of human relationships, loyalty and the corruptive nature of desire.

Bom is the ultimate storyteller of sex, politics and power.
Thanks to the therapy of writing, Bom is now 100 % recovered and lives in Italy with her family. Between writing about the mafia and being a mom, she embraces her newfound addiction to photography and chess.

Connect with her via Instagram: @demibom or Litsy: @demibom

Made in the USA
Middletown, DE
04 March 2019